NOT FOR BREAD ALONE

NOT FOR BREAD ALONE

WRITERS ON FOOD, WINE, AND THE ART OF EATING

Edited by
Daniel Halpern

THE ECCO PRESS

THE ECCO PRESS
100 West Broad Street
Hopewell, NJ 08525
Published simultaneously in Canada by
Penguin Books Canada Ltd., Ontario
Printed in the United States of America

First Paperback Edition

Library of Congress Cataloging-in-Publication Data

Not for bread alone : writers on food, wine, and the art of eating /
edited by Daniel Halpern.
p.   cm.
ISBN 0-88001-346-X
1. Gastronomy. 2. Food. I. Halpern, Daniel, 1945–
TX631.N68   1993
641'.01'3—dc20
CIP 93-37160

Cover design by Jeanne Ensor
Cover art: *Bread* by Jasper Johns © Gemini G.E.L., Los Angeles, California, 1969.
The text of this book is set in Baskerville.

CONTENTS

INTRODUCTION

Food as Gesture

There are ways to think about food and its preparation beyond its actual consumption: thus the essays in *Not for Bread Alone: Writers on Food, Wine, and the Art of Eating*. My idea was to put together a collection that celebrated both the nourishing (and necessary) act of eating, as well as that part that goes beyond merely eating to live—that is, the various social, anthropological, psychological, and philosophical gestures in the non-consuming aspects of food and rituals of eating. Eating our slice of daily bread, but not for the intake of that slice alone.

I entered the resplendent realm of cooking one very early Sunday morning in Seattle, circa 1952, at the age of six or seven, when I served eggs I had poached for an hour or two to my sleeping parents. I had watched my mother poach eggs and understood the technique perfectly: the poaching trays, the arrangement, the proper allotment of water. However, the notion of *time* was yet to enter my burgeoning culinary repertoire. Even then, or especially then, it was *gesture* that made an impression on me: the act of serving "the prepared" to another.

But to me cooking did not truly matter until I used food to do my bidding in the court of women. It was the late sixties and I was undergoing a post-puberty period in Los Angeles, a Valley Boy living in a cheap but rustic apartment rented from Apache landlords in Laurel Canyon, just down the street from "the log cabin," where Frank Zappa and The Mothers of Invention posted rent and held extravagant parties, where I turned up many of the young women I nourished during that time. My small kitchen had a square table with a plastic checkerboard tablecloth, two wicker chairs, and a view of what I liked to describe solemnly as "deep forest." My intention was to give the view a kind of eerie mystery—to set my guests on edge, but to what end I now wonder? I had rehearsed a number of good-looking, if moderately accomplished dishes, but settled on two that seemed to win for themselves the necessary regard. The meals began with spicy corn fritters. I served these with a little crème fraîche and, depending on the intensity of my feelings, a splash of red lumpfish caviar. I followed with a leg of lamb, shank half, injected with garlic splinters and rubbed with olive oil and rosemary. And throughout, plenty of inexpensive zinfandel from Napa, finishing with a simple dessert that would not unduly prolong the evening.

A short time later, I found myself living in Tangier, Morocco, where I taught English and began cooking with a certain earnestness. I lived in the apartment below Paul Bowles, who served as a sort of post-graduate mentor to me. On our afternoon walks through the covered food markets of the Socco Grande, where we shopped for our dinners, we discussed music, literature, stateside gossip, and the mysterious Moroccan culture. It was in Tangier that I was first seduced by the richness of the dark spices—cumin, clove, cinnamon, turmeric, paprika, cardamom—and one fresh herb in particular, *kosbour* (coriander), whose aroma still conjures up those intense, profuse, and honest markets, where nothing was masked or disguised.

Paul and I often ate together and one of the dishes he most enjoyed was a chickpea dish I made with my two favorite ingredients: cumin and coriander. We ate this with our favorite *tagine*, a stew of chicken rubbed with freshly ground cumin, prunes stewed with ginger, and onions sautéed with cinnamon and topped with toasted almonds.

When I left Tangier for Italy, to visit my mother and sisters in Florence, Paul suggested I stop in Venice to see Peggy Guggenheim. As her guest at the Guggenheim *palazzo/museo*, it came to pass that I had the opportunity to help her, using the few culinary skills I had managed to acquire. It was one of those languid, mid-summer days on the lagoons of Venice; we were looking at various obscure churches in the small back canals in her chauffeured gondola, talking about her support of Djuna Barnes, one the expatriate stars of the twenties, and of Italian food. She mentioned she had invited a number of friends to dinner, but was going to have to cancel because her chef had taken ill suddenly. Naturally, in a gesture of foolish generosity, I asked if I might help out by preparing a modest meal for her friends.

She and I then put together a list and, via gondola, "shopped." This meant we went from hotel to hotel, where Peggy was friendly with the head chefs who happily supplied her.

An hour after the appointed hour, the guests began to arrive: local artists and politicians, exiled Brits and Americans, a banker, a beautiful Eastern European jeweller, and (Peggy had neglected to prepare me, a hopeful writer of verses), Ezra Pound. Later in the evening, after a quantity of Veneto red (an Amarone produced by Quintarelli), I reminded him that we had met once ten years earlier on a *vaporetto* plying through a rainy December night from San Marco to Accademia. I had asked, innocently, if he might be the poet Ezra Pound and he had replied, "Nope", in perfect English, keeping things simple. He now said, quietly, "Yes, but you see that wasn't me."

I prepared the meal. Red and yellow peppers stuffed with a purée of tuna and various aromatics and followed by simple but enthusiastic *fusilli* tossed with sausage and three kinds of tomatoes. For a meat dish, I grilled pork tenderloin (the kind that in this country comes packaged in cellophane) marinated, à la Tangier, in a blizzard of brown spices. To close, I presented with immodesty a local thigh-food specialty known as *tiramisu*.

Peggy told me the dinner was well-received. She knew by the invitations at meal's end—gesture for gesture. I left the next day after a lunch on her terrace overlooking the Grand Canal, sitting in the shadow of Brancusi's *Bird in Flight*. As we ate (leftovers), Peggy told me the story of its painful acquisition from the artist himself. They had been "seeing each other in a serious way," as Peggy put it. When the moment eventually arrived for them to break up—which I gathered, from the stories she told me about her many close encounters with the most important men of the first half of this century, was something she got rather used to—she agreed to purchase his *Bird in Flight*. At the appointed hour, she went to fetch the piece. Brancusi came out of his house carrying it in his arms. I asked Peggy if it weren't too heavy for him to carry alone and she replied, "Oh no, he was an extremely strong man." And she added, "You know, he had tears in his eyes, it was very moving. But to this day I don't know whether those tears were for me because I left him or because he was losing his beloved *Bird in Flight.*" I like to think, these many years later (and given this context), their final encounter was like a last supper, bird in hand— betrayed first by his love-in-flesh, who in turn robbed (albeit *purchased*) him of his love-in-silver, both now in flight.

But this is not the gesture I wish to end with. Not with a gesture of parting, but one of arrival. As in introduction. It is reported that Genghis

Kahn said the first thing one man gives another is his hand. I'm thinking of gatherings of friends and relations, and how the hand and cheek are certainly the first to be put forward. But we expect this gesture of formal greeting (among friends) to be quickly followed by the question that makes coming together such a welcome thing, that pregustatory interrogative we have come this distance to be offered by our good and thoughtful hosts: "What can I get you?"

DANIEL HALPERN

NOT FOR BREAD ALONE

ROSE MACAULAY

Eating and Drinking

Here is a wonderful and delightful thing, that we should have furnished
ourselves with orifices, with traps that open and shut, through which to
push and pour alien objects that give us such pleasurable, such delicious
sensations, and at the same time sustain us. A simple pleasure; a pleasure
accessible, in normal circumstances and in varying degrees, to all, and
that several times each day. An expensive pleasure, if calculated in the
long run and over a lifetime; but count the cost of each mouthful as it
comes, and it is (naturally) cheaper. You can, for instance, get a delicious
plate of spaghetti and cheese, or fried mushrooms and onions, for very
little; or practically anything else, except caviare, smoked salmon, the
eggs of plovers, ostriches and humming-birds, and fauna and flora completely out of their appropriate seasons, which you will, of course, desire,
but to indulge such desires is Gluttony, or Gule, against which the
human race has always been warned. It was, of course, through Gule
that our first parents fell. As the confessor of Gower's Amans told him,
this vice of gluttony was in Paradise, most deplorably mistimed.

We shall never know what that fruit was, which so solicited the
longing Eve, which smelt so savoury, which tasted so delightful as
greedily she ignored it without restraint. The only fruit that has ever
seemed to me to be worthy of the magnificently inebriating effects
wrought by its consumption on both our parents is the mango. When
I have eaten mangoes, I have felt like Eve.

> Satiate at length,
> And hightn'd as with Wine, jocund and boon,
> Thus to her self she pleasingly began.
> O sovran, vertuous, precious of all trees
> In Paradise, of operation blest. . . .

And like both of them together:

> As with new Wine intoxicated both
> They swim in mirth, and fansie that they feel

Divinitie within them breeding wings
Wherewith to scorn the Earth: but that false Fruit
Farr other operation first displaid. . . .

And so on. But, waking up the morning after mangoes, one does not feel such ill effects as was produced by that fallacious fruit when its exhilarating vapour bland had worn off. One feels, unless one has very grossly exceeded, satiate, happy and benign, turning sweet memories over on one's palate, desiring, for the present, no more of anything. The part of the soul (see Timæus) which desires meats and drinks lies torpid and replete by its manger, somewhere between midriff and navel, for there the gods housed these desires, that wild animal chained up with man, which must be nourished if man is to exist, but must not be allowed to disturb the council chamber, the seat of reason. For the authors of our race, said Timæus, were aware that we should be intemperate in eating and drinking, and take a good deal more than was necessary or proper, by reason of gluttony. Prescient and kindly authors of our race! What a happy companion they allotted to mankind in this wild animal, whom I should rather call a domestic and pampered pet. How sweet it is to please it, to indulge it with delicious nourishment, with superfluous tit-bits and pretty little tiny kickshaws, with jellies, salads, dainty fowls and fishes, fruits and wines and pasties, fattened and entruffled livers of geese, sturgeon's eggs from Russia, salmon from the burn, omelettes and soufflés from the kitchen. I have always thought the Glutton in Piers Plowman a coarse and unresourceful fellow, who, on his way to church and shrift, was beguiled merely by a breweress's offer of ale. (How ungenteel Mr. H. W. Fowler must have thought her, and all of her century and many later centuries, for using this word, which he so condemns, for beer!) The Glutton asked, had she also any hot spices? and she assured him that she had pepper, paeony seeds, garlic, and fennel. And with this simple and unpleasing fare, Glutton was content, and made merry globbing it until night. Glutton was no gourmet, no Lucullus. Nothing recked he of rare and dainty dishes; nothing out of the ordinary entered his imagination. Not for him the spitted lark, the artful sauce, the delicate salad of chopped herbs and frogs.

There are some sad facts concerning eating and drinking. One is that the best foods are unwholesome: an arrangement doubtless made by the authors of our being in order to circumvent gluttony. It is a melancholy discovery made early by infants, and repeatedly by adults. We all have to make it in turn, only excepting the ostrich. No doubt the Lady in Comus made it later, after she had more fully grown up, though as an adolescent we find her remarking, sententiously and erroneously, to the enticing sorcerer,

> And that which is not good is not delicious
> To a well-govern'd and wise appetite.

Even the untutored savage knows better than this. They of Dominica, said Antonio de Herrera, that elegant Castilian chronicler of Spanish travels in the West Indies, they of Dominica did eat, one day, a Friar, but he proved unwholesome, and all who partook were ill, and some died, and therefore they of Dominica have left eating human flesh. This was a triumph for Friars, which must be envied by many of the animal world.

Another sad comestive truth is that the best foods are the products of infinite and wearying trouble. The trouble need not be taken by the consumer, but someone, ever since the Fall, has had to take it. Even raw fruit was, to the exiles from Eden, hard to come by.

> Their meanest simple cheer (says Sylvester)
> Our wretched parents bought full hard and deer.
> To get a Plum, sometimes poor Adam rushes
> With thousand wounds among a thousand bushes.
> If they desire a Medler for their food,
> They must go seek it through a fearfull wood;
> Or a brown Mulberry, then the ragged Bramble
> With thousand scratches doth their skin bescramble.

And, did they desire anything better, they could not have it at all. Slowly they learned, we suppose, about planting seeds and reaping ears and grinding flour and welding it into that heavy substance we call bread. Rather more quickly, perhaps, about the merits of dead animals as food, but how long it took them to appreciate the niceties of cooking these, we know not. That is to say, no doubt the students of the history of man know, but I do not.

Once learnt, this business of cooking was to prove an ever growing burden. It scarcely bears thinking about, the time and labour that man and womankind has devoted to the preparation of dishes that are to melt and vanish in a moment like smoke or a dream, like a shadow, and as a post that hastes by, and the air closes behind them, and afterwards no sign where they went is to be found.

Still, one must keep one's head, and remember that some people voluntarily undertake these immense and ephemeral labours, for pay or for a noble love of art even at its most perishable, or from not being able to think of a way of avoiding it. All honour to these slaves of baked-meats: let them by all means apply themselves to their labours; so long as those who do not desire to prepare food are not compelled to do so. If you are of these, and can get no one to cook for you in your home, you should eat mainly such objects as are sold in a form ready for the mouth, such as cheese, bread, butter, fruit, sweets, dough-nuts, maca-roons, meringues, and everything that comes (if you have a tin-opener) out of tins. If you can endure to apply a very little and rudimentary trouble to the matter yourself, eggs are soon made ready, even by the foolish; bacon also. I would not advise you to attempt real meat; this should only be cooked by others; so should potatoes.

But, whatever has been prepared for you, and whoever has had the ill chance to prepare it, there comes the exquisite moment when you push or pour it into the mouth. What bliss, to feel it rotating about the palate, being chewed (if this is required) by the teeth, slipping, in chewed state, down the throat, down the gullet, down the body to the manger, there to find its temporary home. Or, if it is liquid, to feel it gurgling and gushing, like the flood of life, quite down the throat with silver sound, running sweet ichor through the veins. Red wine, golden wine, pink wine, ginger beer (with gin or without), the juice of grape-fruit or orange, tea, coffee, chocolate, iced soda from the fountain, even egg nogg—how merrily and like to brooks they run!

My subject runs away with me: I could, had I but time and space, discourse on it for ever. I could mention the great, the magnificent gourmets of history; I could dwell on the pleasures experienced by Lucul-lus, Heliogobalus, those Roman Emperors, those English monarchs, those Aldermen, who, having dined brilliantly and come to sad satiety, had their slaves tickle them with feathers behind the ears until this caused them to retire in haste from the table, to which they presently returned emptied and ready to work through the menu again. These are the world's great gluttons; to them eating and drinking was a high art.

But they are beaten by one Nicholas Wood, a yeoman of Kent, who, in the reign of James I, "did eat with ease a whole sheep of 16 shillings price, and that raw, at one meal; another time he eat 13 dozen of pigeons. At Sir William Sedley's he eat as much as would have sufficed 30 men; at the Lord Wotton's in Kent, he eat at one meal 84 rabbits, which number would have sufficed 168 men, allowing to each half a rabbit. He suddenly devoured 18 yards of black pudding, London measure, and having once eat 60 lbs. weight of cherries, he said, they were but wastemeat. He made an end of a whole hog at once, and after it swallowed three pecks of damsons; this was after breakfast, for he said he had eat one pottle of milk, one pottle of pottage, with bread, butter, and cheese, before. He eat in my presence, saith Taylor, the water poet, six penny wheaten loaves, three sixpenny veal pies, one pound of sweet butter, one good dish of thornback, and a sliver of a peck household loaf, an inch thick, and all this within the space of an hour: the house yielded no more, so he went away unsatisfied. . . . He spent all his estate to provide for his belly; and though a landed man, and a true labourer, he died very poor in 1630.''

And this is the third snag about good eating and drinking.

Nevertheless, expensive, troublesome, and unwholesome though it be, it is a pleasure by no means to be forgone.

WENDELL BERRY

The Pleasures of Eating

Many times, after I have finished a lecture on the decline of American farming and rural life, someone in the audience has asked, "What can city people do?"

"Eat responsibly," I have usually answered. Of course, I have tried to explain what I meant, but afterwards I have invariably felt that there was more to be said than I had been able to say. Now I would like to attempt a better explanation.

I begin with the proposition that eating is an agricultural act. Eating ends the annual drama of the food economy that begins with planting and birth. Most eaters, however, are no longer aware that this is true. They think of food as an agricultural product, perhaps, but they do not think of themselves as participants in agriculture. They think of themselves as "consumers." If they think beyond that, they recognize that they are passive consumers. They buy what they want—or what they have been persuaded to want—within the limits of what they can get. They pay, mostly without protest, what they are charged. And they mostly ignore certain critical questions about the quality and the cost of what they are sold: How fresh is it? How pure or clean is it, how free of dangerous chemicals? How far was it transported, and what did transportation add to the cost? How much did manufacturing or packaging or advertising add to the cost? When the food product has been "manufactured" or "processed" or "precooked," how has that affected its quality or nutritional value?

Most urban shoppers would tell you that food is produced on farms. But most of them do not know on what farms, or what kinds of farms, or where the farms are, or what knowledge or skills are involved in farming. They apparently have little doubt that farms will continue to produce, but they do not know how or over what obstacles. For them, then, food is pretty much an abstract idea—something they do not know or imagine—until it appears on the grocery shelf or on the table.

The specialization of production induces specialization of consumption. Patrons of the entertainment industry, for example, entertain themselves less and less and have become more and more passively dependent on commercial suppliers. This is certainly also true of patrons of the food industry, who have tended more and more to be *mere* consumers—passive, uncritical, and dependent. Indeed, this sort of consumption may be said to be one of the chief goals of industrial production. The food industrialists have by now persuaded millions of consumers to prefer food that is already prepared. They will grow, deliver, and cook your food for you and (just like your mother) beg you to eat it. That they do not yet offer to insert it, prechewed, into your mouth is only because they have found no profitable way to do so. We may rest assured that they would be glad to find such a way. The ideal industrial food consumer would be strapped to a table with a tube running from the food factory directly into his or her stomach. (Think of the savings, the efficiency, and the effortlessness of such an arrangement!)

Perhaps I exaggerate, but not by much. The industrial eater is, in fact, one who does not know that eating is an agricultural act, who no longer knows or imagines the connections between eating and the land, and who is therefore necessarily passive and uncritical—in short, a victim. When food, in the minds of eaters, is no longer associated with farming and with the land, then the eaters are suffering a kind of cultural amnesia that is misleading and dangerous. The current version of the "dream home" of the future involves "effortless" shopping from a list of available goods on a television monitor and heating precooked food by remote control. Of course, this implies, and indeed depends on, a perfect ignorance of the history of the food that is consumed. It requires that the citizenry should give up their hereditary and sensible aversion to buying a pig in a poke. It wishes to make the selling of pigs in pokes an honorable and glamorous activity. The dreamer in this dream home will perforce know nothing about the kind or quality of this food, or where it came from, or how it was produced and prepared, or what ingredients, additives, and residues it contains. Unless, that is, the dreamer undertakes a close and constant study of the food industry, in which case he or she might as well wake up and play an active and responsible part in the economy of food.

There is, then, a politics of food that, like any politics, involves our freedom. We still (sometimes) remember that we cannot be free if our minds and voices are controlled by someone else. But we have neglected to understand that neither can we be free if our food and its sources are controlled by someone else. The condition of the passive consumer of food is not a democratic condition. One reason to eat responsibly is to live free.

But, if there is a food politics, there are also a food aesthetics and a food ethics, neither of which is dissociated from politics. Like industrial sex, industrial eating has become a degraded, poor, and paltry thing. Our kitchens and other eating places more and more resemble filling stations, as our homes more and more resemble motels. "Life is not very interesting," we seem to have decided. "Let its satisfactions be minimal, perfunctory, and fast." We hurry through our meals to go to work and hurry through our work in order to "recreate" ourselves in the evenings and on weekends and vacations. And then we hurry, with the greatest possible speed and noise and violence, through our recreation—for what? To eat the billionth hamburger at some fast-food joint hell-bent on increasing the "quality" of our life. And all this is carried out in a remarkable obliviousness of the causes and effects, the possibilities and the purposes of the life of the body in this world.

One will find this obliviousness represented in virgin purity in the advertisements of the food industry, in which the food wears as much makeup as the actors. If one gained one's whole knowledge of food—as some presumably do—from these advertisements, one would not know that the various edibles were ever living creatures, or that they all come from the soil, or that they were produced by work. The passive American consumer, sitting down to a meal of pre-prepared or fast food, confronts a platter covered with inert, anonymous substances that have been processed, dyed, breaded, sauced, gravied, ground, pulped, strained, blended, prettified, and sanitized beyond resemblance to any part of any creature that ever lived. The products of nature and agriculture have been made, to all appearances, the products of industry. Both eater and eaten are thus in exile from biological reality. And the result is a kind of solitude, unprecedented in human experience, in which the eater may think of eating as, first, a purely commercial transaction between him and a supplier, and then as a purely appetitive transaction between him and his food.

And this peculiar specialization of the act of eating is, again, of obvious benefit to the food industry, which has good reason to obscure the connection between food and farming. It would not do for the consumer to know that the hamburger she is eating came from a steer that spent much of its life standing deep in its own excrement in a feedlot, helping to pollute the local streams, or that the calf that yielded the veal cutlet on her plate spent its life in a box in which it did not have room to turn around. And, though her sympathy for the coleslaw might be less tender, she should not be encouraged to meditate on the hygienic and biological implications of mile-square fields of cabbage, for vegetables grown in huge monocultures are dependent on toxic chemicals just as animals in close confinement are dependent on antibiotics and other drugs.

The consumer, that is to say, must be kept from discovering that, in the food industry—as in any other industry—the overriding concerns are not quality and health but volume and price. For decades now the entire industrial food economy, from the large farms and feedlots to the chains of fast-food restaurants and supermarkets, has been obsessed with volume. It has relentlessly increased scale in order to increase volume in order (presumably) to reduce costs. But, as scale increases, diversity declines; as diversity declines, so does health; as health declines, the dependence on drugs and chemicals necessarily increases. As capital replaces labor, it does so by substituting machines, drugs, and chemicals for human workers and for the natural health and fertility of the soil. The food is produced by any means or any shortcuts that will increase profits. And the business of the cosmeticians of advertising is to persuade the consumer that food so produced is good, tasty, healthful, and a guarantee of marital fidelity and long life.

It is, then, indeed possible to be liberated from the husbandry and wifery of the old household food economy. But one can be thus liberated only by entering a trap—unless one sees ignorance and helplessness, as many people apparently do, as the signs of privilege. The trap is the ideal of industrialism: a walled city surrounded by valves that let merchandise in but no consciousness out. How does one escape this trap? Only voluntarily, the same way that one went in—by restoring one's consciousness of what is involved in eating, by reclaiming responsibility for one's own part in the food economy. One might begin with Sir Albert Howard's illuminating principle that we should understand "the whole problem of health in soil, plant, animal, and man as one great subject." Eaters, that is, must understand that eating takes place inescapably in the world, that it is inescapably an agricultural act, and that how we eat determines, to a considerable extent, the way the world is used. This is a simple way of describing a relationship that is inexpressibly complex. To eat responsibly is to understand and enact, so far as one can, this complex relationship.

What can one do? Here is a list, probably not definitive:

Participate in food production to the extent that you can. If you have a yard or even just a porch box or a pot in a sunny window, grow something to eat in it. Make a little compost of your kitchen scraps, and use it for fertilizer. Only by growing some food for yourself can you become acquainted with the beautiful energy cycle that revolves from soil to seed to flower to fruit to food to offal to decay, and around again. You will be fully responsible for any food that you grow for yourself, and you will know all about it. You will appreciate it fully, having known it all its life.

Prepare your own food. This means reviving in your own mind and life the arts of kitchen and household. This should enable you to eat more cheaply and give you a measure of "quality control." You will have some reliable knowledge of what has been added to the food you eat.

Learn the origins of the food you buy, and buy the food that is produced closest to your home. The idea that every locality should be, as much as possible, the source of its own food makes several kinds of sense. The locally produced food supply is the most secure, the freshest, and the easiest for local consumers to know about and to influence.

Whenever you can, deal directly with a local farmer, gardener, or orchardist. All the reasons listed for the previous suggestion apply here. In addition, by such dealing, you eliminate the whole pack of merchants, transporters, processors, packagers, and advertisers who thrive at the expense of both producers and consumers.

Learn, in self-defense, as much as you can of the economy and technology of industrial food production. What is added to food that is not food, and what do you pay for these additions?

Learn what is involved in the *best* farming and gardening.

Learn as much as you can, by direct observation and experience if possible, of the life histories of the food species.

The last suggestion seems particularly important to me. Many people are now as much estranged from the lives of domestic plants and animals (except for flowers and dogs and cats) as they are from the lives of the wild ones. This is regrettable, for these domestic creatures are in diverse ways attractive; there is much pleasure in knowing them. And, at their best, farming, animal husbandry, horticulture, and gardening are complex and comely arts; there is much pleasure in knowing them, too.

And it follows that there is great displeasure in knowing about a food economy that degrades and abuses those arts and those plants and animals and the soil from which they come. For anyone who does know something of the modern history of food, eating away from home can be a chore. My own inclination is to eat seafood instead of red meat or poultry when I am traveling. Though I am by no means a vegetarian, I dislike the thought that some animal has been made miserable in order to feed me. If I am going to eat meat, I want it to be from an animal that has lived a pleasant, uncrowded life outdoors, on bountiful pasture, with good water nearby and trees for shade. And I am getting almost as fussy about food plants. I like to eat vegetables and fruits that I know have lived happily and healthily in good soil—not the products of the huge, bechemicaled factory-fields that I have seen, for example, in the Central Valley of California. The industrial farm is said to have been patterned on the factory production line. In practice, it invariably looks more like a concentration camp.

The pleasure of eating should be an *extensive* pleasure, not that of the mere gourmet. People who know the garden in which their vegetables have grown and know that the garden is healthy will remember the beauty of the growing plants, perhaps in the dewy first light of morning when gardens are at their best. Such a memory involves itself with the food and is one of the pleasures of eating. The knowledge of the good health of the garden relieves and frees and comforts the eater. The same goes for eating meat. The thought of the good pasture, and of the calf contentedly grazing, flavors the steak. Some, I know, will think it bloodthirsty or worse to eat a fellow creature you have known all its life. On the contrary, I think, it means that you eat with understanding and with gratitude. A significant part of the pleasure of eating is in one's accurate consciousness of the lives and the world from which food comes. The pleasure of eating, then, may be the best available standard of our health. And this pleasure, I think, is pretty fully available to the urban consumer who will make the necessary effort.

I mentioned earlier the politics, aesthetics, and ethics of food. But to speak of the pleasure of eating is to go beyond those categories. Eating with the fullest pleasure—pleasure, that is, that does not depend on ignorance—is perhaps the profoundest enactment of our connection with the world. In this pleasure we experience and celebrate our dependence and our gratitude, for we are living from mystery, from creatures we did not make and powers we cannot comprehend. When I think of the meaning of food, I always remember these lines by the poet William Carlos Williams, which seem to me merely honest:

There is nothing to eat,
       seek it where you will,
             but the body of the Lord.
The blessed plants
       and the sea, yield it
           to the imagination
intact.

CHARLES SIMIC

On Food and Happiness

Sadness and good food are incompatible. The old sages knew that wine lets the tongue loose, but one can grow melancholy with even the best bottle, especially as one grows older. The appearance of food, however, brings instant happiness. A *paella*, a *choucroute garnie*, a pot of *tripes à la mode de Caen*, and so many other dishes of peasant origin guarantee merriment. The best talk is around that table. Poetry and wisdom are its company. The true Muses are cooks. Cats and dogs don't stray far from the busy kitchen. Heaven is a pot of chili simmering on the stove. If I were to write about the happiest days of my life, many of them would have to do with food and wine and a table full of friends.

> Homer never wrote on an empty stomach.
> —RABELAIS

One could compose an autobiography mentioning every memorable meal in one's life and it would probably make better reading than what one ordinarily gets. Honestly, what would you rather have? The description of a first kiss, or of stuffed cabbage done to perfection?

I have to admit, I remember better what I ate than what I thought. My memory is especially vivid about those far-off days from 1944 to 1949 in Yugoslavia when we were mostly starving. The black market flourished. Women exchanged their wedding rings and silk underwear for hams. Occasionally someone invited us to an illicit feast on a day everyone else was hungry.

I'll begin with the day I realized that there was more to food than just stuffing yourself. I was nine years old. I ate Dobrosav Cvetković's *burek*, and I can still see it and taste it when I close my eyes.

Burek is a kind of pie made with fillo dough and stuffed with either ground meat, cheese, or spinach. It is eaten everywhere in the Near East and Balkans. Like pizza today, it's usually good no matter where you get it, but it can also be a work of art. My father said that when Dobrosav retired from his bakery in Skopje, the mayor and his cronies, after realizing that he was gone, sent a police warrant after him. The cops brought him back in handcuffs! "Dobrosav," they said visiting him in jail, "how can you do a thing like that to us? At least make us one last *burek*, and then you can go wherever your heart desires."

I ate that famous *burek* forty-four years ago on a cold winter morning with snow falling. Dobrosav made it illegally in his kitchen and sold it to select customers who used to knock on his door and enter looking like foreign agents making a pickup. The day I was his guest—for the sake of my poor exiled father who was so good to Dobrosav—the *burek* came with meat. I ate every greasy crumb that fell out of my mouth on the table while old Dobrosav studied me the way a cat studies a bird in a cage. He wanted my opinion. I understood this was no fluke. Dobrosav knew something other *burek* makers did not. I believe I told him so. This was my first passionate outburst to a cook.

Then there was my aunt, Ivanka Bajalović. Every time I wiped my plate clean she shook her head sadly. "One day," she'd say to me, "I'll make so much food you won't be able to finish it." With my appetite in those days that seemed impossible, but she did it! She found a huge pot ordinarily used to make soap and filled it with beans to "feed an army," as the neighbors said.

All Serbians, of whatever gender or age, have their own opinion as to how this dish ought to be made. Some folk like it thicker, others soupier. Between the two extremes there are many nuances. Almost everybody adds bacon, pork ribs, sausage, paprika, and hot peppers. It's a class thing. The upper classes make it lean, the lower fatty. My aunt, who was educated in London and speaks English with a British accent to this day, made it like a ditchdigger's wife. The beans were spicy hot.

My uncle was one of those wonders of nature everybody envies, a skinny guy who could eat all day long and never gain any weight. I'm sad to admit that I've no idea how much we actually ate that day. Anywhere between three and five platefuls is a good guess. These were European soup plates, nice and roomy, that could take loads of beans. It was summer afternoon. We were eating on a big terrace watched by nosy neighbors who kept score. At some point, I remember, I just slid off my chair onto the floor.

I'm dying, it occurred to me. My uncle was still wielding the spoon with his face deep in the plate. There was a kind of hush. In the beginning, everybody talked and kidded around, but now my aunt was exhausted and had gone in to lie down. There were still plenty of beans, but I was through. I couldn't move. Finally, even my uncle staggered off to bed, and I was left alone, sitting under the table, the heat intolerable, the sun setting, my mind blurry, thinking this is how a pig must feel.

On May 9, 1950, I asked all my relatives to give me money instead of presents for my birthday. When they did, I spent the entire day going with a friend from one pastry shop to another. We ate huge quantities of cream puffs, custard rolls, *dobos torta*, rum balls, pishingers, strudels with poppy seed, and other Viennese and Hungarian pastries. At dusk we had no money left. We were dragging ourselves in the general vicinity of the Belgrade railroad station when a man, out of breath and carrying a large suitcase, overtook us. He wondered if we could carry it for him to the station and we said we could. The suitcase was very heavy and it made a noise like it was full of silverware or burglar's tools, but we managed somehow to get it to his train. There, he surprised us by paying us handsomely for our good deed. Without a moment's thought we returned to our favorite pastry shop, which was closing at that hour and where the help eyed us with alarm as we ordered more ice cream and cake.

In 1951 I lived an entire summer in a village on the Adriatic coast. Actually, the house my mother, brother, and I roomed at was a considerable distance from the village on a stretch of sandy beach. Our landlady, a war widow, was a fabulous cook. In her home I ate squid for the first time and began my lifelong love affair with olives. All her fish was grilled with a little olive oil, garlic, and parsley. I still prefer it that way.

My favorite dish was a plate of tiny surf fish called *girice*, which were fried in corn flour. We'd eat them with our fingers, head and all. Since it's no good to swim after lunch, all the guests would take a long siesta. I remember our deliciously cool room, the clean sheets, the soothing sound of the sea, the aftertaste and smell of the fish, and the long naps full of erotic dreams.

There were two females who obsessed me in that place. One was a theater actress from Zagreb in the room next to ours who used to sunbathe with her bikini top removed when our beach was deserted and I was hiding in the bushes. The other was our landlady's sixteen-year-old daughter. I sort of tagged along after her. She must have been bored out of her wits to allow a thirteen-year-old boy to keep her company. We used to swim out to a rock in the bay where there were wild grapes. We'd lie sunbathing and popping the little blue grapes in our mouths. And in the evening, once or twice, there was even a kiss, and then an exquisite risotto with mussels.

He that with his soup will drink,
When he's dead won't sleep a wink.

—OLD FRENCH SONG

In Paris I went to what can only be described as a school for losers. These were youngsters who were not destined for further glories of French education, but were en route to being petty bureaucrats and tradespeople. We ate lunch in school, and the food was mostly tolerable. We even drank red wine. The vegetable soup served on Tuesdays, however, was out of this world. One of the fat ladies I saw milling in the kitchen must have been a southerner, because the soup had a touch of Provence. For some reason, the other kids didn't care for it. Since the school rule was that you had to *manger* everything in your plate, and since I loved the soup so much, my neighbors at the table would let me have theirs. I'd end up by eating three or four servings of that thick concoction with tomatoes, green and yellow beans, potatoes, carrots, white beans, noodles, and herbs. After that kind of eating, I usually fell asleep in class after lunch only to be rudely awakened by one of my teachers and ordered to a blackboard already covered with numbers. I'd stand there bewildered and feeling sleepy while time changed into eternity, and nobody budged or said anything, and my only solace was the lingering taste in my mouth of that divine soup.

Some years back I found myself in Genoa at an elegant reception in Palazzo Doria talking with the Communist mayor. "I love American food," he blurted out to me after I mentioned enjoying the local cuisine. I asked him what he had in mind. "I love potato chips," he told me. I had to agree, potato chips were pretty good.

When we came to the United States in 1954, it now seems like that's all my brother and I ate. We sat in front of the TV eating potato chips out of huge bags. Our parents approved. We were learning English and being American. It's a wonder we have any teeth left today. We visited the neighborhood supermarket twice a day to sightsee the junk food. There were so many things to taste, and we were interested in them all. There was deviled ham, marshmallows, Spam, Hawaiian Punch, Fig Newtons, V-8 Juice, Mounds, Planter's Peanuts, and so much else, all good. Everything was good in America except for Wonder Bread, which we found disgusting.

It took me a few years to come to my senses. One day I met Salvatore. He told me I ate like a dumb shit, and took me home to his mother. Sal and his three brothers were all well employed, unmarried, living at home, and giving their paychecks to Mom. The father was dead, so there were just these four boys to feed. She did not stop cooking. Every meal was like a peasant wedding feast. Of course, her sons didn't appreciate it as far as she was concerned. "Are you crazy, Mom?" they'd shout in a chorus each time she brought in another steaming dish. The old lady didn't flinch. The day I came she was happy to have someone else at the table who was more appreciative, and I did not spare the compliments.

She cooked southern Italian dishes. Lots of olive oil and garlic. I recollect with a sense of heightened consciousness her linguine with anchovies. We drank red Sicilian wine with it. She'd put several open bottles on the table before the start of the meal. I never saw anything like it. She'd lie to us and say there was nothing more to eat so we'd have at least two helpings, and then she'd bring some sausage and peppers, and some kind of roast after that.

After the meal we'd remain at the table, drinking and listening to old records of Beniamino Gigli and Feruccio Tagliavini. The old lady would still be around, urging on us a little more cheese, a little more cake. And then, just when we thought she had given up and gone to bed, she'd surprise us by bringing out a dish of fresh figs.

My late father, who never in his life refused another helping at the table, had a peculiarity common among gastronomes. The more he ate the more he talked about food. My mother was always amazed. We'd be done with a huge turkey roasted over sauerkraut and my father would begin reminiscing about a little breakfast-like sausage he had in some village on the Rumanian border in 1929, or a fish soup a blind woman made for him in Marseilles in 1945. Well, she wasn't completely blind, and besides she was pretty to look at—in any case, after three or four stories like that we'd be hungry again. My father had a theory that if you were still hungry, say for a hot dog, after a meal at Lutece, that meant that you were extraordinarily healthy. If a casual visitor to your house was not eating and drinking three minutes after his arrival, you had no manners. For people who had no interest in food, he absolutely had no comprehension. He'd ask them questions like an anthropologist, and go away seriously puzzled and worried. He told me toward the end of his life that the greatest mistake he ever made was accepting his doctor's advice to eat and drink less after he passed seventy-five. He felt terrible until he went back to his old ways.

One day we are walking up Second Avenue and talking. We get into an elaborate philosophical argument, as we often did. I feel like I've understood everything! I'm inspired! I'm quoting Kant, Descartes, Wittgenstein, when I notice he's no longer with me. I look around and locate him a block back staring into a shop window. I'm kind of pissed, especially since I have to walk to where he's standing, for he doesn't move or answer to my shouts. Finally, I tap him on the shoulder and he looks at me, dazed. "Can you believe that?" he says and points to a window full of Hungarian smoked sausages, salamis, and pork rinds.

My friend, Mike De Porte, whose grandfather was a famous St. Petersburg lawyer and who in his arguments combines a Dostoevskian probity and his grandfather's jurisprudence, claims that such obsession with food is the best proof that we have of the existence of the soul. Ergo, long after the body is satisfied, the soul is not. "Does that mean," I asked him, "that the soul is never satisfied?" He has not given me his answer yet. My own notion is that it is a supreme sign of happiness. When our souls are happy, they talk about food.

JOYCE CAROL OATES

Food Mysteries

Appetite is a kind of passion, and bears the same relationship to food and drink as passion bears to the "loved object." Borne along irresistibly by the momentum of both, we never question our destination, still less its mysterious source. Nor should we.

Food doesn't exist, but can only be invented. Eating is one of the very few volitional human activities—perhaps it is the single one—that continues uninterrupted from birth to death, its source "infantile" and its refinements "adult."

The invention of food as "food"—the "loved object"—is the imagination's attempt to (re)create the act of eating as, not passive, not infantile, but active, "adult." The instinctive physical act is appropriated by the conscious self, made into a kind of artwork. A kind of poetry.

A hypothesis: Civilization is the multiplicity of strategies, dazzling as precious gems inlaid in a golden crown, to obscure from human beings the sound of, the terrible meaning of, their jaws grinding.

The meaning of man's place in the food cycle that, by way of our imaginations, we had imagined might not apply to *us*.

* * *

He said, and truly he did not mean to astonish, or offend, or disturb me: "What I think about—what I *really* think about are sleeping, and eating. In that order." And there came then a long pause, a pause of years.

(He was a poet, a distinguished American man of letters. Never famous beyond the literary world, which honored him with every prize you can think of, he had a reputation that seemed at the time inviolable, peaking in the late 1950s when his species of poetry—mandarin, allusive, elegantly and always ironically crafted—seemed all that poetry might be. Decades later this poetry, though still politely admired, is probably not much read. What haunts me about the man, gazing up benignly at me out of his obituary-image in this morning's *New York Times*, is that remark he made so casually, so quietly, in a way so intimately, to a very young woman writer, an undergraduate admirer of his work, as if to dispel the myth in another's eyes of his brilliance, his talent, his vocation for poetry, his very identity. "What I think about—what I *really* think about are sleeping, and eating." So I saw then that there might be some solace after all—some respite, given us by nature, by our own nature, from the fascination and the tyranny of the imagination.)

*   *   *

Alienation. At the periphery of the solemn communal feast at which the dead tribesman (or -woman) is being ritually dismembered, cooked, and devoured, there are surely those mourners who, this time, would just as soon *not* partake of the sacred food . . . but content themselves with the more ordinary grubs, crocodile eggs, pemmican-mash.

The gourmet. Newly returned from a year's visiting professorship at Berkeley, our friend reminisced dreamily of the 1989 earthquake: he'd felt tremors; by chance, he'd happened to see a section of the Bay Bridge collapse, at a distance; he'd hurried to see early, frightening reports of the disaster on television. His immediate response was to telephone Chez Panisse—"I had a hunch I could get reservations there for the next night, for dinner, and I was right."

Wittgenstein, who is said to have said that he didn't care in the slightest what he ate—so long as it was the identical food every day.
    Either one understands this without question, or one does not.

*   *   *

Food is love, as the truism has it. And so to offer food to others may be to offer love; consequently some of us are shy, in the anticipation of being rebuffed.

*   *   *

For the writer, the writing offered to other people is a kind of food. Thus the writer's peculiar vulnerability, risking rebuff, misunderstanding. *What nourishment!* some may exclaim. *What garbage!* others may exclaim.

Which is why, for sheer delight, writers turn to real food.

Poets make the best cooks. Prose writers, the most appreciative friends of poets.

For some, the crucial test of character is, or will one day be: *Can I eat alone?*

*   *   *

American nostalgia. There are adults of middle age in whom the sudden acrid smells of cafeteria food (scorched macaroni-and-cheese casserole, canned spaghetti with tomato sauce, grease-encrusted french fries, "beef doves," "shepherd's pie," "Texas hash," et al) galvanize taste buds dormant since eighth grade, with a hungry violence rarely experienced since eighth grade: but it is better not to be one of these.

Betrayal. He said, out of earshot of the others, "When I hear the word 'cuisine,' I reach for my revolver." And his friend, married to a woman as devoted to cooking, dinner parties, as the hostess of tonight's party, was taken by surprise, and laughed—but guiltily.

ORANGE: the poem. I was sick with what was called the Hong Kong flu, and I had lost my ability to taste, and to smell; and so I'd lost my appetite. So sick, so miserably sick, we have all been sick in exactly this way yet how to speak of it? how to indicate the dull dead weight of the malaise? when, in a nightmare cocoon of aching head, aching joints, fever, chills, intermittent nausea and diarrhea, when simply to speak is an effort that isn't worth it, simply to turn your head on a pillow can require twenty minutes, and you discover yourself on a plane of being that, though wretchedly physical, is simultaneously metaphysical, as if gazing down in horror and pity at your own bodily predicament—how to speak of it?

We have all been sick in this way, and will surely be sick in this way again, unable to taste food, unable to smell food thus to taste food, bereft of appetite, yet, once we regain our health, our presumed normality, we quickly forget: nothing seems so natural to us as *taste, smell, appetite*.

Yet, how to define such phenomena, though we inhabit them. Their presence, their absence. Their mysterious return.

When what you eat tastes like paper pulp, it is very difficult to take eating seriously. The ritual of meals, the preparation and presentation and consumption; the "little touches" that make us civilized, thus not merely two-legged appetites, anonymous bearers of DNA to the future—candlelight, linen napkins, good cutlery, good company. The condition of being human depends upon being able not merely to eat, chew, swallow, digest food, but to stand in a relationship vis-à-vis food that makes it a substance of value and not "food"—a substance that, when chewed, is indistinguishable from paper pulp.

Without appetite, why live?—for life *is* appetite. That lovely flickering upright flame that, lacking other fuel, will consume itself.

Without appetite, you wake up to find yourself in an eerie zone of existence inhabited, analogously, by the color-blind, the tone-deaf, the illiterate; the one-eyed, who are said to experience the world flat, as animated wallpaper.

Without appetite, you begin to lose not only yourself but your memory and conception of yourself, your personal mythology, so intimately bound up with rituals of eating, sharing food, sociability. To sit at a table with others, even those you love, revulsed by the food they eat, and seem actually to enjoy, you feel the chill of the abyss as never before.

Without appetite, steadily losing weight and noting with a grim pleasure how readily flesh melts from your bones, you experience the anorexic's fatally sweet revelation: *I* am not *this*, after all.

The vanity of being without human wishes.

The vanity of "fasting" to no purpose—that ostensibly religious/spiritual activity whose intention is to detach the mind from the body, as if that were possible, or in any way desirable.

Yet, for many, how seductive! How sweetly fatal.

For our relationship to food makes us human, and our repudiation of a relationship to food is a repudiation of our humanity as well. We come to imagine ourselves superior to others—those with appetites!—as, growing ever sicker, weaker, we deteriorate physically. As the deluded "mystic" Simone Weil prayed, "May God grant that I become nothing"—even as, with a martyr's angry zeal, she methodically starved herself to death.

Yet, in such states, in the radiance of a hunger beyond hunger, every instant flashes with the feel of eternity; the most wayward of light-headed thoughts is an epiphany; consciousness, heightened to the point of pain, makes the subject a razor, scintillating, deathly sharp, cutting through the dull surfaces of the world. Who has not been in this place, and who does not recall it, half-shamefully, as one of the radiant regions of the soul, a lure into the abyss, and into death . . . ? Though it may be called by other names. Of course, it is always called by other names.

In time, naturally, the Hong Kong flu ran its course, in thousands of others in North America (this was in the mid-1970s), and in me. What marked the beginning of health, health's shaky return, for me, was such a small thing: an orange: the sharp, pungent smell of the citrus fruit, and its peel—the first thing I had been able to smell in about two weeks. The smell of an orange! the smell of orange peel! And then by degrees, almost shyly at first, the taste of the orange . . . the vivid, acetic, miraculous *taste*.

Nothing else had the slightest taste, it seemed, except this orange, which I ate slowly, haltingly, as one might grope in the dark, or try to walk after a long illness. And suddenly I was tasting, not *nothing*, to which I had become accustomed, but *something*—and feeling, not nausea, but hunger. Again.

It seemed to me then, and seems to me now, that there is nothing more delicious than an orange. The very sound of the word, the dazzling exotic color that shimmers inside the word, is a poem of surpassing beauty, complete in this line:

Orange

*   *   *

He must have been . . . memorable. The Boston University professor of biology and German who, year after year, until his death in 1940, horrified his captive audience of students with a laboratory demonstration meant to expose their irrational attitude toward food: he skinned a dead rat in front of them, sliced some meat off the bones, sautéed the meat in a pan, and ate it, with the commentary that rat meat might be commonly considered disgusting and inedible in our society, but "it is really no different from rabbit meat, which people have eaten as a delicacy for centuries."*

He *must* have been memorable, the posthumous "Daddy," Dr. Otto Plath, of Sylvia Plath's poem.

*   *   *

The secret memoir that is a compilation of those persons with whom you have shared a great intimacy: preparing food together.

The secret memoir that is a compilation of those persons, friends, relatives, acquaintances, strangers whom you would invite to the dinner that is *the* dinner of your life as a cook. And the seating arrangement.

The secret memoir that is a compilation of the foods you once ate, and ate with zest, now banished from your life, denied, or, with the passage of time, simply lost: . . . Tootsie Rolls and Mallow Cups and Milky Ways and Mars Bars . . . Juicy Fruit and Dentyne . . . Hostess Cupcakes . . . pies that fit into the palm of your hand, to be eaten on the sidewalk outside the store . . . pop-, fudg-, and creamsicles of all lurid flavors . . . peanut butter sandwiches on soft white pulpy Wonder Bread . . . The Royale (hot fudge banana split with cherries, walnuts, whipped cream, decorated with a crown of sugar wafers—the specialty of the ice cream parlor) . . . glazed doughnuts, grease-saturated doughnuts, frosted doughnuts, Freddie's Doughnuts (specialty of a Buffalo bakery: immense, sweet, doughy, covered in confectioner's sugar and filled to bursting with whipped cream) . . . the shamelessly salty, greasy hamburgers, cheeseburgers, hot dogs, and french fries sold for human consumption in the Lockport, New York, area . . . the shamelessly salty, greasy, and stale popcorn sold in theater lobbies everywhere . . . pizza (of all varieties) . . . triple-layer devil's food cake with fudge frosting . . . strawberry-banana cream pie with "Nabisco-wafer crust" . . . southern fried chicken, and sweet-glazed ham steaks baked with canned pineapple rings . . . homemade chicken soup brimming with globules of fat . . . all red meats, but especially fat-webbed roasts and 8-oz. sirloins . . . breaded things (fish, fowl, animal) . . . fish sticks dipped in catsup . . . Planter's Peanuts, so greasy and salty your fingers began to smart, eaten directly from the can . . . Royal Crown Root Beer, especially when insufficiently cold . . . cheese omelets the size of automobile hubcaps . . . canned pork and beans . . . canned applesauce . . . canned salmon

---

*Paul Alexander, Rough Magic: A Biography of Sylvia Plath (New York: Viking, 1991), p. 12.

. . . iceberg lettuce wilting beneath dollops of "Russian" dressing . . . the specialty (canned) fruit cup that is served only as a first course at formal, institutionally catered meals in your honor . . . the Parker House rolls that accompany the fruit cup . . . and the excruciatingly sweet, cloying, thick blueberry pancakes I prepared as a young wife, Sunday mornings in Detroit, in our single-bedroom uncarpeted apartment south of Palmer Park, festive concoctions out of a Pillsbury mix, presumably delicious, for, otherwise, how could we have eaten them?

*   *   *

The literary acquaintance whom we met for lunch at a small Greek restaurant in Soho, the several of us visiting Americans in London, who opened a menu, glared at it, sipped his drink, said, "Anything's all right with me—it's all the same garbage." And I thought, I never want to see this man again, and I never did.

*   *   *

Food taboos. Food customs. Our ancestors' curious conviction that *God cares what we eat, and when, and how prepared.*

Food doesn't exist, but can only be invented. And reinvented.

So many unexamined taboos and customs surround food—the selection, the preparation, the serving, the eating, even the speaking of it afterward—it is virtually impossible to know what food *is*, other than that we are defined by it and obsessed by it.

From the rituals of food no less than from food itself, there is no escape. Not so long as we remain human.

This is being composed in Princeton, New Jersey. Where the mere glimmer of the mere possibility of a *new restaurant* will be discussed as avidly as the recent Gulf War in the early days of the war.

Where, at painstakingly prepared, elegant, delicious, multicourse meals, men and women will dreamily reminisce of other meals, often in French or Italian restaurants.

Where the late R. P. Blackmur is best remembered, or remembered exclusively by some, for his quip about watching Edmund Wilson eat spaghetti: "It was enough to make you lose your faith in human nature."

Where some gourmet practitioners choose their menu, and the date of their dinner party, and bring together a haphazard assortment of guests to fill the seats at the table—mere afterthoughts.

Food mysteries are so primary, so stark, they may strike us as juvenile. Why food on the plate is aesthetically pleasing, yet, once masticated, repulsive to contemplate. Why actual, ravenous hunger, at a dinner party for instance, would be terrifying to see, deeply disturbing to those for whom the food ritual is primarily social and rigidly controlled. Why, as Dr. Otto Plath scornfully taught, there are foods that are considered "disgusting and edible" that are in fact "delicacies"—in the proper context.

The ingesting of food is a social ritual; the elimination of food, by any means, is a social taboo, however it may be a private, universal necessity. Why?—the child may ask.

To which the adult can only reply, Don't ask.

For there is no answer, only custom. Taboo.

It will evoke disgust in my readers if I describe one of the most peculiarly memorable experiences I've had at any public, ceremonial meal; memorable in the primary sense, it cannot be dislodged from my memory. And, yes, it *is* disgusting. It was.

A prominent American poet, a patrician elder, having drunk too much at an elaborate luncheon at the American Academy and Institute of Arts and Letters (you know the setting: idyllic, beneath tents, on the flagstone terrace, in May), suddenly vomited onto his plate of food, while a table of twelve or thirteen others looked on in helpless disgust. The poet patted his mouth with his napkin, mumbled a vague apology, made no effort to leave. A uniformed young waiter with a carefully composed face hurriedly carried the quivering mess away; there was a brief embarrassed silence; then conversations resumed. In my memory, everyone, except the poet, began talking at once, loudly.

Unfazed by what another might have seen as mortifying behavior, especially in the company of such fellow Olympians, the poet asked for another drink, and more food—and, a few minutes later, incredibly, again having made no effort to leave the table, he again vomited onto his plate; again everyone looked on, with expressions ranging from dismay to revulsion to disbelief to embarrassment to impatience to outright disgust. Another time, the poet patted his mouth with his napkin, and mumbled an apology. His face was pale, his eyes rather bloodshot. A waiter came forward to carry the quivering mess away . . . but by this time I had made my escape from the table, drifting off into the interior as if seeking a ladies' room, as one must do in any case at these tedious formal gatherings that so test our capacity for sitting! sitting! sitting to no purpose, as if adulthood, achieved at last, were but a child's malicious parody of adulthood after all.

In the corridors of the old, poorly ventilated Academy building, perspiring waiters were piling trays of dirtied plates and glasses onto carts; what remained uneaten of the gourmet poached salmon, the vegetables julienne, the crusty rolls was most unceremoniously being scraped off as garbage; even as, borne aloft on spotless trays, the bavarian cream, or chocolate rum charlotte russe, or blitz tortes, whatever, were being carried in to the luncheon guests—the final course of the multicourse meal. If there is a gourmet food, is there a gourmet garbage? Or is garbage sheerly democratic, like vomit? I don't remember now if, like some others at our table, I was offended by the poet's behavior—not his being sick, which perhaps could not have been prevented, but his curious insouciant behavior regarding his sickness; or whether I was simply . . . struck by it. I certainly never forgot it. It seemed to me a melancholy thing that a man of such distinction should behave in such a way, but, who knows, perhaps that was the way he liked to behave, flaunting not merely convention but taboo; his poetry has much anger in it, and deep misanthropy, for all its formalist precision.

He was the very man who, years before, had told me that what he *really* thought about was sleeping, and eating. In that order.

Sleeping, and eating. The mystery at the heart of our human existence seems to me inextricably bound up with these phenomena. How to formulate it except to hypothesize, somewhat awkwardly, that it has to do with the relationship between our highly developed, unique personalities and the purely physical, impersonal, and even anonymous beings that contain them; the paradox that there is a *not-I* upon which the *I* floats, like a ball at the top of a jet of water—when the jet of water ceases, the ball topples down. Though the perspective from the top may be splendid, perspectives are relative.

Not just the physiological self, the perpetually hungry, eating, food-besotted self, but the nighttime, dreaming self as well—these rebuff our attempts to understand them, let alone define and control them. Mysterious as we are to one another, we are equally mysterious to ourselves. And this mystery deepens with time, when we see that answers to our questions are in continual retreat, like desert mirages.

Sleeping, and eating. The perimeters of the self. One third of a lifetime spent in, surrendered to, sleep. One third! As if there existed a nighttime self, a dreaming self only tenuously related to the daytime self: the *not-I* we inhabit. And eating: how many hundreds of thousands of hours out of a lifetime are spent in eating—in the choosing of food, the preparation of food, the chewing, swallowing, digesting of food. And the talk. Talk of food. Endless. Inexhaustible. Recipes, restaurants. Talk of meals past, passing, or to come. (As for wine—a complete galaxy, with its own vocabulary.) For some, food is so boring as to constitute the greatest of challenges for the writer—how to say anything interesting about it at all. For others, food is an obsession, a fetish, and all daytime activities are ways of filling in time between meals. There may even be those for whom food is both boring and obsessive. And those who gamely try, in our gastronomically sophisticated culture, to pass as if they are sophisticates too—gourmets like their friends and colleagues. Food writers, even.

*   *   *

There is an intimate, methodical, deeply engrossing and rewarding activity I do, and have done, with only one person in my lifetime: this is the activity of cooking, and I do and have done it only with my mother, Carolina Oates.

Now, it happens that the cooking we do together is nearly always done in my kitchen, in Princeton, New Jersey. In the past, of course, it was done in my mother's kitchen, in Millersport, New York, and my earliest memories of preparing meals have to do with helping my mother. For a small child, preparing meals is serious play, adult play; for me to have been initiated into it, on even the most modest terms (setting the oven, getting out utensils, rubbing a stick of butter on a sheet of waxed paper, frosting a cake with a knife) was enormously exciting. Though I have virtually no memory of myself as a little girl, I remember vividly the kitchen in our old house, a farmhouse long since razed, where we prepared and ate our meals for many years: It was upstairs in my parents' half of the house (my mother's adoptive parents, whose house it was, lived downstairs), walls painted a light cheery yellow, a big round electric clock over the stove, shiny linoleum tile on the floor, counter, cupboards, and drawers built by my father running the length of one wall.

So much of the house, the interior in particular, was built, or refashioned, by my father, it was as if we'd lived in his handiwork—though that was hardly a perception I would have had at the time.

The foods I helped my mother prepare are quite commonplace, for the most part, probably identical with the foods of most of my contemporaries, given similar economic backgrounds. We were not what one would call well to do, but living on a farm, even a small farm, had its obvious advantages. We had chickens, Rhode Island Reds, thus a steady supply of eggs, and chicken for special occasions; there was a mad interlude, rather like the pilot for a doomed situation comedy, when my father, a city boy by nature, tried to raise pigs; we had our own potatoes, corn, carrots, tomatoes, et al, in summer; we had pear, apple, and cherry trees, which seemed to have produced fruit as rapidly as my father could pick it. My memories of the old farmhouse in Millersport have much to do with the aromas of cooking—the long hours of simmering spaghetti sauce on the stove, made of course with our own tomatoes, but considerably "spiced up"; the scalding, eviscerating, feather-plucking of chickens, and the long hours, too, of the cooking of chicken soup; the sugary-syrupy smell of fruit being prepared for canning, or made into jams and jellies. (How tedious canning was! And how to recall such childhood foods while acknowledging that, for my mother and grandmother, who did all this cooking, day following day and year following year, the experience could hardly have been an idyllic one.) My grandmother, who was from Budapest, made rich, heavy, sour cream–dolloped goulashes and a dish whose anemic American analogue is chicken paprika; she made her own noodle dough, of course, rolling the stiff dough into flat layers on the kitchen table, stacking the layers carefully together, cutting them briskly with a long-bladed knife into noodles, which were then set aside, on cloth, to dry. Her most intricate specialties were Hungarian pastries that required such patience and skill that my mother, a very capable cook, never learned to make them: one consisted of thin, large pancakes prepared in a big iron skillet, and filled with fruit and sour cream; another, yet more complicated, was rolled to airy thinness on her round kitchen table, filled similarly with fruit and sour cream, then rolled up tight, baked, cut, and served in small dishes.*

I never learned to prepare any Hungarian dish. I never learned a word of Hungarian.

We were Roman Catholic and, on Fridays, at that time meatless by a decree of the Church, we ate "fish dishes"—salmon patties fried in a skillet, creamed tuna with peas on toast. Except for the toast, these ingredients came out of cans; I must have been fairly grown by the time I grasped the concept that salmon and tuna *are* in fact fish, and quite sizable.

*Variations on the traditional Hungarian pancakes and strudels—almás palacsinta, egri félgömbpalacsinta, and rétesek.

Does God care what we eat? I used to wonder. Even when I seem to have accepted my elders' vague belief in God (of Whom in any case we never spoke), I thought this not a very likely prospect.

My Hungarian grandfather began his day, at his early breakfast, with swigs of hard cider from a stoneware crock placed on the floor by his heel. That was just the beginning.

It must have been my grandfather who beheaded the chickens, but I have no memory of these bloody scenes. As a child I was entrusted with some of the care of the chickens, feeding, egg gathering, and I even made a pet of one of them, I was sensitive and tenderhearted . . . I think. Certainly the eviscerating, feather-plucking, and diligent cleaning of the carcasses with their pale, pimpled skin turned my stomach, as did the smell, *the awful smell!* of the procedure. Yet I can't seem to recall a single visual image of a chicken being butchered, the frenzied wing-flapping and squawking as the bird is brought to the chopping block, the swing of the ax, the headless neck spouting blood in the dirt, and the body still twitching as if animated, sometimes running in spasmodic circles—I know that this is what must have happened, and must have happened many times during my childhood, but my mind is blank, as with an amnesia wash. This too may be a food mystery in my life, and helps account for the fact that I find unacceptable the idea of eating any living creature, but especially the more highly developed warm-blooded creatures, while, at the same time, I don't really want to think about it. At least not in a recollection of those playful sessions when my pretty young mother, years younger than her daughter is now, taught me how to cook.

* * *

She was naturally an articulate, fluent young woman, and she was certainly a very attractive young woman, and these were friends of hers genuinely interested in why she had broken off what had appeared to be a serious relationship with a man; but she was having difficulty explaining herself. She still felt very strongly about her former lover, she said, but there was something about his past, he'd been a foster child, living in a series of foster homes, and in some of the homes he and the other children and the adults of the household would sit together at the table and pass around bowls of food and sometimes, not all the time but sometimes, enough to have lodged deeply in his memory, there wasn't enough food to go around . . . and, at mealtimes even now, in certain circumstances, he was susceptible to sudden attacks of anxiety, panic, stomach cramps, even nausea. This wasn't why, she said quickly, she had decided to break off with him, she really didn't know why she'd decided to break off with him except she knew, she said, she would never be able to give him "as much as he'd want."

JUDITH B. JONES

A Religious Art

One day this summer I found that my husband had posted on the refrigerator door—a catchall for all food notes in our house—this quotation:

> Cooking is one of those arts which most requires to be done by persons of a religious nature.
>
> —DIALOGUES OF ALFRED NORTH WHITEHEAD

Evan knew that that thought would delight me because I have always felt that the preparation of food is one of the most joyous and inwardly satisfying of all activities that we as human beings are peculiarly privileged to indulge in daily. Other creatures receive food simply as fodder. But when we take the raw materials of the earth and work with them— touch them, manipulate them, taste them, revel in their heady smells and glorious colors, and then through a bit of alchemy transform them into delicious creations—we do honor to the source from whence they sprang. Cooking demands attention, patience, and, above all, a respect for the gifts of the earth. It is a form of worship, a way of giving thanks.

The first time you make a loaf of bread, you usually experience, particularly if you are a child, an exciting sense that you are actually giving life to an inert lump of flour and water. You watch the dormant yeast become active (it's even more thrilling if you've done your own fermentation from scratch and captured the wild yeast cells that may be lurking in your kitchen). Then you knead the dough and feel it transformed from a sticky, lumpy paste to a cohesive mass that is smooth and resilient and bouncy under the heels of your hands. When you poke it, it springs back at you. It is alive. Sometimes it forms bubbles and blisters in its eagerness to expand; it doubles, triples in volume. And then after it has been punched and tamed, it responds to the heat of the oven, rising again, settling into the shape you have given it, and sending forth the most tantalizing aroma as it bakes. No wonder that through the ages we've endowed bread with symbolic meaning: the staff of life, the bread of heaven, the body of Christ.

Often when I look at the carts at the supermarkets laden with frozen dinners and other quickie foods that need only be heated in the microwave, which doesn't even give forth any smell as the food is zapped, I feel sorry for the people who are missing out on the rewarding experience of cooking. Wendell Berry wrote in *The Unsettling of America* that "If you take away from food the wholeness of growing it or take away the joy and conviviality of preparing it in your own home, then I believe you are talking about a whole new definition of the human being." I know in my bones exactly what he means.

I think of evenings in northern Vermont, where we live part of the year, running across the lawn to gather salad greens. I always wait to do it just before dinner because the light at that moment is so beautiful—the grass, the herbs, the various shades of the greens so luminous in the intensity of the setting sun. I feel deeply connected to these things that we have grown and that will now nourish us.

The first year we bought our place, before we had planted anything, we were fortunate to meet Adele Dawson, who gives workshops around the state on medicinal herbs and wild edibles (she's a gifted dowser, too). We asked her to walk the woods and pastures with us so we could recognize some of the wild plants around us. I learned about the little tongues of sorrel that spring up all over, about the shoots, flowers, and pods of milkweed, each stage a different taste and texture, which kinds of ferns made fiddleheads, how the poisonous chokecherry turns benign when cooked, and many more mysteries. The woods, I discovered, were full of raspberries and blackberries, and I would go picking deeper and deeper into the dark stillness of our mountain forest, reaching for yet one more plump, juicy berry to add to my hoard. I felt at one with the musty earth and grateful for the treasures it yielded; even the fear of coming face to face with a black bear abated because I was certain that with such abundance he couldn't begrudge me my small share of his supper.

I think, too, of the many months of the year in New York when I am far removed from the sources of our food and how much pleasure a few herbs grown on a sunny windowsill or a sack of stoneground flour, still smelling of the granary, can bring to our ninth-floor kitchen. These days in most cities we can all browse in farmers' markets, talking to the families who have grown the fruits and vegetables, exchanging information. I remember once being asked what I was going to do with a big bunch of basil I'd bought (that was years ago; now everyone knows). I learned that Brussels sprouts are at their best, still clinging to their tall stalks, after a frost has touched them, and that gooseberries should be green and hard to yield the best flavor when cooked. Once I took home live eels. The fishman from Long Island said he didn't have time to kill them (or was he testing me?); fortunately, by the time I got home they had smothered in the bag so we didn't have to whack them on the head.

But what about all the time it takes, one is constantly asked—all the shopping, tracking down of choice produce, hours of attention lavished on the preparation of a meal? I guess to many people in our world of modern conveniences, it is irrational. But then most pursuits "of a religious nature" are irrational. In addition, there's the complaint that the results of our cooking labors disappear so rapidly, gulped down in a matter of minutes, that it hardly seems worth it. Jane Grigson, however, regarded this quick consumption as a blessing. "Cooking something delicious," she wrote in *Good Things*, "is really much more satisfactory than painting pictures or making pottery. At least for most of us. Food has the tact to disappear, leaving room and opportunity for masterpieces to come. The mistakes don't hang on the walls or stand on shelves to reproach you forever. It follows from this that the kitchen should be thought of as the centre of the house. It needs above all space for talking, playing, bringing up children, sewing, having a meal, reading, sitting, and thinking. . . . It's in this kind of place that good food has flourished. It's from this secure retreat that the exploration of man's curious relationship with food, beyond the point of nourishment, can start."

But even though our efforts disappear, we do derive great pleasure from them. We enjoy the sharing, the bustle and mess of that kitchen Jane Grigson describes, children licking the bowl, a guest pitching in, someone setting a table nicely—all the rituals that precede the main event. It is fun to tease and tempt another's palate with what we have created. We love to feel, as we hear appreciative murmurs and smacks of approval, that we have contributed in such a fundamental way to someone else's well-being.

Recently Ed Giobbi, the painter and wonderful Italian family cook, gave me a new insight into the nurturing aspect of cooking, particularly for a man. He told me that when his wife was pregnant many years ago and more recently when his daughter was about to give him his first grandchild, both times he felt left out and frustrated that he couldn't participate somehow in the process of birth. But he discovered that he could: all he had to do was cook for them, prepare naturally healthy foods that would nourish both the mother and the child she was carrying, bring tempting dishes to the hospital at the time of birth, and then make wholesome meals at home as she nurtured the infant. In fact, we are talking about his doing a cookbook on the husband/father as nurturer and about the proper feeding of the young.

Ed would deny, I'm sure, that all this had anything to do with "a religious nature," just as Julia Child hooted when I showed her the Whitehead quotation. But I've been pursuing the root of the word "religious" and I find that it is thought to spring from *religare,* meaning to bind, to tie fast, to reconnect. Isn't that exactly what we do when we cook? We connect again to the earth, to the source of our food, and we bind to one another in the sharing of it, in the breaking of bread together, the celebrating of life.

M.F.K. FISHER

One Way to Give Thanks

There could not be a better place for Thanksgiving than the vineyards of northern California, where we were. There could not, in truth, be more to give thanks for: two of the sisters and their families living within calling distance over the bright leaves of the plucked frost-nipped vines, in the valley rimmed with blue mountains, and another sister not more than a hundred miles away. All of us were friendly to the point of open enjoyment, a good rare thing in a family and especially to be savored at this turn-point of the year.

Norah would have us all at her house for the solemn, giddy festival. Anne would bring the wines. I would, I said, roast two birds of proper age and size.

Norah would set out the long table, which with help from lendings could stretch from the middle of the farmhouse kitchen through the big folding doors into the living room, with my red-checked tablecloths, her glasses, a general assemblage of plates and silver. Anne would assemble, too, a colossal pile of greenery for the salad, and keep it mixed, in batches as needed: all the children are part rabbit. I would make Elsa's Orange Torte, for a light, delicately dry dessert with coffee.

We would meet at midday, all the friends. . . .

I found that a mind of rebellion teased me, about the turkeys. It was because of the peculiarly poignant setting in the wine valley with all of us there: I did not want to do what any fool could do time and again, as I had often done, with oysters and dry bread and sage. I wanted to roast our dainty birds as they would never have been roasted before, and still keep them simple and succulent enough for the children, those perceptive creatures of unsullied palate, innocent of nicotine and alcohol and God knows what other decadent titillators. I wanted to produce something that they would smile on, and their parents, too.

Then, as I knew I would, I got out Sheila Hibben's *Kitchen Manual*, which remains for me the simplest and most sensible essay ever written in good English on the proper behavior when faced with a fish, fowl, or cut-off-the-joint. (It is the only cookery book I own which I've marked and added to, and from which clippings spew out.)

Stuck in at page forty-seven, where Mrs. Hibben gets off to a fine start on the subject of roast chicken by taking a ladylike poke at Brillat-Savarin, was a chipped yellowing sheet from an Iowan collection of "The Ladies' Guild's Best," which had fairly brutal directions for the Thanksgiving rites (dated 1879): ". . . place in hot oven, but not too hot at first until flour dredgings blacken; look in often and you will be able to tell if your fire is too brisk or too slow."

There was a column torn from a supermarket throwaway, which gave some good tips on tempering deep-freeze birds to the local winds. One of the best ones, from frozen turkeys or those caught on the hoof, was to let the roasted beauty "set" for half an hour or so before carving it.

Then there was a colored card about trussing a bird, which I think I cut from a dime-store set of skewers I once bought. I have since located the same excellent directions in several good cookbooks, but it is nice to know, in my own private filing system, just where they are for *me:* pasted in the back of Mrs. Hibben's *Manual.* I always follow them as if they were new to me, armed with needles, skewers, twine, scissors. . . .

Then there was a Christmas card printed years ago by Ward Ritchie, with a Landacre woodcut on it . . . "How to Cook a Turkey," by Morton Thompson. The method is as odd as the text, and all of Thompson's pseudo-real quotations from sages like Gisantius Praceptus and so on are not as true as his own dictum, "If you want a well-cooked dinner the labor of preparing must be equal to the pleasure of your enjoying."

This is my theory too, for ceremonial feasting at least, and this is how I proved it, in a somewhat tedious but never-faltering pattern, with all the children and several friends and now and then Norah and Anne wandering about me in the kitchen, sniffing, yearning, exclaiming, doubting, commenting. . . .

The two birds weighed about twelve pounds each. I gave them my best attention and tweaked out even more than the usual number of feather ends, both before and after I had washed them well in cold running water and dried them gently. I swished out the insides with a cup of *vin rosé*, unnecessarily but all to the good, and salted them lightly, and laid them away in a cool, airy place until the next day, to be stuffed and roasted.

The stuffing, or dressing as you may call it, depending on how and by whom you were raised, is enough for these two trim little birds or one big one, and would as far as I know be as good in a goose, if you are of the stuffed-goose school. It might even be good with a domestic duck. It is robust and yet light and subtle, like some Chinese dishes, and its preparation is, as Mr. Thompson and many another cook would recommend, a finicky and odorous one.

TURKEY STUFFING

8 slices lean bacon
3 cups chopped mild onions
3 cups chopped celery stalks and tops
½ orange and ½ lemon, finely chopped (skins and all)
1 large green pepper, chopped
Livers, hearts, and so on of the bird(s), coarsely chopped
½ cup butter
8 cups cooked rice

1 cup slivered blanched almonds or whole pine nuts
1 cup chopped fresh parsley or 2 tablespoons dried
1 teaspoon dried marjoram (optional)
2 pounds cooked cleaned, peeled shrimp (or prawns)
½ teaspoon cayenne pepper
Butter and cream
Salt, pepper to taste

Sauté the bacon, drain on paper, and crumble. Sauté the onion in the bacon fat until golden. Pour off the excess fat into another skillet. Add the celery to the onions, and sauté gently. Add the orange and lemon and the green pepper, return the bacon to the mixture, and set aside.

Sauté the chopped livers and so on in the butter, and add to the mixture.

How much raw rice will make 8 cups of cooked rice depends on whether it is polished, brown, precooked, and so on, but no matter what kind you use, it is best browned slightly in the bacon fat left from the first step, and then cooked in the Italian style, with adequate chicken stock or water in a tightly covered pan, until done and fluffy. Then add the nuts and parsley and (if you wish) the marjoram to it, toss all together lightly, and combine in the same manner with the main mixture.

Cover the fresh or frozen shrimps (or prawns) deeply with cold water, add the cayenne pepper, bring to a quick boil, and let cool in the water. Peel and clean, and cut into bite-size pieces. Sauté until golden in adequate butter, and add to the mixture.

Toss all together very lightly, and let stand for a few hours, or overnight in a cool place.

Allowing plenty of time before the roasting should begin, pack the stuffing lightly into the bird(s), adding some melted butter or cream if it seems too dry. Correct seasoning to taste, using salt and freshly ground pepper if wished. Truss with string and skewers, according to custom and common sense, and rub all the skin well with soft butter. Then weigh it, and put it in a 300-degree oven, counting between ten and twelve minutes for each pound.

It should be basted every ten or fifteen minutes, with its own juices and a warm mixture of one part butter, one part good olive oil, and one part sherry or vermouth. (Very sweet vermouth adds to the fine glaze. . . .)

And that was the basic formula, a kind of distillation of what a dozen cooks had hinted to me in their pages, and what I myself was hoping for. I went on from there, realizing my limitations and accepting my blessings. I found that in my electric oven I did not need to cover the birds with butter-soaked cloths as I would have done in a gas oven, especially if they had been older. I found that my somewhat inexpert trussing presented several little holes where I could squirt the juices from my glass baster. I found that every time I opened the oven several people wanted to look, so I added fifteen minutes to the cooking time.

I did the two birds separately, because of my small stove and because of the general enjoyment of the slow, demanding ritual. The children would drift in and out, from the vineyards or the redwood trees, to watch the ceremony and to breathe the smells, which grew by the minute into a kind of cloud of herb and orange peel and turkey-ness. They leaned forward and then away, stunned and tempted, and the dance went on.

We took the birds up to Norah's in the back of the station wagon, past the blazing vines, and there was the long table, three different patchy shapes under the stretch of red and white cloths and three different heights, but with chairs all around it for us the diners, so varied too in shapes and heights and even purposes. One thing we all did know: we wanted to sit down together and eat and drink.

We had sipped Wente Brothers Dry Semillon all morning, slowly and peacefully. Gnats fell into it whenever we stepped outside the two little farmhouses we moved between: the vineyards and indeed the whole valley still gave off a winey, rotting perfume of discarded grapeskins and forgotten raisins.

Inside Norah's place the children prepared and then presented some sort of pageant about Pilgrims and Indians sitting down together to a feast of corn pudding and baked pumpkins and firewater. Anne patted the ten thousand leaves of a series of "tossed green salads" and stirred a large bowl of dressing made firm but mild for the young palates. On the sideboard Norah put the Danish coffee mugs, the dark rum for them as wished it, and the handsome torte dusted with white sugar.

Down the table marched breadbaskets, and ripe grapes on their flat bright leaves, and the wine bottles, a noble motley for the various tastes, but all from the valley where we stayed so thankfully: Charles Krug and Louis Martini had made the whites, and Inglenook, Beaulieu, and Krug again the reds; and there were pitchers of milk for the children. . . .

The birds were noble and enough, thus bolstered. Their juices followed the course of the knife, as Mrs. Hibben had said they would, and the meat fell away like waves before a fine ship's bow. All down the table the people held up their plates as fast as the server could carve again, and their eyes shone, and they reached happily for bread, salad, wine, milk, the silver bowl of cranberry sauce in honor of the Pilgrims, and a stone jar of ancient jelly, which one of us three sisters had brought dutifully from our childhood home.

I sat near the carver. I was hot and weary and exalted. I looked down the long gay table, into the living room from the kitchen and past the hearth and out through the big window toward the mountains. The grapes were harvested. The vines were starting, brilliantly, a short beneficent sleep, and in here in the warm cluttered rich room were my sisters and those they loved and those I did too. It was a good moment in life.

Everything was fine, and so was the dressing. It was light, tantalizing, essentially Oriental. And before we ever tasted it, through the long exercise of our senses while it was prepared and while it fumed slowly in the dainty birds, we all as one (and that is an important fine thing to happen at least a couple of times in anybody's life), we all as one bowed our heads in thanksgiving. It was part of the pageant that none of us had rehearsed. . . .

BARBARA KAFKA

Tempest in a Samovar

My father loved storms, water pounding into already muddy earth, the rich scent of the wet ground carrying a hint of mold, god-bearing cracks of lightning and body-shaking thumps of thunder. He would sit on an awninged terrace to be spectator, possessed and possessor of nature's big effect. Frightened, I would join him, trying to live up to his exhilaration. I loved my father, was an acolyte trying to share his vision and not be afraid of his storms. I have never been ill on a boat; he boasted of his years on ocean liners when only he and the captain arrived for dinner. In the wind's shout, I heard his voice and tensed against alarm.

This is how I learned about food, amid the alarms of the dinner table, his pleasure surrounded by the family fights. The food sheltered me; I grew round as I built a wall against their anger, which sought to shred me between the talons of competing ambitions, assign me roles and set goals that if achieved could only displease one while satisfying the other. The food covertly put me on my father's side. He took the steak bone from the platter and gnawed it, smearing his mouth with fat and flecks of charred bone, his teeth grating into the hard surface, his tongue seeking out bits of marrow and shreds of sweet flesh, to my mother's flesh-fearing disgust. I learned that the sweetest meat lies near the bone.

He drank and his many brothers drank. Together they drank, challenging each other with their ice-cold native vodka. The clear liquid was a booby trap, hot with long-soaked small red peppers, but clear as rainwater. Who would gag, who would reel? When he drank with them, the bitter arguments, the arm wrestling were softened by love and shared memories. They listened to news from the Russian front and ate herring in cream with sliced onions, smoked salmon, sturgeon, and a fish they called *kipchunkie* (which I later learned to call sable) and, finally, smoked black cod. There were bagels too hard for me to bite, black Russian pumpernickel, and what they called cornbread, a throwback to Europe where wheat was "corn." The bread was dense and heavy and has disappeared. No one will any longer make the dough, too thick for machines. He ate the heel, the crumb of bread was for the effete, along with white meat of chicken and desserts.

He taught me to eat pickles from the barrel, the juice running down my arm, and took me to restaurants when I was mother-abandoned. She was out of town, often in Washington, doing important work—beyond objection—for the government during the great war. His was the ultimate revenge and seduction. We had lunch at Lüchow's. His office was nearby, and he was proud of his charge card: number 1. We ate herring in dill mustard sauce and puffy, plate-sized apple pancakes, boiled beef with lots of horseradish, and I sipped his beer.

At Chambord, we sat outdoors on a spring night, beyond the copper-pot view of the kitchen, a kitchen where they would prepare, if you would wait, any dish from the classic French repertoire, and my father ordered—the whole restaurant stopped to stare—a nineteen-dollar bottle of wine in 1945 when I was twelve. I remember the bottle shape, a Bordeaux, the year a '29; but the name is clogged in memory. I fell in love with the idea of France, the country vital to my father's business but whose language remained arcane to him. Later, that was my victory, my French.

My mother did not, does not cook. Like learning to type, it was something for servants. She scrambled to success with education as grappling tool and was moving always upward, bringing sometimes a memory of a tasted recipe for Rachel, a recipe reflecting the ever-increasing image of the better life, first, *moules marinière*, then fillet of sole *bonne femme*. She liked chocolate ice cream and tried French with a clumsy accent. I learned that food was part of travel and distant places.

Rachel was not a nice person, and why should she be, a black woman living in a tiny room—a maid's room—in the Fifth Avenue apartment without a view of self-proclaimed liberals? But she was a superb natural cook and always there from the time I was four until the apartment with the view could be bought and she didn't fit. My mother fought her leaving. My father was remorseless and Rachel went to work in his factory. I didn't miss her. By then I was leaving as well, glad to escape the escalating sound of fighting, the several glasses of Scotch too many, and the disappointment of a woman whom the end of Depression and war left without a clear cause.

I didn't spend time in the kitchen with Rachel. I lived in Barsetshire, Jane Austen's Hampshire, Joyce's Dublin, Swann's attar-of-roses Paris, and Stendhal's provinces. I swallowed the sentimental sour of Edna St. Vincent Millay and Dorothy Parker. I gobbled Yeats, Eliot, and Mallarmé and wandered lonely through picture galleries learning the strange green faces of gold-framed madonnas, the melodrama of red in El Greco, the tear-provoking repose of Cézanne's solid geometry, and the liquid geometry of Dali. I danced, and a savage in music, I could hear only the insistent beat of ballets, the enticements of my father's gypsy records, and the voice-carried sweetness of opera. And what I wrote I hid.

But Rachel did teach me that cooking was an improvisation and a response. My mother's hints of dishes produced, from Rachel's pots, wonderful flavors, and, for the few people Rachel liked, there were mysteriously good chocolate cakes to eat late at night with whole bottles of milk.

Refuge in the mind-world of college brought no relief. I courted favor, writing other people's papers, better than my own. To produce was too frightening, a challenge to my father's fragilely male repudiation of my mother's achievement, a challenge to my mother's expansive competition, her flight through six degrees. It was to risk annihilation, and I graduated with a cum, summa generals, and a summa thesis written late at night in the last hurried hours before the deadline in the less frightening, public space of my dorm's living room.

I worked, I married, and I fled again from my parents' house as I tried to learn, awkwardly, what a home might be, a place that was not perpetually neat and ready to be viewed, one filled with the smell of onions and garlic and welcoming to hoped-for friends. I learned to cook. It was not frightening. It was all there in my friends the books, often wrapped in the festivity of French. I spread six or seven on the floor and learned of food as I had learned to learn. Comparing recipes, I tried to see through them to the times when they were written, the personalities of the cooks, and to an ultimate version of whatever dish I would serve, a try at loving, too late at night. I was still not able to judge the time and space of recipes, had not yet learned to listen to the changing sound of bubbles in the pot, the varying smells from the oven.

I had found the way to invert and supersede my father's intrusive pleasures, avoid my mother, and reject their worlds. I worked with my hands. I was a cook. I learned a new language, recipes.

In this new language I found work. I had wanted to write great poetry, but my fears of competing in my parents' worlds crippled my ambition. As if by happenstance, but surely by the intuition of others, I found that people would pay me to write about food, about what I had traveled and tasted, what my hyperacuity—honed in staying short of danger in those nightly dinner-table battles—made me taste and replicate and feel. In that work, everything I knew and the ways I had learned to see was of use. If we look, food has the structure of linguistics and religion. It is sociology and economics, politics and cultural definition; it is history, memory, and passion interwoven with style as clearly as painting, literature, dance, music, and architecture. Yet it is without the risks of high art.

Food is about loving and giving and performance and applause. It is polymorphous, combining what had been the professional work of men with what had been the largely invisible, perhaps because ubiquitous, labors of women. It is essential and sensuous. I found a home where my father's storm could be tamed to the bubbles and steam of my grandmother's samovar.

COLETTE

TRANSLATED FROM THE FRENCH BY DEREK COLTMAN

Wines

I was very well brought up. As a first proof of so categorical a statement, I shall simply say that I was no more than three years old when my father poured out my first full liqueur glass of an amber-colored wine which was sent up to him from the Midi, where he was born: the muscat of Frontignan.

The sun breaking from behind clouds, a shock of sensuous pleasure, an illumination of my newborn tastebuds! This initiation ceremony rendered me worthy of wine for all time. A little later I learned to empty my goblet of mulled wine, scented with cinnamon and lemon, as I ate a dinner of boiled chestnuts. At an age when I could still scarcely read, I was spelling out, drop by drop, old light clarets and dazzling Yquems. Champagne appeared in its turn, a murmur of foam, leaping pearls of air providing an accompaniment to birthday and First Communion banquets, complementing the gray truffles from La Puisaye . . . Good lessons, from which I graduated to a familiar and discreet use of wine, not gulped down greedily but measured out into narrow glasses, assimilated mouthful by spaced-out, meditative mouthful.

It was between my eleventh and fifteenth years that this admirable educational program was perfected. My mother was afraid that I was outgrowing my strength and was in danger of a "decline." One by one, she unearthed, from their bed of dry sand, certain bottles that had been aging beneath our house in a cellar—which is, thanks be to God, still intact—hewn out of fine, solid granite. I feel envious, when I think back, of the privileged little urchin I was in those days. As an accompaniment to my modest, fill-in meals—a chop, a leg of cold chicken, or one of those hard cheeses, "baked" in the embers of a wood fire and so brittle that one blow of the fist would shatter them into pieces like a pane of glass—I drank Château Lafites, Chambertins, and Cortons which had escaped capture by the "Prussians" in 1870. Certain of these wines were already fading, pale and scented still like a dead rose; they lay on a sediment of tannin that darkened their bottles, but most of them retained their aristocratic ardor and their invigorating powers. The good old days!

I drained that paternal cellar, goblet by goblet, delicately . . . My mother would recork the opened bottle and contemplate the glory of the great French vineyards in my cheeks.

Happy those children who are not made to blow out their stomachs with great glasses of red-tinted water during their meals! Wise those parents who measure out to their progeny a tiny glass of pure wine—and I mean "pure" in the noble sense of the word—and teach them: "Away from the meal table, you have the pump, the faucet, the spring, and the filter at your disposal. Water is for quenching the thirst. Wine, according to its quality and the soil where it was grown, is a necessary tonic, a luxury, and a fitting tribute to good food." And is it not also a source of nourishment in itself? Yes, those were the days, when a few true natives of my Burgundy village, gathered around a flagon swathed in dust and spiders' webs, kissing the tips of their fingers from their lips, exclaimed—already—"a nectar!" Don't you agree that in talking to you about wine I am describing a province I know something about? It is no small thing to conceive a contempt, so early in life, not only for those who drink no wine at all but also for those who drink too much.

The vine and the wine it produces are two great mysteries. Alone in the vegetable kingdom, the vine makes the true savor of the earth intelligible to man. With what fidelity it makes the translation! It senses, then expresses, in its clusters of fruit the secrets of the soil. The flint, through the vine, tells us that it is living, fusible, a giver of nourishment. Only in wine does the ungrateful chalk pour out its golden tears. A vine, transported across mountains and over seas, will struggle to keep its personality, and sometimes triumphs over the powerful chemistries of the mineral world. Harvested near Algiers, a white wine will still remember without fail, year after year, the noble Bordeaux graft that gave it exactly the right hint of sweetness, lightened its body, and endowed it with gaiety. And it is far-off Jerez that gives its warmth and color to the dry and cordial wine that ripens at Château Chalon, on the summit of a narrow, rocky plateau.

From the ripened cluster brandished by its tormented stem, heavy with transparent but deeply troubled agate, or dusted with silver-blue, the eye moves upward to contemplate the naked wood, the ligneous serpent wedged between two rocks: on what, in heaven's name, does it feed, this young tree growing here in the South, unaware that such a thing as rain exists, clinging to the rock by a single hank of hemplike roots? The dews by night and the sun by day suffice for it—the fire of one heavenly body, the essence sweated by another—these miracles . . .

What cloudless day, what gentle and belated rain decides that a year, one year among all the others, shall be a great year for wine? Human solicitude can do almost nothing, it is a matter in which celestial sorcery is everything, the course the planets take, the spots on the sun.

Simply to recite our provinces and their towns by name is to sing the praises of our venerated vineyards. It is profitable both to the spirit and the body—believe me—to taste a wine in its own home, in the landscape that it enriches. Such a pilgrimage, well understood, has surprises in store for you that you little suspect. A very young wine, tasted in the blue light of its storage shed—a half bottle of Anjou, opened under a barrel vault dusted with pale light by a violent and stormy summer afternoon—moving relics discovered in an old stillroom unaware of the treasures it contains, or else forgetful of them . . . I once fled from such a stillroom, in the Franche-Comté, as though I had been stealing from a museum . . . Another time, among the furniture being auctioned off on a tiny village square, between the commode, the iron bedstead, and some empty bottles, there were six full bottles being sold: it was then, as an adolescent, that I had my first encounter with an ardent and imperious prince, and a treacherous one, like all great seducers: the wine of Jurançon. Those six bottles made me more curious about the region that produced them than any geography teacher ever could have done. Though I admit that at such a price geography lessons would not be within the reach of everyone. And that triumphant wine, another day, drunk in an inn so dark that we never knew the color of the liquid they poured into our glasses . . . Just so does a woman keep the memory of a journey, of how she was surprised one night, of an unknown man, a man without a face, who made himself known to her only by his kiss . . .

The present snobbery about food is producing a crop of hostelries and country inns the like of which has never been seen before. Wine is revered in these places. Can wisdom be born again from a faith so unenlightened, a faith professed by mouths already, alas, armored with cocktails, with venomous apéritifs, with harsh and numbing spirits? Let us hope that it can. As old age approaches, I offer, as my contribution, the example of a stomach without remorse or damage, a very well-disposed liver, and a still sensitive palate, all preserved by good and honest wine. Therefore, wine, fill up this glass I now hold out to you! A delicate and simple glass, a light bubble in which there play the sanguine fires of a great Burgundian ancestor, the topaz of Yquem, and the balas ruby, sometimes with a paler purple tinge, of the Bordeaux with its scent of violets . . .

There comes a time of life when one begins to prize young wine. On a Southern shore there is a string of round, wicker-covered demijohns always kept in store for me. One grape harvest fills them to the brim, then the next grape harvest, finding them empty once more, in its turn fills them up again. Perhaps you have a hoard of fine old wines in your cellar, but do not disdain these wines because they give such quick returns: they are clear, dry, various, they flow easily from the throat down to the kidneys and scarcely pause a moment there. Even when it is of a warmer constitution, down there, if the day is a really hot one, we think nothing of drinking down a good pint of this particular wine, for it refreshes you and leaves a double taste behind, of muscat and of cedarwood. . . .

MICHAEL FRANK

The Underside of Bread:
A Memoir with Food

Nearly a century ago in Safed, a small town in what was then known as Palestine, a slice of bread slipped out of a young girl's hand one morning, and five children, all sisters, began to riot. Skirts were hiked up over knees and sleeves were bunched above elbows. Big ones trampled little ones, little scratched big, some bit and others pummeled until the bread was pulverized and chins were scraped and a great emotion descended over the girls, rage and sorrow and jealousy, much jealousy: for the underside of the bread had been covered, in secret, with a thick golden icing, upholstery as bright as the sun that hung over their village. The bread, it was apparent the moment it dropped, had been buttered.

There was a sixth girl present that morning, and she alone knew about the subterfuge and grasped its purpose. She was my maternal grandmother, Sylvia Ravetch, née Shapiro, and this is one of the few stories she told me about her childhood in Palestine. At approximately thirteen, Sylvia understood that her sister Leah was ill with polio and that the doctor had ordered her to be given butter with her bread, to make her fit and plump. Sylvia also understood how poor her family was, seven daughters in all born to a lacy-bearded, Talmud-studying rabbi and his stout, dark-dispositioned, tirelessly domestic wife. It fell to Sylvia to soothe the younger girls, to explain. She did not weep at this injustice, she told me proudly; she reasoned through it and helped her mother pacify the children. With the marriage and departure of her older sister, she had assumed the place of the firstborn, and firstborns are responsible and perspicacious, natural mediators between parents and siblings. Once Sylvia interceded, Leah was able to eat her bread with the buttered side facing up.

Actually, now that I've put it down, I realize that this is the *only* story my grandmother told me about her childhood in Palestine, and I don't think it's by accident that it centers on a memory of food, even if the food, in this case, went unconsumed. Food has a rare ability to carry you back. It's not dissimilar to scent in this, though for me taste is more powerful than smell; more dependable too, since with few exceptions (a recipe botched or forgotten, a vegetable common to one garden, uncultivable in another) food can be counted on to produce a sensation in time present that will duplicate a sensation from time past. With its myriad connections to the nurturing and sustenance of mothers and grandmothers, nannies and governesses, food is an uncanny defogger of early memory. But not only of early memory: its habits and associations, the ritual of its acquisition and preparation, the quarrels it can provoke and the solace it can provide have a way, I think, of recovering and linking a good deal of lost history.

Can you distill someone in food? It is my contention, or at least my experiment here, that if you capture the bread and butter, you capture the life. First, some terms. "Distill" and "capture" locate this endeavor squarely in the realm of memoir, not biography. Memoir is impressionistic, selective, idiosyncratic, a concatenation of scenes—ingredients —that, when artfully combined, add up, if you will, to a recipe that works. I know this woman, you think when you come to the last sentence, even as you recognize that there are a great many facts you haven't learned about her. In a memoir, you can mount your subject behind all sorts of very specific frames: food, travel, reading, medicine; if you tried this in a biography, you would not be doing your job. Although the goal of both is to "shape a likeness of the vanished figure," as Leon Edel has put it, the biographer, he explains, "seeks to restore the very sense of life to the inert materials that survive an individual's passage on this earth." In a memoir, if you have no letters or books or documents of consequence, no collections of butterflies or drawers full of military decorations, no inert materials to draw on, as I haven't with my grandmother, you still have the slice of buttered bread, figs and kumquats and a sponge cake, diaphanous sheathes wrapping airy blintzes, endless glasses of pulpy orange juice, Sylvia's foods all and all richly storied. Food is a language that is spoken, one way or another, in every life.

By the time I knew her, my grandmother was deracinated, "pluck[ed] and [torn] up by the roots" *(OED)* and worse; it seemed as if her roots hadn't been left dangling to surface again, as they do in so many transposed lives, in the anecdotes, artifacts, and customs that mark immigrant grandparents as exotic and old-worldly. With Sylvia they were chopped off. While it's true that she spoke, read, and wrote Hebrew fluently, she never did so with me, the son of her unobservant daughter and son-in-law. Her vocabulary had the occasional thread of Yiddish running through it, but the threads were much fainter than they would have been had she been born in Eastern Europe or Russia. All but one of the few photographs that were taken of her family in Safed were taken after Sylvia left. If she had carried so much as a hairpin with her from Palestine, it had long since disappeared. But it's not merely the lack of goods and chattels that marked Sylvia as cut off from her origins. She never celebrated her birthday; indeed, she did not know it, a fact I had great difficulty understanding as a child—it made Sylvia seem like a figure out of a fairy tale or a myth when in reality she was merely another girl child fathered by a man who, longing for sons to follow him in his Talmudic studies, couldn't be bothered to mark down the date any of his daughters was born. My grandmother suffered from what my mother calls immigrant shame, though I wonder if it is not more specific to Sylvia than this categorizing suggests. She was embarrassed by her accent, which she believed gave her away as a greenhorn (my mother never heard it; nor did I). She thought her handwriting looked foreign and unlettered (it didn't; she wasn't), so that when I wrote to her during my summer vacations she refused to write back. She hated most photographs taken of her and often tore out her head, leaving a long series of decapitated bodies to embrace children and grandchildren, husband and friends. Even though she'd been married for decades to a man who had his citizenship, because she'd entered this country illegally, she never let herself return to her homeland; she remained convinced, in middle age, in old age even, that if she left America she would not be allowed back in.

Out of this self-abnegation, the blankness of Sylvia's past, the story of the bread and butter had the luster of a single wick shining on an enormous black sea. "Unfortunately, one only remembers what is exceptional," Virginia Woolf observes in her loose, honest, speedily written late memoir, "A Sketch of the Past." If this is true, and if the bread and butter incident was indeed exceptional for Sylvia, it was, I believe, because it represented the moment when she became conscious of her autonomy. Sylvia stood apart from her sisters that morning. She read her mother and comprehended, if she did not condone, her duplicity; by interpreting for an adult, she joined her ranks. The bread and butter presaged the dramatic turn Sylvia's life was to take two years later, when the girl who did not weep at being denied this gustatory treat was deemed sufficiently mature to travel West, to Montreal, where she would go to work as a Hebrew teacher and earn enough money not only to keep herself but to help bring the rest of her family to North America.

When Sylvia married my grandfather, Shalom Ravetch, in New Jersey, he was studying to become a pharmacist, a nice, dependable occupation that would take Sylvia far away from the butterless penury she knew as a rabbi's daughter. But her new husband had a crisis; pills and ointments bored him; he went back to school and then on to the Jewish Institute of Religion; and now it's, say, 1942, and Shalom is the rabbi of Temple Sinai in Long Beach, California, where he delivers sermons with such titles as "Anti-Semitism—the Remedy" and "Chanukah Challenges the Jew." Sylvia is the rebbetzen, leading the kind of public life she never anticipated. With endless orchid corsages pinned to her collar, her hair waved and shellacked, suits and stockings donned and pumps polished, she occupies a regular front-row seat at the synagogue, beams at bar mitzvahs, and is brave at funerals. She teaches in the Sunday school, attends banquets and fund-raisers and sisterhood meetings. She sits on committees; she performs good works. At home the pumps are replaced by slippers and an apron covers the good suit while Sylvia kneads and braids dough for each week's challah and prepares sedulously kosher meals. She can't cheat because members of the congregation are fond of stopping by, unannounced, to check up on the rabbi's wife. She can't skimp because her family, two sons now and a daughter, rarely eats alone. The Ravetches' door stands permanently open, the leaves in their dining room table stuck in place to make room for mayors and business-men and fellow rabbis, scholars bearded and scholars shaven, fathers with children in crisis, wives with husbands on the run; anyone, it seemed to my mother, watching this panorama as a young girl, who passed through Long Beach and needed a kosher meal.

Week after week, the braids on Sylvia's challahs grew to Rapunzel-lian length. They were laborious loaves, and I could easily let them stand for this period of my grandmother's life, but the impulse to render the past as fairly as I can compels me to reach into Sylvia's larder and find her sponge cake. I tasted it, in its later incarnation, many times in my childhood, and I always had the sense that this was Sylvia's happiest dish, not merely because it was party food, though party food it certainly was, but because I detected an unfamiliar levity in the way she composed its aromatic batter. Was it a child's fascination with the mystery of the egg white, that runny mucous liquid that a grandmother's deft wrist can transform into a mountain of frothy snow? I think not. This dish provoked a ruminative look in Sylvia. She inclined her head as she prepared it, almost as if she were leaning, smiling into another world, peering at what I never knew or thought to ask. Thanks to my mother, I know now that Sylvia's sponges date from the height of her kitchen drudgery but that they did not often grace the table jammed with its uninvited guests. No. She saved them for the sudden marriages her husband performed during the war: soldiers or sailors who had fallen in love and found a bride and, on a day's leave, far from home, appeared in Shalom's study to be wed. Some died in battle, some lived long lives, but all who had no family nearby were launched in marriage with a slice of sponge and a glass of berry wine. They were Sylvia's pastry of celebration, of goodwill, and whenever she turned one out of its pan she seemed to be revisiting, briefly, a vanished festivity.

My mother marries, my grandfather dies, I am born, the pancake wars begin. Until I am ten years old, when I visit one grandmother, I visit the other. I do not think there is anything odd about this—don't all grandmothers live together? Mine do. Well, to be precise, my mother's mother lives *with* my father's mother. After Shalom's death, Sylvia was deemed incapable of living on her own. She'd never maintained a checking account or managed her affairs or been by herself. She was lonely and grieving. The children convened and decided it would be best if she took up Huff's offer and moved into the back bedroom of her apartment in Los Angeles. Finally the leaves were yanked out of Sylvia's dining room table; her household was disbursed; she arrived at Ogden Drive with two suitcases and two cartons of books.

In the kitchen, as elsewhere, these two women could not have been more incompatible. Huff was chocolate, Sylvia vanilla. Huff prepared dense, meaty soups, Sylvia chicken broth with matzo balls floating through them. Huff brewed coffee; Sylvia preferred Sanka. Their polarities were as clear to me, their shared grandson, as their different perfumes. Huff drove, Sylvia rode the bus. Huff had worked in the world of Hollywood and had the wardrobe and jewelry and bearing to prove it; Sylvia had remained in the synagogue and at home. . . . But there was one place where at least their culinary worlds intersected, a dish both women made: the thin papery delicacies Huff called either crepes or German pancakes and Sylvia interpreted in a more utilitarian way, as shells for her blintzes. Huff larded her version with butter, in the batter and in the pan, where she left them over the flame until they were crisp and brown; afterwards she accumulated them in the oven, in a square Pyrex dish coated with still more butter; then they were eaten with syrup or powdered sugar or jam. Sylvia's were prepared with the scantest amount of shortening. Her batter was scarcely poured into the scalding pan until it congealed, and the pancake was turned out onto the counter-top, pale as the tiles on which it cooled. Later it would envelop a filling of hoop and cream cheese, eggs and vanilla and sugar, all mixed with the fingers of her right hand.

If "pancake wars" has an overly melodramatic ring, consider the battleground: the affections of an eight-year-old boy who is about to be awakened from the childish notion that tension, conflict, hurt, and loss are the stock-in-trade of the school yard, never of grandma's—grand-mas'—house. I can travel back and open the door to the apartment on Ogden Drive so easily, so vividly, that I have trouble believing it no longer remains intact: the living room with its Flemish mirror, its brown and beige curtains and sofa, the Queen Anne table, the Welsh dresser arranged with Chinese ceramics, the reverse paintings on glass; Huff's bedroom with its twin beds, the bureau with bunches of carved grapes for pulls, the wallpaper I would finger when I woke in the morning, *wreath-urn-wreath, wreath-urn-wreath;* Sylvia's smaller bedroom down the hall, where one wall is papered with blue toile (revelers picnicking in a generic French garden) and where the Zenith radio by her bed crackles with opera every Saturday morning; the kitchen with its pegboard, its whistling tea kettle, its flame-darkened frying pans, its spoon rest. Who-ever guides this camera will never let me skip the spoon rest. A ladle is slapped down. A bowl jumps. Pancake batter splashes. "Why will a young man ever need to know how to make blintzes?" Grandma Huffy asks Grandma Sylvia sharply, and Sylvia wipes her hands on her apron and abandons her post at the stove. Huff melts a chunk of butter in the pan, enriches Sylvia's batter, and makes me a heap of German pancakes that I eat with syrup and powdered sugar and . . . appetite. I would like to be able to say the pancakes turned to paper—dust—wood in my mouth, but they didn't. They were delectable.

The moment, however, was not. The first of several complex pair-ings of women in my life had revealed itself to me. By some obscure alchemy of consciousness, the sting of Sylvia's hurt feelings turned on, or more accurately turned me on to, the rivalry between my two grandmothers. The beautiful museum of their apartment was never quite so beautiful or quite so like a museum again.

Huff dies, and Sylvia has a handful of fairly good, fairly independent years—bookending her youth, she even resumes teaching Hebrew at a synagogue in Los Angeles—before she becomes ill and a paid companion moves in to care for her. During the in-between period, Sylvia spins a cocoon that relieves the considerable pain of my early adolescence. Its dominant motif, the images that linger most palpably two decades later, all contain food: glasses of fresh-squeezed orange juice that were Sylvia's idea of a cure-all for every cough and shiver; bowls of warm, fragrant, milky tapioca; the ubiquitous blintzes, which she would send home stacked between sheets of waxed paper; figs and kumquats, which we would buy on our excursions to the Farmer's Market, Fairfax and Third, and which, I now suspect, must have summoned her childhood in Palestine; the celebratory sponge cakes, of course; her crisp *mandelbrot* cookies, which I never tasted again until I went to live in Florence and encountered them under a different name, *biscotti di Prato;* and the Friday Night Meal: a plate of glistening T-bone steak, a pool of peas, a sour-creamed and chived baked potato for me and for Sylvia a scoop of cottage cheese and half a pear. I was being given the buttered bread, while she made do with the plain.

The last time I saw Sylvia I'd come to the apartment for one of my Friday nights and was given the choice of staying as usual or accompanying my younger brothers to the movies. Sylvia encouraged me to go. "There'll be another Friday," she said. We embraced—in the dining room, of course. I saw us, I see us still, in the mirror that hung on one wall: an ungainly dry-haired boy standing over his grandmother, her eyes large and moist, the color of skim milk. Holding—fitting. She died at five o'clock the next morning. Later that same afternoon, a United Parcel truck parked at 1648 North Ogden Drive, and a large squat man in a brown uniform delivered a tinned fruitcake ordered by my mother, an out-of-season surprise for my grandmother, who was fond of them. Mom and I opened the cake, prepared two glasses of tea, and sat down to the familiar table in the familiar room, but neither of us could swallow a bite.

Other than a handful of birthday cards, the only examples I have of Grandma Sylvia's handwriting are her recipes. Among them is one for the sponge cake. I tried to make it once, about five years ago. It was a disaster: limp, heavy, off. Unlike the fruitcake, which I don't believe I will bother to taste again, I will return to the sponge one day, only not, I think, until I am an old man, and I am able to tell my grandchild some stories about bread and butter and pancakes and orange juice and a long-ago woman in a long-ago time. Surely then the cake will rise.

JAMES SEAY

Our Hands in the History of It

When she wrung the necks of chickens for our Sunday meals, my grandmother summoned an uncommonly nimble articulation in her wrist that allowed her, after about three quick rotations of the bird, to cast it far enough from her to avoid spotting her apron with blood. It was a motion of the wrist that I don't remember in even the younger women of our family, nor in any of the men, including my father, gathered for our Sunday visits, but then again age and gender aren't the controlling factors here. There's also the fact that I've never seen anyone else wring the neck of a chicken, so what I guess I'm saying is that I can't imagine anyone even coming close to the smooth, articular motion that my grandmother introduced into her final rotation of the bird to send it in headless flight from her.

Usually she would have taken two pullets from the chicken yard and put them in a raised frame-and-wire coop for special feeding during the week before our visit. At some point in the past my grandfather had brought in some White Leghorns to mix with the flock, but her choice for these special occasions continued to be her "Dominickers" (Dominiques), because the Leghorns were too small to satisfy her protocol for a full serving on each plate—man's, woman's, or child's. Even if Leghorns were allowed to grow beyond pullet size, for laying purposes, their eggs were too little for her use, she said. So it was the favored Dominicker that she would take from the coop, gather partly under her arm, one hand over its neck and head, the other around its legs, and carry to the middle of the backyard. Releasing its legs and holding it by the head, she would rotate it quickly in the air by the weight of its body for as many turns as she judged the thickness of the neck to require. The image that I carry, nearly half a century later, is of that particular motion—to say flick is to suggest too sharp and radical a motion—of her wrist in the conclusion, along with a casting away and a simultaneous stepping back while still in an almost graceful stoop, a half bow. The headless chicken, thrashing in the grass, is a blur to me and my cousins standing agape on the back porch or draped over one of the low limbs of the apple tree.

We are waiting to watch her take the other Dominicker from the coop and wring its neck.

The food and wine I remember and celebrate most fondly is that which I've been close to the source of. It's probably sentimental to think that these experiences actually are more intense and resonant the closer we are to the place of the sowing or gathering or preparation—and in the degree to which we have had a hand in any of this—but my own narratives of eating and drinking seem to favor that notion. The baker, dusty with flour, has just handed me a *bâtard* fresh from the oven, and I am eating it outside his shop. The Provençal village is bright with promise all around me. It is the best bread I have ever eaten. In another story it is a local wine and a train window in Tuscany letting onto the changing crosshatch of vineyard rows. My wife-to-be and I might think vaguely of the cheese and olives we have wrapped in wax paper, but for now there is nothing close in pleasure to this wine and the fleeting landscape of its origin. It's not that all of this is better than sex, but there are other passengers sharing our sleeping compartment. Also the nuns have a habit of looking into compartments, regardless of whether the curtains are open or drawn, in search of better seats and privacy.

O lost, and by the wind grieved, ghost thigh, drumstick, wishbone, come back again. Obviously, the chicken that my grandmother is about to fry is going to be the best that I have ever eaten. As I said, these narratives of memory and celebration have for me an emotional signal-to-noise ratio that relies on both the hands-on and the close-source quotients. My bread in Provence, even though I am at several removes from any chance at having a hand in its creation, is caught in the light of all its sources. Or at least I have romanticized it as such, and that generates a nearly optimum signal for the scope of things here. Likewise with the Tuscan wine, where the sense of source is even keener. It is late summer and the vines are heavy with grapes. The speed of the train accentuates the gradations of texture in the vineyards and gives the illusion of an actual winemaking already at work in the vines. As we pass through Chianti, the Gallo Nero (black rooster) logo of that region's wines flashes occasionally by our window, each image doubling and deepening the impression of those same road-side signs that we carry in memory from our recent drives into the countryside for lazy picnics among the olive groves or under the slender cypresses, all a part of the taste and texture of the soft wine and cheese and olives in brine and herbs, the fresh loaves of bread. We drink more of the wine and look out of the window now with the mild sadness of such departures. It is the best wine we have ever drunk.

I have my hands on the Dominicker's scaly though surprisingly smooth legs and am carrying it to the black cast-iron pot under which my grandfather has a fire going. My grandmother will dip the headless chicken into the hot water to loosen its feathers and then let me or one of my cousins take it to the back porch while she is scalding the other one. We have spread newspapers for her. If she is not in too big a hurry she will let us help with the plucking. Everybody gets a tickle-feather to take home later, despite the fact that the air of the car will be tinctured with wet chicken. That odor, though, is nothing compared to the smell of the recently lit kerosene stove blending with the stench of burning pin feathers as my grandmother singes the plucked Dominickers in the kitchen. She would normally dip them in melted paraffin to remove the pin feathers, but the store was out of stock. On the kitchen counter there is a blue and white paper carton of Humko Vegetable Shortening out of which she scoops a large portion of shortening for the hot skillet, and it's not until the butchered and dredged chicken is settled in this, sputtering and popping, that the kitchen becomes a place my cousins and I want to spend any time in. My grandfather has butchered a hog recently and given her the lard he rendered, but she adds it to the melted shortening only sparingly and has never fried a chicken in it exclusively, as some of the neighbors do. Too greasy, she says. Throws the flavor off.

Proust may have written the book on this kind of thing, but the typically Gallic quality of his treatment of his Aunt Léonie's tea and *petites madeleines* is much too delicate and highly nuanced to handle the imprint that is forming in my brainpan now that the true frying has commenced in my grandmother's kitchen.

Don't misunderstand; it would suit me to do a lot less cooking than I do, and I'm sure my grandmother would have said the same for herself. If I were a boulevardier, I would be one with a proven weakness for good restaurants and cafés. If I were an especially rich boulevardier, I'd leave the boulevards once a week and jet to such places as the west coast of Ireland and be at Moran's of the Weir before the landing gear cooled, drinking one of their lighter draughts and eating salmon from the waters of history. This is not to say that I am backing down from my claim that the best food and drink for me is not only close-source but also a part of the work of my own hands. The family Moran's salmon, close to its source, is of the first order, but in the final reckoning I cannot honor it in the way that I honor, say, the flounder that my friend Tom Huey and I caught and pan-fried in butter, dill weed, and lemon over an open fire on Cape Lookout one summer evening at sunset.

They were the best flounder I have ever eaten. One reason is that they were fresh out of the water. We had been drift-fishing in Lookout Bight and hooked them in the late afternoon after an otherwise luckless day, except for sighting some of the wild horses running at a canter along Shackleford Banks. In the slackness of the afternoon Tommy kept mixing Cuba Libres for us. By differing degrees our marriages were failing, and this was something I guess we thought we could do to stave off what was coming. Besides the Cuba Libres, all we had for dinner was the flounder and half a loaf of Pepperidge Farm, which made the moment seem sort of scriptural and beatific. When we woke the next morning and stumbled out of the tent, we found my Boston Whaler beached, dead weight on the sand with its heavy seaworthiness and an old forty-horse Evinrude that was about three times the weight of present models. We had neglected to factor in the low tide line in anchoring it, so there it was, thirty yards from the water, and we had to move it, foot by dark Bacardi foot, over the drying sand. All of that—the dead weight and sweat and near nausea, the beautiful emerald water we fished on, the recurring dread beneath the surface of our happiness, the wild horses, the fish finally taking our bait, the driftwood fire—is why it is the best flounder I have ever eaten. We had our hands in the history of it, and its provenance was all around us.

These stories of fish eaten fresh out of water—including those from sushi lovers—are implicitly competitive, and I give the prize to a group of Oriental tourists that a charter boat captain working out of Alligator Point, Florida, told my group about. After boating a nice Spanish mackerel that one of the Orientals had caught, the captain busied himself rigging an extra line and getting bait ready, only to look around and find the Orientals sitting in a circle on the deck by the fish box. They had quit fishing, taken the Spanish out of the box, cut strips from it, and were happily, ceremoniously, feasting. Those little fellas had brought along a bottle of some kind of brown sauce, the captain said, and were putting it on that fish and eating it raw!—smiling and jabbering in a language he'd never heard. Happy as they could be. It was the best fish they had ever eaten.

I am going to the garden to pick collards after first frost. Even while tilling and working the compost into the ground and planting the small seeds, I knew the mature plants would take up too much space for the limited plot I had, but I wanted to feel the heft again in the harvesting and taste the taste I remember from country dinners. I plan to cook them for several hours with an unhealthy-sized piece of fatback in the pot. My boat is in the water and I am playing out line to troll along tide rips for blues. When they start striking we'll double back and try to cast without spooking them. The farm family, friends of my sister, calls to say come pick some Silver Queen; the tassels are turning. There are doves simmering in a broth of red wine, shallots, herbs, a little olive oil. Maybe a pinch of fennel. Even in a brief cataloging such as this, we begin to read our lives, and in this sense food also takes on a political shading, though that would have to be the most remote of motives and associations. My father is home on leave before shipping out for the Pacific. He has put on his red and black buffalo plaid shirt and is up in the pecan tree shaking a limb that we can't reach with the shaker pole. The pecans shower down on me. When I have filled another pail or two, we will take them inside and pick them, passing the nutcracker back and forth across the table as my mother gets ready to toast them with salt and butter. We will eat them fresh out of the oven early in the evening, and then tomorrow my father will go to war. My greatest fear, though, is that a limb will break or he will lose his purchase as he climbs higher. But he calls down to me and says to crack some of the pecans and make sure these higher ones aren't too green.

One Sunday we showed up at my grandparents' house unannounced. Maybe because the phones were out. I don't remember. At any rate, my grandmother had not put any Dominickers up for special feeding, and besides she said there weren't any really big enough to cook. We'd have to go with one of the Leghorns. I don't think that this was a terribly unsettling event for her—the substitution of a Leghorn—but I do think that our surprise visit and the need she felt to set a decent table for company, though not a two-chicken crowd, flustered her a bit. Still and all, she took her usual steady course to the chicken yard, singled out a shiny white Leghorn, and began to work it toward a corner. This was a hot summer day in Mississippi, and the Leghorn, smaller and more agile than her Dominickers, tested her further, but she caught it and brought it to the middle of the yard to wring its neck.

At the critical moment during the wringing, something apparently failed to engage in the small bones and musculature of her wrist, with the result that the chicken was not propelled as far from her as usual.

In the bird's first wild flailing loop on the ground, several drops of blood from the neck stump came flying back at her and were absorbed in the white cotton of her apron, just off center between her breasts. She had forgotten to change to her work apron before coming to the chicken yard and was still wearing the clean white apron that she had put on when we arrived. I can see her now, pulling the bib of the apron slightly away from her body and looking down at the stains on the clean cotton: three bright and neatly tailed meteors of red, seeming to be in a state of tension, still resisting their arrest in flight.

It was not a particularly dramatic mishap for her, though, as well as I can remember. She took note and went on with the work at hand. My grandfather later commented on the stains, but she explained it as a simple matter of not having cast the chicken far enough and then not being able to dodge the spattering of blood. The nuisance was in the prospect of having to wash and iron the apron again so soon. I am not making this out to be a badge for anything or a mark of my grand-mother's mortality. It was a measure of her failing strength and facility of motion possibly, but she went on to wring the necks of scores of chickens and serve up the platters by which I continue to judge all fried chicken put before me.

After we ate the Leghorn that day, along with hot buttered biscuits, mashed potatoes and gravy, pole beans, creamed corn, sliced tomatoes, pickled watermelon rind relish, iced tea, and fried peach pies, my grand-father and I walked to town to visit Mr. Woolfork's ice cream parlor, which we often did during my visits. The unusual thing, though to me it seemed providentially arranged and was a time-honored combination in Mr. Woolfork's parlor, was that Mr. Woolfork sold used pocket knives along with his ice cream. He kept them in cigar boxes under the counter and would bring them out if someone wanted to buy or trade knives. The strangeness of that union, ice cream and knives, did not register on me until much later, but the realization seemed only to deepen the mystery that I somehow sensed as a child.

A pocket knife was as essential as a shoe or a hat. My grandfather would whittle, lance a boil, cut an apple, or trim his toenails all with the same pocket knife. Mine was perhaps more a token knife, though I would find ways to use it in the woods, on fishing trips, and so on. I don't want to push the implications here, but obviously our knives—their size, sharpness, relative elaborateness—were a subject of compari-son for me and my friends. But so also were our dogs, our bicycles, our new winter coats. For whatever meaning, they were fascinating objects—knives—and it was an enthralling piece of action for me to walk into Mr. Woolfork's with my grandfather, order White House Ice Cream, and sort through the knives offered there for sale or trade. Probably my hope each time was that my grandfather would get me a different knife, but he did that only a couple of times during my entire childhood. As for his own knife, he would wear down a blade maybe every ten years or so and have to trade the knife and some money with Mr. Woolfork or go to the hardware store for a new one.

The thought of this particular hardware item in an ice cream parlor comes back to me on occasion, its force field of mystery as strong as ever. I call them the ice cream knives, and somehow I am trying to bring them to bear on the image of my grandmother and her ability to deal so summarily with her Dominickers and Leghorns. There are affinities, but the two images—the ice cream knives and my grandmother with her chickens—are bound to a time and a culture and I have to leave them there in a loose and tentative circling. They seem to want to join in what might be a redefining of sacrament and sacrifice that I could understand, but it is a closure that I am finally incapable of forcing.

Besides, that would be asking too much of a motley assortment of used pocket knives in a cigar box, and also my grandmother would look back at me through the years, puzzled at such a farfetched notion. At the moment she is looking down at me as I reach under the thin cover-cloth she has spread over the leftovers on the table. There is not much fried chicken left except for a neck and a back with its vestigial tail pucker that she refers to as the preacher's nose. She knows I am full of White House Ice Cream but does not say anything. I am telling her about the ice cream knives. As I pick at the last of the nuggets of meat on the chicken back, I look up at her and see that she still has on the stained apron. She looks down at the bloodstains and then back to me without any comment. I don't say anything either. I am eating the best chicken I have ever eaten.

WILLIAM CORBETT

To Carol Braider's Kitchen

I first saw shelves of cookbooks, hanging copper pots, an overflowing spice rack—first drank wine and first ate garlic, olive oil, kosher salt, and soups made with homemade stock—in Carol Braider's kitchen. I was fifteen at the time and because of my upbringing expected kitchens to be sterile as hospital rooms. You went into them carefully for snacks, made no mess, and at dinner you cleaned your plate, did the dishes, and did not linger. It was a high compliment to declare some housewife's kitchen floor was clean enough you could eat off it.

Carol Braider's kitchen smelled of food and cooking; there was no attempt to hide what took place there. Her stove was crusted with spilled food and her refrigerator crammed with leftovers—it was what my grandmother called a pigsty. As she cooked Carol drank wine, and dishes were as much improvised as built from recipes. Her aprons were spotted and stained, and she was constantly hovering, tasting, stirring, adding pinches of this and that.

When you dined at Carol's table you were expected to smoke between courses, to drink a few glasses of wine, to talk over coffee. Carol's husband, Donald, was my teacher, and when I came into their house as a baby-sitter and had my first meal there, I was appalled and fascinated. We ate spaghetti with a sauce that was *not* meatballs, and their poodle, Bucky, ate with us—I can still see the strands of pasta disappearing one after another into his curly black muzzle. Growing up, I was usually put off by the strange odors in friends' kitchens. But Carol's kitchen did not repulse me. There was so much life and so many mysteries in the place that I was drawn to it.

My awareness of food as more than sustenance, of the lore of cooking, eating, and drinking, began in the Braider kitchen. Carol's kitchen meant freedom to me; although I was fed liberally, as any middle-class child of the fifties, I was confined to a dull menu and a tense dinner hour.

My mother must have felt similar constraints, for as she got to know Carol she began to consult French cookbooks, use wine in sauces, and generally let her kitchen and her cooking go. She had always loved to eat and had, until the ten days it took her to die from a fall down the stairs, a lumberjack's appetite—she was forever going on a diet tomorrow. Yet before Carol's influence my mother's cooking was bland as her kitchen was spotless, and her dinners had as much to do with discipline as food.

My father was a doctor, a general practitioner, and five nights a week he held office hours, first in a room off the kitchen and then at his office in a local shopping center. When he came home at sundown he wanted food on the table. He often teased in a crude way that he expected his wife to be a slave and wanted things just like they were in the old country, where the wife served the husband, then satisfied herself on what scraps were left over. His diatribe was interrupted by the ring of his office phone. "Take two aspirins and call me in the morning." "Give him a bath in Epsom salts." "I'll be out to see her after office hours." If my mother served us a dish fixed—she never "prepared" a meal—in a new way, he ate it without comment in an ostentatious silence. In response to her asking if he liked it, he'd snap, "I'm eating it ain't I!" He half meant this to be funny, but he had so little gift for humor that the effect was most often deadening.

About his own father he said little, but his most repeated anecdote had to do with food. His father and mother had a miserable marriage, one of such acrimonious contention his father frequently stayed away from home for days at a time. When he came back at lunchtime he found waiting, as expected, a mound of cold stuffed cabbage. He sat down to this plate and wordlessly polished off every one, as many as twenty-five stuffed leaves at one of these sittings. Then he retired to his chair in the living room and snored off his gluttony. For my father his surly father embodied some otherwise indefinable male prerogative. The apple, as Hungarians say, does not fall far from the tree.

Of course, there were many nights when my father was not the "moody Hungarian," and on these occasions my brother and I sometimes suffered as well. During the day my mother used the rod of my father's coming home to dinner to try to keep us in line. By the time he arrived, and we were seated, my mother served up our crimes with the casserole, and the meal quickly became a court in which we were lectured and punished—so many nights early to bed, so many afternoons doing yard work, etc. As he harangued us, we either wolfed our hamburgers, hot dogs, or tuna casseroles so as not to be hectored about our lack of appetite or, baleful night, pushed our food around our plates, food we had to force down even on an ordinary night: liver, broccoli, or lima beans! Frozen Ford Hook lima beans cooked in a pressure cooker resembling the Kaiser's helmet! Limas that were a stomach-turning green, mealy *and* slimy and even drowned in catsup . . . impossible to force down. My brother and I could not be members of the clean plate club no matter the threats that rained down on us: "You'll stay here and finish your dinner even if it takes until hell freezes over." It took years before we could laugh at this and years before we could deflect some of the unwanted parental scrutiny through jokes and mockery, but it's no wonder I still inhale my food, as if to escape the table.

We were so ceaselessly sullen and sharp with one another, so angry and in tears so often, that the family battles over dinner are more memorable than the dinners themselves, save for my mother's desserts. She had a sweet tooth and a gift for pies and cakes, inherited from her mother. Her cherry pie or butterscotch cream pie, chocolate pudding, her black cake with white mint frosting, or even her thin-sliced ice-box cookies kept my attention on any number of mushlike stews from the pressure cooker.

At restaurant tables my father could be expansive and, to restaurateurs, charming. Thursdays were his day off, and if he and my mother didn't drive to New York City for dinner and a show, we dined out at Manero's Steakhouse, The Clam Box, or the Algonquin Club with its glass boats of celery and olives. My father liked to have his steak burned black, but what he liked best in restaurants was to diagnose illnesses he could see in another diner's walk, posture, or complexion.

Most dinners out calmed our fractious temperaments, and we even enjoyed ourselves. If I wasn't always crazy about the food in these restaurants, I did fall in love with eating out. I think it was the staginess of restaurants, their rituals that first appealed to me. There was so much to pay attention to, so much to consider and to master. I imagined a curtain going up revealing a world arranged to surprise, test, and delight me.

As my parents got to know the Braiders and their interest in food developed, so did their taste in restaurants. During the late fifties and early sixties, good cooking began to mean French cooking. They were not adventurous eaters, and we sampled none of the ethnic restaurants in working-class Bridgeport. Indeed, their tastes must have been formed in part by their rejection of the ethnic cooking of their childhoods.

My father's mother was a hilariously rotten cook. We went there twice a year for the same lunch: stuffed cabbage (I still can't stomach even one!), chicken paprikash, a *bland* dish, noodles that came to the table in a clump, green beans in a red sauce named "lurch" by my mother, and a dessert of hard curls of pastry dusted with confectioner's sugar. We ate this meal in her kitchen with the windows closed even for the summer lunch, and we sweated like pigs as we groaned through the courses.

My mother's mother was more gifted. We still use her recipes for spinach or Swiss chard with hot bacon dressing and for shoofly pie, a Pennsylvania Dutch molasses-based breakfast pie she called crumb pie. She had a small vegetable garden behind her Pennsylvania home, and she put up vegetables and the huckleberries my grandfather and I gathered while stream fishing. She could bake a superb huckleberry pie and cursed them if they came out "runny buggers." And she could make a good dish of sauerkraut and roast pork. But she hated the mess of cooking, and her meals seemed less important than the cleanup to quickly restore her kitchen to apple-pie order. Outside of the lunches she made for her bridge club, she never served a guest in her house. And her husband refused to eat out after being served cake on a dirty plate at his sister's.

Throughout my childhood I heard women complain of slaving over a hot stove, of working their fingers to the bone fixing dinner, and of men who wouldn't lift a finger and if they did have a mind to wouldn't know what to do if you told them ten times. "Get out of the road," my grandmother shooed my grandfather out of her kitchen. Cooking, for the cooks of my childhood, and eating for all of us, was a form of labor. Given the extraordinary plenty of this country, it seems strange we did not enjoy ourselves more, but we did not seem to know how. Certainly my grandparents, three of whom were immigrants, sustained no peasant traditions. Perhaps we had so much we took food for granted and did not want to remind ourselves of how much we had.

The food at meals was often secondary, secondary to discipline, to cleanliness, and to shortcuts, bargains, and the new improved world of timesavers. Food, it seems, would take care of itself or be taken care of by ever-new marvels of processing. In my house meals were used to dispense justice, or they were finished speedily so the mess of cooking could be tamed and order restored.

In Carol Braider's kitchen I experienced a mixture of leisure and total attention. Every move Carol made mattered and could be enjoyed in itself; and every cheese, cut of meat, sauce, piece of fruit, or hunk of bread had a history, imparted some knowledge, and therefore possessed a presence. I remember watching once as Carol made *cassoulet* with its traditional goose fat, mutton, and pig's hocks. It was a snowy March afternoon, and she cooked from a thick book, warped by butter, oil, and a hundred different sauces. And I remember another *cassoulet* at her table twenty years later. Its texture, grainy and smooth, is in my mouth as I write. And I remember Carol's *crème caramel*, a slippery blond denseness, taste, color, and texture in each mouthful.

Certainly there was turmoil and sometimes sharp words as Carol cooked, but there was also the intense pleasure of watching someone in love with her work. And the special pleasure of listening and talking while you are doing something else at the same time. Carol seemed to be free to do as she pleased, and this sense of freedom was liberating for me. Carol made food that tasted good, sometimes great—but the greater pleasure came from enjoying food for its own sake. In this way the humblest sausage or a dish of leftover *cassoulet* has dignity. And so does the man or woman who sits down to savor it.

MICHAEL DORRIS

The Quest for Pie

One of my seminal childhood books was *Mickey Sees the U.S.A.*, a travel extravaganza in which Mickey, Minnie, and the two nephews, Morty and Ferdy, set out in a convertible and traverse the country. Every place they pass offers adventure, new sights, tasty treats—the ultimate all-American family vacation on wheels.

That was a while ago—so far in the past that Disneyland didn't yet exist as an promotional destination—but the high concept of that fictional journey took root in my imagination and informed each family outing. We had relatives scattered from Tacoma to Miami, from New York to San Francisco, from Tensed, Idaho, to Henderson, Kentucky, and every summer my mother, my aunt, and I managed to visit some of them. (Occasionally my cousin Frank would join us, but not for the long hauls. He had a tendency to become carsick, and once my aunt had to bathe his forehead in milk from the thermos just to keep him pacified until we reached a picnic ground.)

I was too young to drive, of course, so I became the navigator. In deep winter I would begin to clip coupons from the *National Geographic*, soliciting maps and lodging brochures from the tourist bureaus in states along our potential routes. These packets, as they were invariably called, arrived in impressively lumpy envelopes, extolling the "enchantment" of New Mexico, the "surprises" of Missouri, the "discovery" potential of New England. Sometimes, once I had learned to type, I wrote letters to accompany the clippings, broadly hinting that I had more than just a passing interest in this or that region and was in fact contemplating relocation. This line of correspondence yielded even more substantial harvests of mail when the respective state office of economic development got into the act. For one heady week in 1959 I received, absolutely free, a daily subscription to the Fort Worth *Star-Telegram*, forever establishing in my mind a loyalty to that plucky city in its underdog rivalry with Dallas—which was apparently above wooing my business.

Over the spring I would cull through my colorful stash, making short lists of state parks, petting zoos, and inexpensive motels that promised heated kidney-shaped swimming pools. I mail-ordered a wonderful little device that looked like a cross between a ballpoint pen and a thermometer. By merely adjusting a setting to correspond to the scale of a map and running the little metal wheel on the tip along the route of any highway, one got an instant reading of the approximate mileage involved. Then it was a matter of simple calculation. The distance from starting point A to destination B divided by fifty miles an hour (my family's average speed) times eight hours a day (their joint capacity behind the wheel) equaled the range of my accommodations search.

There was a limit, however, to the discretion I enjoyed. I was, after all, a child, a passenger, and my mother and aunt—the women who drove the car and paid the bills—had their own priorities that any proposal of mine necessarily had to incorporate. And those were, in a word, pie.

Looking back, I realize now that our journeys could quite accurately be described as a quest for pie. For instance, like experienced surfers who chart odd itineraries (Laguna to Capetown by way of The Big Island) in order to snag a reliable wave en route, I always had to include Paoli, Indiana, in any cross-country trip. There was a café off the square in that otherwise undistinguished hamlet where was found, according to my mother the connoisseur, a lattice crust like no other. Woven in intricate patterns across a sea of blueberry or peach, each segment was crisp and melting, studded with just the right amount of sugar, laced with a subtle jolt of almond extract, and browned to perfection. If I brought us through Paoli too soon after a major meal, we might order our twenty-five-cents-apiece slices for the crust alone, reluctantly leaving the fruit on the green plastic plates.

An innocuous-looking lunch counter in New Ulm, Minnesota, was the polar opposite: a decent pastry, nothing to complain about, but a truly spectacular chess or lemon or coconut cream within. The baker wouldn't tell, but my grandmother back home, upon hearing my aunt describe the airy yet smoothly substantial and satisfying volume of the filling, put her money on whipped egg whites and a dash of mace. Yet no amount of research was too exhaustive in pursuing the solution to so important a mystery, and that was fine with me. New Ulm was also the site of my favorite motel in the world: a swimming pool, a playground, and a fully made bed that folded down from a door in the wall—for eight dollars a night. I always finagled for us to hit town just as the sun was about to set, and consequently in New Ulm we ate pie for dinner, and then again for breakfast.

The pie map of the United States bears little resemblance to standard demographics. The New Yorks and Clevelands and Milwaukees are mostly etched in light print, marked with tiny dots, while the big black circles and capital letters are reserved for Brattleboro, Vermont, Tyler, Texas, Shelby, Montana, and Hays, Kansas. There are other features as well: On the west side of an invisible line, running roughly correspondent to the Appalachian Mountains, people prefer their doughnuts with icing. The South is The South when you leave a restaurant and instead of "good-bye" the waitress says, "Come back," unless it's New Orleans and she says, "Enjoy." The hallmark of the Midwest is an all-you-can-eat salad bar with at least one hundred items, most of them encased in jello. The Rocky Mountain states feed in pure volume, no matter what the course—the byword there is "Refill?"—whereas the Pacific Rim overdoes with fruit, as in a wedge of orange on the plate next to your pizza.

A culinary relief map of the country pretty much inverts the standard topological zones. Rather than the vaguely camel-back shape of North America (the humps represented by the two major north-south mountain chains), portion size translates into a more hammock effect. Sea level becomes the highest instead of the lowest part, and major sags and droopings are found inland from the coast. The state of Utah, for instance, constitutes the sleeping giant's hip, for it's a place that compensates for an arid and rather spartan environment by distributing ten-cents-a-pop soft ice cream machines at the exit door of most restaurants with large parking lots. Nebraska, home, at rest stops beckoning from the endless Interstate 80, of a particularly high-density food called potato meatloaf, accounts for the mid-depression of the continent, and the Old South—arbitrarily centered in Gadsen, Alabama, birthplace of the bottomless grits—is its lolling head, which, as any chiropractor will tell you, is the heaviest part of the body.

European tourists, with their effete tradition of teeny-tiny glasses of no-ice Coca-Cola, must be flabbergasted by the proffering of "20 oz. Thirst Busters" at each K-4 convenience store in the western steppes, and Japanese honeymooners, coming from a context of hundred-dollar steaks, must believe they've found paradise in the hefty "full-pound burgers" of rural Texas. Dietary largesse is patriotic, an entitlement protected, coterminous with individual ownership of automatic weapons, by the Constitution. We fought Iraq for the right to drive-thru an emporium boasting thirty-six oil-based flavors of frozen nondairy dessert. We celebrate Christmas with Federal-Expressed boxes of the world's weightiest Oregon pears or Idaho potatoes or California onions, or by sending each other baskets, their overflowing contents of dense Edams and Goudas barely contained by protective cellophane, shipped from Wisconsin—a state whose highway signs proclaim more often than historic markers or scenic vistas simply CHEESE. Less specific, but no less commanding, is the banner permanently overhanging Tower City, North Dakota, visible from five miles in any direction, reading FOOD, and followed by an enormous arrow pointing straight down to the rich, loamy landscape.

For Americans of a certain age and class, food is the punctuation of life, a commercial break between those bothersome segments of work or play that require the use of our hands, thus prohibiting their availability for unwrapping, unpeeling, or defrosting. Eating certifies leisure, the coffee 'n' Danish break a defiance of the time clock, the snack a voluntary intrusion into a routine not of our own making. And yet eating is also a kind of defensible duty, a recreation we can shrug off as a need, excuse ourselves for, indulge in with some righteousness. Researchers tell us that diners' pupils narrow to pinpoints when plates are set before them. Our beings concentrate, focus, rivet to the task at hand. We *need* to eat, we tell ourselves. Our parents mandated it, and it made them happy when we complied. It made us good. It made us grow. Unlike masturbation or pleasure reading or a midmorning nap, determined consumption carries a cultural cachet of respect, equaled only, on occasion, by refraining from eating, an appositive ingestive practice during which, if anything, our minds are even more firmly fixed on what's *not* for dinner. We read cookbooks as literature, copy and exchange exotic recipes, devote on the average (if we can afford it) one technology-laden room of our homes for the sole purpose of food storage and preparation, and another, plus deck or patio, for its display prior to disappearance. We support an entire industry of pressure-sealed leftover containers because we invariably prepare more of everything than we can swallow.

What is this obsession with jumbo helpings? Is it the aftershock of the Great Depression, a kind of chipmunk-drive to hoard unto and into ourselves so that in the event of lean days we can feed off our own stored fat—the ultimate convenience: we don't even have to leave home or microwave! Is it an assertion of Manifest Destiny, the ultimate reward for the transoceanic migration of our starving ancestors? Do we eat "because it's there"? Certainly for most of us the urge to stuff normally arises from habit, not from hunger. Early on we were initiated into the clean plate club by a ritual that normally culminated by a final swipe of every eating surface with Wonder Bread, a final lip-smack cleansing of each utensil, the lick of fingertip or lips so that no available morsels escape our digestive tract. Is it an instinctive urge toward bulk-signifying-power, a thumbed-nose at death, an insistence on closure before the hunt begins afresh?

Once food has been elevated to the category of Symbol, it begins to serve other, quasi-existential functions. Pie, for my mother, is much more than pie. It's the icing on the doughnut of a life challenged with disappointments in love and expectation, an affordable, slightly illicit luxury, a thing for which her addiction is coyly confessed. Pie has served as a staple of barter in her dealings with the universe—raised, as she was, in a complex Roman Catholic economy of indulgences and leveraged buy outs. The standard micro-system was fairly straightforward: three hundred days grace in the afterlife for the trifling price of a whispered ejaculation, more for a whole rosary or a novena. Attending mass on the first Friday of nine consecutive months purchased an insurance policy that guaranteed a happy death. Remaining resolutely still during the reading of the long gospel of Palm Sunday or Easter sprang the soul of your choice from Purgatory on early parole. Good works produced results, and there was no more potent form of good works than sacrifice, no sacrifice more expensive than one involving abstention from the thing most cherished. Abraham anted up Isaac. St. Elizabeth of Hungary abdicated her royal throne. St. Teresa, obviously on my family's wavelength, forwent all nourishment save a daily communion wafer.

It's little wonder that my mother's devotion to pie became a valuable commodity, her own personalized bargaining chip with a shrewd divinity so omniscient that no thumb-weighting of the scale or inflated price gouging would ameliorate. Pie, like the coin of the realm, came in various denominations, depending on my mother's sliding preference. Value was purely subjective, and all contracts were accepted or rejected on a single best-bid basis—no haggling allowed. In my mother's metaphysical accounts payable department, apple and cherry were nickel-and-dime, the stuff one threw on the table in exchange for the finding of lost car keys, but God *knew* how much she loved pecan. When she negotiated to voluntarily forgo it for, say, six months in reciprocation for my receipt of a college scholarship, it was a serious offer He couldn't ignore. My aunt once saved herself and an entire busload of other tourists from vaulting over the guardrail of a twisting Mexican highway by eliminating, curve by treacherous curve, every type of liquor, nut, and cake from her repertoire. There was something my grandmother wanted enough to warrant her giving up all candy—for life—at the age of forty-two, but she would never tell me what it was. Obviously "no publicity" was part of the deal.

At the other end of the spectrum from deprivation lies submission, and my family, *in extremis*, has been known to combine the two: not eating potato chips, for instance, is all the more negotiable when supplemented by a contract to consume salad without dressing. For every declined satin negligée among the major food groups, there's a hairshirt waiting to be donned, and doing with can easily double the value of doing without. But if comestibles are the hard currency of divine transaction, they're also clearly the reward for virtue. Dinner is to a day what dessert is to dinner.

Such philosophizing is a perfectly respectable way to wile away the minutes between breakfast and brunch. Think about the issue intensely enough, however, and the automatic biological response is hunger—an insight no stranger to the fast-food industry, whose stationary signs must convey, in staccato shorthand, a metalanguage that can be scanned, judged, and braked for by people hurtling past at seventy miles per hour. Inevitably in transit, where having enough fuel is an ever-present concern, there's a spillover from gas tank to stomach, and thus the vocabulary of a menu must communicate more than simple information, especially to a target audience. No type vehicle is more desirable than a station wagon or van, preferably one that carries a suction-cupped yellow window message announcing CHILD ON BOARD. Not only do such chariots transport multiple hungry passengers, but they are likely to be commanded by juveniles who experience no hesitation in making a snap decision. In casting their net for such prey, restaurateurs lay a double bait. To the recently literate young they dangle, "Fried!" and to the long-suffering parents they whisper, "Relief."

"Homemade" is a basic code word of such establishments, along with "Family Style" and "E-Z Access," but these phrases are simply substitutes and stand-ins for their true meaning: double-burgers, grilled cheese, and peanut butter. "Don't worry," parents are assured. "They won't gag. And we won't complain when they spill their drink." In many of these places, pictographs replace writing on the laminated menus. Standardized, no-surprises photographs beckon diners seeking the reassurance of an homogenized national cuisine. Adults are lured by the supposed economy of "platters," with their suggestion of balanced nutrition coupled with volume, and proprietors compete against each other with ingenious "extras." "Boy Have We Got Chicken!" brags a

Kountry Kitchen in Great Falls, Montana, whereas a Denny's in Bellevue, Washington, simply exclaims, "Canadians!" Certain nouns, masquerading as other grammatical forms, are especially in evidence —country, purveyor, family, kitchen, dining—and ersatz symbols as decor ("antique" or quilted wall-hangings, oak-grain coat hooks, and wood-burned slogans) also contribute to a sense of the predictable and familiar "away from home."

Exceptions from this type of lingo often signal promising gastronomical finds, for even as a chef might err on the billboard, being slightly off the mark in comprehending the lowest common denominator, so too might the side dishes retain a regional or idiosyncratic signature. "Eggroll and Barbecue Take Out" could spell disaster, but at least it will probably be a memorable one. "Live Bait and Ice Cream" indicates a particular sensibility. The old-fashioned word "café" is often a plus, especially when preceded by the cook's first name, and surrounded, at six A.M., by a semicircle of parked police cruisers and pickup trucks bearing local license plates. Once inside, listen for a bell attached to the door, look for day-of-the-week specials listed on a blackboard in illegible penmanship, and keep an eye out for real plants in the windows. If actual herbs or tomatoes are growing, settle yourself upon a round stool at the lunch counter. And if the owner confesses, with some pride, that the well-scrubbed stains on the baby high-chair upholstery were made by her very own grandchildren, contemplate permanent residence. You may have stumbled into an eatery where children are regarded as people with smaller appetites and not as a separate, cholesterol-crazed subspecies.

It's the kind of joint Mickey and Minnie were always pulling into during their journey of forty years past, the Americana full of Frank Capra faces, bottomless cups of coffee, and in-the-booth jukeboxes with selections drawn from local favorites rather than MTV. It flourished when geography meant more than a printout of bills from the same motel chain, when the Mississippi River divided—except for Pittsburgh—the radio stations whose call letters began with a W from those that started with a K, when every small town produced its own version of a newspaper reporting its own version of the news. And it still exists.

In 1986 my wife and I drove across country with our daughters to visit my grandmother. We probably appeared to be the ideal demographic—the nuclear family feeding group—but in our hearts we were Kerouac, ready to be transformed by the bizarre, the offbeat, the unknown. We eschewed major highways, fine family dining that provided crayons with the place mats, and set our radar for hand-stitched curtains in the windows of establishments with names like Betty's. We spent a night in the Atlasta Motel because it advertised "in-room clock radios" and "heat." And late one afternoon we came by chance upon the café of our dreams in an otherwise ordinary little town in the Pacific Northwest. A mimeographed sheet, tucked between the salt and pepper shakers, informed us that a "pie war" was presently under way with a rival establishment, one block down Main Street, and as a result, a slice from any of the sixteen varieties made fresh on the premises that morning could be had for only thirty-five cents. So confident was the baker that he invited us to sample the competition (naturally, at the same price), then return and get our money back if his was not better. For me, it was Paoli squared—Parsifal had found the Holy Grail—and five years later we didn't just come back to that town to order more pie. We came back for good.

EVAN JONES

Delmonico's

In the early nineteenth century, the first American menu to list all its selections in two languages—translating the names of French classic dishes in an adjoining column—was that of the Restaurant Français des Frères Delmonico. Among the scores of entrées presented on its eleven crowded pages were a dozen kinds of simmered beef, seven variations of grilled steak, and thirty-eight chicken dishes, including *euisse de poulet en papillot*, or drumsticks in paper sleeves. Once, this menu, in a puffed-up phrase, was declared to be "the Magna Carta of sophisticated and gracious dining in America." Whatever the encomium, the beginning of Delmonico's was the start of something good, a first effort to assure New York diners that they could eat as stylishly as bon vivants across the Atlantic.

The man behind this bill of fare (it translated "ham and eggs" as *jambon de Virginie aux oeufs*) was twenty-eight-year-old Lorenzo Delmonico, whose family made its surname a part of the American language, analogous with eating in splendor. Astonishingly, none of the family had been trained in *le vrai cuisine*, nor had even waited tables in Paris. The first of the clan was John Delmonico, a retired sea captain whose three-masted schooner had engaged in trade between the West Indies and New York, and who had grown up in the wine country of the southern Alps. Fed up with life at sea and impressed with the boom-town tempo of Manhattan, John brought over from their home in the Swiss province of Ticino his elder brother Peter, who was a confectioner, as glad to shake off the dust of the Old World as he. Together they began to operate a small shop near the Battery in which they sold wine from barrels, and offered a place to sit for patrons who bought fancy cakes and ices. When it opened it was as unpretentious as any one-room hamburger joint—about a half-dozen wooden tables with primitive chairs to match, and a counter along one side that was laden with the newly baked pastries, napkins of white cloth, and pottery cups and plates. But soon the café developed a reputation for hospitality and "the prompt and deferential attendance" that could not be had, as one young diner recalled, at any other New York eating place of the period. The unimpressive shop caught on, and became known in advertisements as "Delmonico & Brother, Confectioners and Restaurant Français," for John and Peter had found that they could hire French cooks from the steady stream of immigrants arriving in pursuit of American dollars.

Yet however prosperous the brothers may have been as entrepreneurs, neither of them suspected when they welcomed their nephew Lorenzo that the family's success for the next hundred years was assured. Under their proprietorship, and with the chance to learn from the French emigrés in the kitchen, the nephew turned himself into an astute and sensitive master of Parisian-style dining.

It was a time when there were virtually no places in Manhattan that could be called restaurants. The average public dining room, according to a firsthand report, served little else but "very rare roast beef in thick slices, or a beefsteak barely warmed through, English plum pudding, and half-and-half ale . . . customers helped themselves, bolted the food, and rushed out. . . ." On the other hand, the same observer noted, Delmonico's offered "delicious dishes and moderate charges [which] suited the pockets of Knickerbocker youth. . . ." James Fenimore Cooper drew the contrast in sharp distinction when he returned from living abroad. "The Americans are the grossest feeders of any nation known . . ." he told his readers, "their food is heavy, coarse, and indigestible. . . ."

It was plain to the Delmonicos that their rescue squad had arrived in time. The family of uncles, nephews, and cousins soon decided to take on New York, and they found the competition guilty as charged by Cooper. A few blocks from the brothers' café on South William Street was Daniel Sweeney's "six-penny house." Here a small plate of stringy meat and tepid vegetables could be had for sixpence, and rice or corn-meal mush went for ninepence—Sweeney's may have been the first self-declared "fast food" dining room in the U.S. Not much different was Brown's Ordinary in Water Street, likened by a *Tribune* reporter to an English-style chophouse, one which—hard to believe—dealt every day with up to two thousand customers. The quality of Brown's food may have been a cut above Sweeney's, but there was nothing to appeal to New Yorkers who wanted to dine in leisurely style.

More and more of them were becoming interested in nightlife. There were "pleasure gardens" for food and frolic, and there was, at last, John Jacob Astor's elegant hotel, which attracted people who had learned not to bolt their food. The more serious eaters among them discovered Delmonico's, and the interest in the café's novel menu persuaded the brothers in 1829 to open a second place, and to bring over Lorenzo, then only nineteen. For a decade, while New York developed into a city often praised by travelers ("situated on an island . . . it rises, like Venice, from the sea [and] receives into its lap tribute of all the riches of the earth") Lorenzo saw the opportunities in the same rosy terms. He became convinced that Delmonico's should attract all those New Yorkers who had acquired cultivated appetites as well as purse strings open to expensive, even luxurious dining. When a fire forced the construction of a new Delmonico's, the family imported two Pompeian columns to frame the corner doorway of the impressive three-story building at 2 South William Street, which had a café, lobby, and dining room on the ground level, and ballrooms and lounges above. The word "Delmonico" was chiseled in stone above the Italian pillars.

As the family supply sergeant, Lorenzo ensured the best of ingredients for the kitchen by rising daily before dawn to check out the open-air market on the Hudson River side of town. Here was a sprawling scene of sheds, stalls, piers, patched and rebuilt structures filled with game and much pork, and almost as much beef, some produce from the nearby countryside, bananas from the Caribbean, seafood from the Atlantic, and delicacies from Europe and the Mediterranean. A dark-haired, stocky youth distinguished by full sideburns and a good wardrobe, Lorenzo knew how to get the best from farmers and merchants, or any other suppliers. By midmorning daily he was on his way back, his carriage loaded with *garde manger* booty. If the vegetables that day had been less than choice, he could meet the chef's needs most often with the produce the family had planted on the two-hundred-acre farm it maintained near what was to become Atlantic Avenue in Brooklyn.

Like other Manhattan eating places, Delmonico's prided itself on wild food served in sophisticated style. The visiting British writer Captain Marryat, a satisfied patron who was impressed by the New York market bounty, wrote that "the great delicacy . . . are the terrapin and the canvasback ducks. . . . They have sheeps' head, shad . . . their salmon is not equal to ours . . . oysters are very plentiful, very large, rather insipid . . . [but] there are plenty of good things for the table. . . ." Nineteenth-century travelers often based their judgments of American restaurants on the taste of food that was not domestically raised, for they rightly believed that a knowing chef could distinguish himself by his understanding that woodland fish and game draw unique flavors from the nature of the country in which they mature. Like Les Trois Frères Provençaux, which brought to Paris the taste of the Mediterranean,

Delmonico's reflected untamed America. In the era in which pork was considered "common doin's," the choice of red meat was a sign of virility, and status, too. Pigs overran the new country "like vermin," and they were treated as such. They were easy to raise because they fended for themselves. In rural districts a good-sized hog was shared by three or four families. In the towns, pork wasn't considered impressive enough for a home-cooked company dinner, and it was unfit for Delmonico patrons—the stylish restaurant's lengthy menu, which Lorenzo had composed, lists not a single item of pork.

In the British-American tradition, that early bill of fare is dominated by beef, and it wasn't long before Lorenzo's kitchen staff was known for featuring a particular piece of beef—it was the first cut near the head of the short loin, the chunk that is now known variously as a club steak, or a "Delmonico." The cut has always been an expensive choice; home recipes sometimes have cautionary phrases appended: "Delmonico steaks—if the budget allows." In Jeanne Owen's Delmonico recipe, that dynamo of New York Wine and Food Society after World War II stipulated a further qualification. "If an added touch of swank or taste is desired," she wrote, "pour [a pony of brandy] into the pan after the steaks have been removed *'pour glacer'* as the French have it. Then pour the juices of the meat mixed with brandy over the steaks."

"Swank" was a word just coming into usage as Lorenzo Delmonico, taking over after the death of John and the retirement of Peter, began to make the restaurant a synonym for fashion. In the minds of New York's gentry, Lorenzo's immediate competition was the dining room of the Astor House, the nearest contender for the "swank" patronage. In the first half of the nineteenth century, the Astor was enthusiastically touted by Americans and Europeans alike as a "palace" among hotels. But, though it served *de luxe* meals to those who could afford them, its big dining room offered a table d'hôte menu with a mingling of French and colonial items, including boiled cod alongside *ballon de mouton aux tomates, macaroni au parmesan,* and desserts as prosaic as Queen Pudding. As a restaurant without the burden of providing rooms for scores of travelers, Delmonico's stuck to menus that were exclusively à la carte.

Under the system that became known as "the American plan" (a carryover from colonial days of roadside taverns), hotel keepers charged their guests a lump sum that covered three to four meals a day as well as a place to sleep. The custom may have started out with a wayfarer eating whatever his landlord and family were having for breakfast, dinner, or supper, but as hotel competition grew, potluck gave way to something that was described by some observers as "cuisine." Table d'hôte, in its "American plan" version, meant vast tables loaded with dozens of dishes, hot and cold. There were tureens of soup, and platters bearing choices of meat and game, various vegetables, and great bowls of cornmeal pudding and other boiled grains. The common table was perceived as a symbol of democracy, but its days became numbered when society caught on to the Delmonico vision of what a good restaurant could be like.

In the course of his long influence on American eating, Lorenzo presided over a half-dozen establishments bearing the family name. He had a keen sense of New York's residential shifts. When John Jacob Astor moved his family (Astor House remained on lower Broadway) to the Thirty-fourth Street site later occupied by the Empire State Building, Lorenzo watched the trend that made Fifth Avenue a necklace of ornamented mansions. In one of these, the four-story Italianate town house on Fourteenth Street built by a whale-oil tycoon, Lorenzo established at the beginning of the Civil War a splendid complex of restaurants, ballrooms, cafés, and residential suites. He kept the downtown restaurants on South William Street, and one near City Hall, but in the new place the Delmonicos could concentrate on what the *Times* called "the very centre of fashionable life." The newspaper, indeed, expressed doubt that Europe could boast anything to compete with the new Delmonico's in understated elegance.

The ground-floor café on Fourteenth Street, with its marble-top tables and without a bar that pandered to those who might order alcohol, was the first of its kind; the private dining rooms and apartments upstairs were innovations that enhanced the life-styles of powerful men. There were travelers who came to Delmonico's not simply to dine well but to share with Lorenzo their enthusiasm for the fastidious preparation of food. General Winfield Scott was a Mexican War hero who became Chief of Staff, and his career had required him to cover the country on inspection tours from which he returned to check in at Delmonico's. He was the only candidate for the presidency who was defeated (as gossip had it) by charges that he was guilty of luxurious eating. He was notorious for putting on airs, and he was accused of posturing by those who whispered that he lived on "hasty plates of turtle and oyster soup." A bountifully padded soldier, six feet four, he seemingly would rather be fat than President—he carried only four states when he was defeated by Franklin Pierce.

Scott was one of a very few regulars who could get Lorenzo to leave his small office to dine vis-à-vis. As longtime friends, they could discuss the menu, trading expertise about origins of classic dishes. Scott had eaten studiously in Paris, at least once taking his officer's leave time to drink in the mysteries of Chef Baleine's cuisine at Rocher de Canale, or the techniques that distinguished Very's, and La Restaurant Les Trois Frères Provençaux. But, at least as importantly, he brought Lorenzo news of the delights of American gastronomy beyond the New York horizon.

Scott applauded the Delmonico policy of serving only aged southern hams, and those from Charles County, Maryland, stuffed with spring greens, were among his favorites. For his own larder, he had regular shipments to his quarters of barrels in which, packed in the ashes of fruitwood fires, were hams taken only from hogs that ran wild in beechnut woods. Scott once passed on his appreciation of Great Lakes whitefish along with a recipe: "They must be cooked *done*, and immediately rolled up, one after another, in a napkin, doubled and heated almost to scorching. Then they are to be served and eaten immediately, unrolling the napkin as the fish are wanted." The gourmandizing general was as keen about roast canvasback duck as either Lorenzo or their friend Sam Ward (who liked his duck with gooseberries), while the Delmonico kitchen recognized the best of American cooking by serving the bird with fried slices of hominy grits. Unlike other waterfowl, the canvasback of the eastern seaboard fly-way chose to feed on the roots of an aquatic grass known as wild celery, which then was rampant in the Chesapeake Bay region.

As Lorenzo's menus increasingly recognized the best of native provender, Americans felt freer to boast openly of regional dishes. Canvasbacks appealed to nineteenth-century epicures because they lacked the fishy tang characteristic of other wild ducks. European restaurant-goers bolstered local pride. Charles Dickens, in whose honor one of Delmonico's most noteworthy galas was given, told his readers about the skies over the Chesapeake Bay that were blackened by the seasonal flights of canvasbacks, and the Delmonico chef, Alessandro Filippini, later wrote that "no game is more highly praised or more eagerly sought after in Europe," in effect certifying the general American contribution to classic feasting.

Two items of the Delmonico kitchen that evolved into menu classics were *aspic de canvasback* and truffled ice cream, the latter becoming an essential in the minds of New York high livers who liked to have a hand in their own private dinners. Leonard Jerome, the grandfather of Winston Churchill, was one, and so was August Belmont, a Wall Street leader of the new social order. As important as any of numerous others was Lorenzo's longtime admirer, Sam Ward, the so-called King of the Lobby, who at sixteen had become a devotee of the first Delmonico café. Throughout his influential life in New York and his career of political advocacy in Washington, Ward made a practice of eulogizing Lorenzo, once describing him as "the young Napoleon of our future army of restaurateurs," once as one who was shrewd enough to see "the unfolding resources of the mighty West." Sam Ward had gone to California during the gold rush, and had eaten with miners who had made famous the simple combination of oysters and scrambled eggs known as Hangtown Fry. But in the East, Ward became known for his own recipes for such delicacies as wild mushrooms and aged Virginia ham under glass, and for his way with minced chicken and bacon. He was an epicure whose advice on food and wine was sought by contemporaries who, coming into sudden wealth, were in much need of social guidance. Like Winfield Scott, Sam Ward had brought home from his serious study of Parisian kitchens many ideas to enhance the dinner parties that made his name almost as much a household word as that of his sister who wrote "The Battle Hymn of the Republic." And he may have been the only amateur cook permitted by Lorenzo to prepare his own sauces side by side with Delmonico chefs.

In the ballroom of Delmonico's on Fourteenth Street, Ward McAllister, nephew of Sam Ward, established his reputation as the guru of society matrons. He began the custom of exclusive dances, which were known as cotillions and were most often followed by elaborate supper parties; and he also invented the term "the Four Hundred" to designate those he found acceptable as the "society" that counted. He made Newport, R.I., famous for society picnics staged on his country estate. It was his boast that he showed America how to entertain alfresco as ostentatiously as at a meal in Delmonico's indoor opulence. But after a brief period, McAllister found it shocking that in Manhattan fewer than a dozen of the best families had their own chefs, and that the nation in general was being taken over by *nouveaux riches*.

The majordomo of the Four Hundred may not have realized just how times had changed.* But the signs were there. Increasingly, Lorenzo

*Unlike Lorenzo, McAllister refused to see much merit in cooking that wasn't French oriented. At a dinner for sixty in Newport he arranged a "cook-off" between a noted black cook and a

found himself dragooned into providing food and service for people who preferred to entertain at home. Manhattan families summering in Newport prevailed upon Delmonico's to cater country parties, and dozens of waiters were transported north, along with wagonloads of food, as relief for the kitchen staffs of Newport's wealthy vacationers. The middle classes were affected differently by the new tempo. In the 1880s, armed with new culinary technology, more modestly affluent families were beginning to use their kitchens and dining rooms in a renewed effort, an observer said, "to secure or elevate their often shaky status." As servants proved hard to get, Juliet Corson addressed the new interest in food by opening the New York Cooking School in response to requests from some of the city's wealthy hostesses. Dinner parties at home became the vogue. One might not be able to afford Delmonico's or to rival the Astors in elaborate cooking, but guests could be impressed by expensive ingredients when they were prepared with care for your own dinner parties.

Nonetheless, Delmonico's remained the Times Square for itinerant diners-out as well as the Fifth Avenue crowd, and as always it was the place to find the best of new ingredients from everywhere. An habitué named Ben Wenberg, who operated his own coastwise shipping line to the Caribbean and South America, added to the restaurant's aura when he came in from a voyage one day and demanded a brazier and spirit lamp in order to demonstrate a new lobster recipe. His dish was found to be so agreeable that it went on the menu with his name appended. His elegant creamed lobster became even more talked about after Wenberg was turned out of Delmonico's following a fight he caused with another patron—what had been known as Lobster Wenberg was henceforward listed as Lobster Newburg.

Delmonico's was also the place where people first began to speak with some excitement about avocados. Richard Harding Davis, novelist, playwright, swashbuckling journalist, and escort of Ethel Barrymore, made his usual reentry visit to Delmonico's upon return from assignment in Caracas. On this occasion, he showed up bearing a basketful of avocados, which he had eaten for the first time in Venezuela. Although other Americans by then were growing avocados as an exotic fruit, they weren't yet being served at the table. A Florida horticulturist had brought some from Mexico in 1833, and a couple of generations later

---

French chef. The latter, he said in his autobiography, was "very much the victor . . . an educated, cultivated artist"; his competitor had only "a wonderful, natural taste, and the art of making things savory, i.e. taste good."

an avocado grove was planted in Santa Barbara by a California judge named Ord. But Delmonico regulars were the first Americans to encourage a place on the menu for a fruit course of "alligator pears," as they were first known. As listed in the massive Delmonico book of recipes, the fruit was peeled, cut in slices, seasoned with salt, pepper and vinegar, with lemon slices on the side. After some acceptance early in this century, the myriad ways of serving avocados began to develop after World War II, when they were grown in Florida and California as a cash crop that became available in supermarkets. Henry T. Finck, the New York music critic and gastronome, compared his first encounter with avocados to "the discovery of a new song by Schubert or Grieg, or a new painting by Titian." The avocado's firm flesh, "though soft and custardy," he wrote, "has a most exquisite flavor which, with oil and vinegar makes a symphony of flavors." After the early introduction at Delmonico's, avocados became so characteristic of American summer fare that they are available in every small town.

The pervasiveness of the dish called Chicken à la King (the bane of business lunches and sometimes served as a late supper indulgence) has been attributed to one of Lorenzo's guests, but there are also others credited for the first serving of this creamed chicken that is made prettier with chopped green pepper and pimiento. For some reason, claims about its origin are numerous. Foxhall Keene, a rather rich young patron, is said to have brought the idea to Delmonico's, and on Long Island the chef of the Brighton Beach Hotel prepared an almost identical recipe and asked his boss, E. Clarke King, to lend it his name. Charles Ranhofer, who presided over Lorenzo's kitchen for years after his boss's death, is the chef who got the honors for creating Baked Alaska, a dessert conceived to help celebrate the purchase of the territory that is now the forty-ninth state.

As Lorenzo's life as the host of New York raced on, he was given credit for the influence he had on the nation as a whole. "O rare Delmonico!" a literary editorial writer intoned in the *New York Herald*, "we would say [this] of the great king of cuisine, as it was said of Ben Jonson, did it not strike us that a captious world might think that the perfect chef of chefs was in the habit of presenting his viands underdone. Let us rather say *sagacious Delmonico*, for it is the live tradition of nearly a century in Gotham that 'as Delmonico goes, so goes dining.' " Praise for Lorenzo followed him as once more he moved uptown, building in 1876 a lavish new complex of dining rooms on Fifth Avenue and Twenty-sixth Street. The new restaurant was described as "the pride of the nation," by the *Tribune*. The newspaper wasn't shy about its approval: "There is no restaurant in Paris or London or Vienna which can compete with our Delmonico's in the excellence and variety of its fare," the *Tribune* writer continued. "This is mainly the result of keeping the business in the same family. . . ."

As general manager of the four Delmonico establishments, Lorenzo had the help of his brother Sirio, who often came along on his sunrise marketing sorties and who ran Delmonico's on Chambers Street. A cousin was in charge of the Broad Street place, Lorenzo's brother Constant at the old South William Street quarters. Charles, Lorenzo's nephew, took command of the new flagship restaurant on Fifth, and in the kitchen was Chef Charles Ranhofer, the Paris-trained cook who had had stints in New Orleans and Washington, D.C., before Lorenzo hired him. Ranhofer believed, as he once wrote, that the "culinary art should be the basis of all diplomacy." It was a statement Lorenzo might have made. He picked chefs and sous chefs for Delmonico kitchens who were to continue his standards for hospitality and high-quality cooking when they ran restaurants in other regions. Lorenzo and Ranhofer saw eye to eye immediately, and the young chef (he was twenty-six when he took over Delmonico's) got the credit for developing Lorenzo's policy of emphasizing ingredients considered uniquely American. Ranhofer's paupiettes of kingfish and buffalo fish bavarois failed to ignite the public fancy as did Baked Alaska, but his touch with earthy American ingredients was an inspiration of sorts for cooks at home. He took, for example, pumpkins he had cut into matchstick size, parboiled the pieces, and dusted them with flour, then deep-fried them as a forerunner of shoestring potatoes.

Ranhofer was firmly in place when Lorenzo died in 1881, leaving the Delmonico empire to his nephew Charles. The transition proved to be seamless, but across the street from the newest Delmonico address was a former waiter who was to make his name as a rival to all that Lorenzo had initiated in his half-century of restaurant building. Louis Sherry, who earlier quit his job as maître d'hôtel in the dining room of the Hotel Brunswick, began to challenge Lorenzo's reputation as a pacesetter. Delmonico's was a place for serious banquets in honor of visiting firemen from the reigning Prince of Wales to Louis Bonaparte, the future Napoleon III. Sherry's became the same kind of gastronomic institution, housed in equal luster in a four-story mansion designed by Stanford White.

Sherry's was a rendezvous for J. Pierpont Morgan and his set, and for a while the competition was nip and tuck. "The public . . . fickle and uncertain," wrote Frank Chase, the host of the Algonquin Hotel Round Table, "would shift for no apparent reason back and forth across the avenue. One year, Sherry's would have the advantage, until suddenly everyone would begin going to Delmonico's, and continue for a year or so before they suddenly shifted back. If you were taking the reigning favorite of the theater to lunch or supper . . . you would first find out which of these two places was in favor at the moment." The kitchens of both restaurants were considered superlative; the competition was often heated up by Louis Sherry's skillful flattery of society egos and by Charles Ranhofer's mastery of the gala dinner. The feud was inspired publicity, and newspapers and nationally distributed magazines filled columns with what went on in the kitchens and who sat with whom in the dining rooms.

One result was that "Delmonico" became the unchallenged synonym of excellence in the gastronomic world. The family name was appropriated by various hotels and restaurants as new eating places were opened across the country. In downtown Boston's Pie Alley there was a Delmonico café that flourished for years. One of the earliest popular stops in San Francisco was named without apology the Delmonico Hotel. Even restaurant proprietors in cow towns and mining camps composed menus by copying directly from Delmonico's, although these enterprises, said one reporter, "were prepared to serve only a limited selection of frying-pan and boiling-pot victuals." Only a gullible stranger would take such bills of fare seriously. The novelist Owen Wister tells of a traveler who ordered *vol-au-vent* because he saw it listed. As Wister had it, "The proprietor yanked out his six-shooter and said, menacingly: 'Stranger, you'll take hash!' "

In places where the chef (rather than the establishment's name) had been acquired from the original Delmonico's, there was nothing primitive about the menus. Among the most creative of those trained by Lorenzo was Jules Harder, who bemoaned the fact that California's suddenly wealthy mine owners were too ignorant to appreciate his delicate sauces. In San Francisco, after ten years at Delmonico's, Harder was hired to open the kitchens of the celebrated Palace Hotel with its equally impressive Palm Court. A generation later, another Delmonico graduate signed on at the lavishly appointed Broadmore Casino, a Colorado oasis that brought New York's rich to climb Pike's Peak. Meanwhile, simple dishes credited to Delmonico's, like veal hash in St. Louis, potatoes with Parmesan in St. Paul, *capon au vin blanc* in New York State, began to appear in local charity cookbooks and became circulating recipes among home cooks. The spicy dish called Country Captain, a southern version of curried chicken, was a national success after Alessandro Filippini, who had served Delmonico's as both a restaurant manager and chef, included the recipe in his *The Table: How to Buy Food, How to Cook It and How to Serve It* (1889). And the compendious *Buckeye Cookery*, published in the same period, provided housekeepers with instructions for the uncomplicated Delmonico custard ice cream recipe. As late as 1970, James Beard published in his *American Cookery* the beefsteak and oyster pie instructions of Pierre Caron, the Delmonico chef whose book, *French Dishes for American Tables*, had been translated in 1886.

There were bumper crops of recipe manuals of all kinds during the decades in which the Delmonico name was preeminent, and some reflected the influence on home kitchens of professional cooks. Chefs like Victor Hipzler, who gained fame after he left Sherry's to take over the St. Francis Hotel in San Francisco, wrote columns for newspapers. His creations, or his variations on old themes, had such titles as Celery Victor, or Lalla Rhook (a frozen punch named for a Persian fable). Among restaurants that served the dishes—along with Charles Ranhofer's Baked Alaska—was Solari's of Geary Street in San Francisco, where the Drews and the Barrymores might be seated next to the family of M. F. K. Fisher, and where the dramatic Delmonico dessert was considered a "bigger eyecatcher" for the Fishers than Broadway's royal family.

In an assessment of the American appreciation of food served with style and finesse, Charles Ranhofer identified the people who ate Delmonico's food as "by taste and breeding epicureans." Within a decade of Lorenzo's death, Ranhofer published his book called *The Epicurean*, in which he expressed this snide sentiment along with a 1,500-page collection of professional recipes. He dedicated the work to "the Messrs. Delmonico for the interest shown by them in developing the gastronomic art in this country." For some of Lorenzo's faithful, the book was an act of treason. Years after his boss was dead, Leopold Rimmer, who ran one of Lorenzo's dining rooms, branded it "the only mistake ever made against the interest of the Delmonico business [because it] gave away all the secrets . . . every Tom, Dick and Harry who calls himself a cook, and learned his trade in Delmonico's kitchen, can make up the finest dinners with that book. . . . There is hardly a hotel in New York today," said Rimmer bitterly, "whose chef did not learn his trade at Delmonico's."

For Wall Street regulars at the end of the twentieth century, the

Delmonico name remains carved in stone above a pillared entrance at the corner of Beaver and South William Streets, where the first of the family's opulent hostelries opened in 1838. A century after Lorenzo's death, the *New York Times* described the Delmonico corner as "a melancholy sight, so empty and deserted that it seems unhaunted even by ghosts." It is true that the last member of the Delmonico clan left the restaurant business during Prohibition, but the reputation Lorenzo created hasn't been extinguished. I went down to South William Street to have lunch one day not long ago. The restaurant was back in business, and the place was filled with prosperous people, happily eating from a menu that reflects the country's bounty. Perhaps Lorenzo's greatest contribution is that he made the Delmonico name a symbol of American food with a sophisticated edge, not only in restaurants but in average kitchens. Delmonico's helped to push the country away from the idea of food as fodder. Increasingly, most Americans took to Lorenzo's standards as a sign of civilization. Others, like his friend Mark Twain, would still cling—when it came to eating at home—to traditional fare that was simple, untainted, and abundant; and they remained suspicious of anything that seemed to be putting on airs.

ALICE WATERS

The Farm–Restaurant Connection

I have always believed that a restaurant can be no better than the ingredients it has to work with. As much as by any other factor, Chez Panisse has been defined by the search for ingredients. That search and what we have found along the way have shaped what we cook and ultimately who we are. The search has made us become part of a community—a community that has grown from markets, gardens, and suppliers and has gradually come to include farmers, ranchers, and fishermen. It has also made us realize that, as a restaurant, we are utterly dependent on the health of the land, the sea, and the planet as a whole, and that this search for good ingredients is pointless without a healthy agriculture and a healthy environment.

We served our first meal at Chez Panisse on August 28, 1971. The menu was pâté en croûte, duck with olives, salad, and fresh fruit, and the meal was cooked by Victoria Wise, who, together with Leslie Land and Paul Aratow, was one of the three original cooks at the restaurant. The ducks came from Chinatown in San Francisco and the other ingredients mostly from two local supermarkets: the Japanese produce concession at U-Save on Grove Street and the Co-op across the street. We sifted through every leaf of romaine, using perhaps 20 percent of each head and discarding the rest. We argued about which olives we ought to use with the duck and settled without much enthusiasm on green ones whose source I don't recall, agreeing after the fact that we could have done better. To this day we have yet to find a source of locally produced olives that really satisfies us.

We don't shop at supermarkets anymore, but in most respects the same processes and problems apply. Leslie Land recalls, "We were home cooks—we didn't know there were specialized restaurant suppliers. We thought everybody bought their food the way we did." I think that ignorance was an important, if unwitting, factor in allowing Chez Panisse to become what it is. Often, we simply couldn't cook what we wanted to cook because we couldn't find the level of quality we needed in the required ingredients, or we couldn't find the ingredients at all. Our set menus, which we've always published in advance so customers can choose when they want to come, featured the phrase "if available" with regularity during the first seven or eight years. Since we've always felt that freshness and purity were synonymous with quality, there were few guarantees that what we needed would appear in the form and condition we wanted when we wanted it.

If, as I believe, restaurants are communities—each with its own culture—then Chez Panisse began as a hunter-gatherer culture and, to a lesser extent, still is. Not only did we prowl the supermarkets, the stores and stalls of Chinatown, and such specialty shops as Berkeley then possessed (some of which, like the Cheese Board and Monterey Market, predated us and continue to develop from strength to strength) but we also literally foraged. We gathered watercress from streams, picked nasturtiums and fennel from roadsides, and gathered blackberries from the Santa Fe tracks in Berkeley. We also took herbs like oregano and thyme from the gardens of friends. One of these friends, Wendy Ruebman, asked if we'd like sorrel from her garden, setting in motion an informal but regular system of obtaining produce from her and other local gardeners. We also relied on friends with rural connections: Mary Isaak, the mother of one of our cooks, planted fraises des bois for us in Petaluma, and Lindsey Shere, one of my partners and our head pastry cook to this day, got her father to grow fruit for us near his place in Healdsburg.

Although most of our sources in the restaurant's early days were of necessity unpredictable, produce was the main problem area, and we focused our efforts again and again on resolving it. Perhaps more than any other kind of foodstuff, produce in general and its flavor in particular have suffered under postwar American agriculture. Although we've been able to have as much cosmetically perfect, out-of-season fruit and vegetables as anyone could possibly want, the flavor, freshness, variety, and wholesomeness of produce have been terribly diminished. With the notable exception of Chinese and Japanese markets that even in the early seventies emphasized flavor and quality, we really had nowhere to turn but to sympathetic gardeners who either already grew what we needed or would undertake to grow it for us.

Our emphasis—and, today, our insistence—on organically grown produce developed less out of any ideological commitment than out of the fact that this was the way almost everyone we knew gardened. We have never been interested in being a health or natural foods restaurant;

rather, organic and naturally raised ingredients happen to be consistent with both what we want for our kitchen and what we want for our community and our larger environment. Such ingredients have never been an end in themselves, but they are a part of the way of life that inspired the restaurant and that we want the restaurant to inspire. Most of us have become so inured to the dogmas and self-justifications of agribusiness that we forget that, until 1940, most produce was, for all intents and purposes, organic, and, until the advent of the refrigerated boxcar, it was also of necessity fresh, seasonal, and local. There's nothing radical about organic produce: It's a return to traditional values of the most fundamental kind.

It had always seemed to us that the best way to solve our supply problems was either to deal directly with producers or, better still, to raise our own. By 1975, we'd made some progress with the first approach, regularly receiving, for example, fresh and smoked trout from Garrapata in Big Sur. One of my partners, Jerry Budrick, had also set up a connection with the Dal Porto Ranch in Amador County in the foothills of the Sierra Nevada, which provided us with lambs and with zinfandel grapes for the house wine Walter Schug made for us at the Joseph Phelps Winery. Jerry also acquired some land of his own in Amador, and it seemed an obvious solution to our produce needs for us to farm it. In 1977 we tried this, but we knew even less about farming than we thought we did, and the experiment proved a failure.

Fortunately, during the late 1970s some of our urban gardens were producing quite successfully, notably one cultivated by the French gardener and cook at Chez Panisse, Jean-Pierre Moullé, on land in the Berkeley hills owned by Duke McGillis, our house doctor, and his wife, Joyce. In addition, Lindsey Shere returned from a trip to Italy laden with seeds, which her father planted in Healdsburg, thereby introducing us to rocket and other greens still exotic at that time. Meanwhile, we were also learning how to use conventional sources as best we could. Mark Miller, then a cook with us, made the rounds of the Oakland Produce Market each dawn, and we discovered useful sources at other wholesale and commercial markets in San Francisco. Closer to home, we bought regularly—as we still do—from Bill Fujimoto, who had taken over Monterey Market from his parents and had begun to build its reputation for quality and variety.

It's difficult now to remember the kind of attitude to flavor and quality that still prevailed in the mid and late 1970s. When Jeremiah Tower, who was our main cook at Chez Panisse from 1973 to 1977, once sent back some meat he felt wasn't up to scratch, the supplier was apologetic: No one had ever done that before. And Jerry Rosenfield, a friend and physician who has worked on many of our supply problems over the years, caused an uproar one morning when he was substituting for Mark Miller at the Oakland Produce Market: Jerry insisted on *tasting* some strawberries before buying them. Jerry was also a key figure in securing our sources for fish, probably the first of our supply problems that we were able to solve successfully. During the restaurant's first few years, we served very little fish at all, such was the quality available—despite our being across the bay from a city renowned for its seafood. But, in 1975, Jerry brought us some California sea mussels he'd gathered near his home, and they were a revelation. We asked him to bring us more, and in late 1976 he became our fish dealer, buying from wholesalers and fishermen ranging up the coast from Monterey to Fort Bragg. Along the way he began to be assisted by Paul Johnson, a cook from another Berkeley restaurant called In Season, who took over from Jerry in 1979 and who today sells what is arguably the best fish on the West Coast.

Our produce problem, however, remained unsolved, and we decided to have another try at farming. John Hudspeth, a disciple of James Beard who later started Bridge Creek restaurant just up the street from us, owned some land near Sacramento that he was willing to make available to us in 1980 and 1981. In some respects, this farm was a success—producing good onions and potatoes and wonderful little white peaches from a tree John had planted—but we weren't equipped to deal with the valley heat or the land's penchant for flooding. While the farm did produce, it produced unreliably, and we had to continue to obtain supplies from elsewhere. It also finally disabused us of any illusion that we were farmers. We realized that there seemed to be only two solutions available: extending and formalizing the system of urban gardeners we already had in place, and establishing direct connections with sympathetic farmers who could grow what we needed—that is, farmers who, since we didn't know enough farming to do it ourselves, would farm on our behalf.

In the early 1980s, two members of the restaurant staff, Andrea Crawford and Sibella Kraus, and Lindsey Shere's daughter Thérèse established several salad gardens in Berkeley, one of which was in my backyard. These eventually met most of our needs for salad greens, but for other kinds of produce we remained dependent on a hodgepodge of often-unreliable sources. Two things happened in 1982, however, that turned out to be tremendously important. First, Jean-Pierre Gorin, a friend and filmmaker teaching in La Jolla, introduced us to the produce grown near there by the Chino family. And, second, Sibella Kraus became the forager for the restaurant and eventually started the Farm–Restaurant Project. Jean-Pierre happened by the Chinos' roadside stand, tasted a green bean, and arranged to have two boxes sent to us immediately. The beans were exquisite, and I flew down to find out who had grown them. We became good friends, and to this day we receive nine boxes of produce from the Chinos each week.

Meanwhile, as Sibella had become more and more involved with our salad gardens, she decided that she would like to work with produce full-time and proposed that she become the restaurant's first full-time forager, an idea we agreed to with enthusiasm. Sibella spent her time on the road locating farmers, tasting their produce, and, if we liked it, arranging for a schedule of deliveries to Chez Panisse. In 1983, we funded the Farm-Restaurant Project under Sibella's direction, which set up a produce network among a number of Bay Area restaurants and local farmers and culminated in the first Tasting of Summer Produce, now an annual event at which dozens of small, quality-conscious farmers show their produce to the food community and the general public. Sibella left us to work for Greenleaf Produce (from whom we still regularly buy) and has become an important figure in the sustainable-agriculture movement. She was succeeded as forager by Catherine Brandel, who has since become one of the head cooks in our upstairs café. During this period, Green Gulch, run by the San Francisco Zen Center, became an important supplier, as did Warren Weber, whom we continue to work with today. We were also fortunate to have Thérèse Shere and Eric Monrad producing tomatoes, peppers, beans, lettuce, and lamb for us at Coulee Ranch near Healdsburg.

During her tenure as forager, Catherine continued to develop the network Sibella had created, finding, for example, a regular source of eggs for us at New Life Farms. But she was frustrated, as we all were, by the seeming impossibility of finding meat that was both flavorful and raised in a humane and wholesome way. Since the beginning of Chez Panisse, we had been forced to rely on conventional suppliers, a continuing disappointment given how much progress we had made with other kinds of materials. But, in late 1986, Jerry Rosenfield took over as forager from Catherine, and over the next two years he made enormous strides in finding meat sources for us. Jerry had been living in the Pacific Northwest and had discovered a number of ranchers and farmers there who were attempting to raise beef, veal, and lamb without hormones and under humane conditions. In particular, the Willamette Valley between Portland and Eugene, Oregon, became a source for rabbits, lambs, goats, and beef, although Jerry also located producers closer to home, including ones for game and for that most elusive bird—a decently flavored, naturally raised chicken. We still have a way to go, but today, for the first time in our history, we are able to serve meat that really pleases us.

We have made progress on other fronts, too. In 1983, for example, we helped Steve Sullivan launch Acme Bakery, which bakes for us and for many other local restaurants. And, recently, we've realized a close approximation of our dream of having a farm. In 1985, my father, Pat Waters, began looking for a farmer who would be willing to make a long-term agreement to grow most of our produce for us according to our specifications. With help from the University of California at Davis and local organic food organizations, Dad came up with a list of eighteen potential farmers, which he narrowed down to a list of four on the basis of interviews, tastings, and visits. We settled on Bob Cannard, who farms on twenty-five acres in the Sonoma Valley.

Bob is very special, not only because he grows wonderful fruits and vegetables for us—potatoes, onions, salad greens, tomatoes, beans, berries, peaches, apricots, and avocados, to name a few—but also because he is as interested in us as we are in him. He likes to visit the restaurant kitchen and pitch in, and we send our cooks up to him to help pick. He takes all the restaurant's compostable garbage each day, which he then uses to grow more food. He is also a teacher at his local college and a major force in his local farmer's market. He sees that his farm and our restaurant are part of something larger and that, whether we acknowledge it or not, they have a responsibility to the health of the communities in which they exist and of the land on which they depend.

The search for materials continues, and I imagine it always will. We are still looking for good sources for butter, olives, oil, and prosciutto, to name a few. But, even when we find them, the foraging will continue. Ingredients will appear that we'll want to try, and we in turn will have new requirements that we'll want someone to fulfill for us. Whatever happens, we realize that, as restaurateurs, we are now involved in agriculture and its vagaries—the weather, the soil, and the economics of farming and rural communities. Bob Cannard reminds us frequently that farming isn't manufacturing: It is a continuing relationship with nature that has to be complete on both sides to work. People claim to know that plants are living things, but the system of food production, distribution, and consumption we have known in this country for the last forty years has attempted to deny that they are. If our food has lacked flavor—if, in aesthetic terms, it has been dead—that may be because it was treated as dead even while it was being grown. And perhaps we have tolerated such food—and the way its production has affected our society and environment—because our senses, our hearts, and our minds have been in some sense deadened, too.

I've always felt it was part of my job as a cook and restaurateur to try to wake people up to these things, to challenge them really to taste the food and to experience the kind of community that can happen in the kitchen and at the table. Those of us who work with food suffer from an image of being involved in an elite, frivolous pastime that has little relation to anything important or meaningful. But in fact we are in a position to cause people to make important connections between what they are eating and a host of crucial environmental, social, and health issues. Food is at the center of these issues.

This isn't a matter of idealism or altruism but rather one of self-interest and survival. Restaurateurs have a very real stake in the health of the planet, in the source of the foodstuffs we depend on, and in the future of farmers, fishermen, and other producers. Hydroponic vegetables or fish raised in pens will never be a real substitute for the flavor and quality of the ingredients that are in increasing jeopardy today. Professionally and personally, both our livelihoods and our lives depend on the preservation of what we have and the restoration of what we have lost. The fate of farmers—and with them the fate of the earth itself—is not somebody else's problem: It is our fate, too.

There is clearly so much more to do. But ultimately it comes down to realizing the necessity of the land to what we do and our connection to it. Few restaurants are going to be able to create the kind of relationship we have with Bob Cannard, but there are other routes to the same goal. I'm convinced that farmer's markets are an important step in this direction; they also contribute to the local economy, promote more variety and quality in the marketplace, and create community. As restaurateurs and ordinary consumers meet the people who grow their food, they acquire an interest in the future of farms, of rural communities, and of the environment. This interest, when it helps to ensure the continuing provision of open space near cities and the diversity of food produced on it, is to everyone's benefit. Country and city can once again become a mutual support system, a web of interdependent communities. That's why fresh, locally grown, seasonal foodstuffs are more than an attractive fashion or a quaint, romantic notion: They are a fundamental part of a sustainable economy and agriculture—and they taste better, too. Of course, people respond, "That's easy for you to say: In California you can have whatever you want all year round." I tell them that's true, but I also tell them that most of it tastes terrible. And, while there's no reason to forgo all non-locally-produced ingredients—I wouldn't want to give up our weekly shipment from the Chinos—local materials must become the basis of our cooking and our food; this is true for every region of the planet that has produced a flavorful, healthy cuisine.

What sometimes seem to be limitations are often opportunities. Earlier this year, in the lee between the early spring vegetables and those of mid-summer, we had an abundance of fava beans, which we explored in the kitchen for six weeks, served in soups, in purees, as a garnish, and, of course, by themselves—and we discovered that we had only *begun* to tap the possibilities. There was a stew of beans with savory and cream, a fava-bean-and-potato gratin, fava bean pizza with lots of garlic, a pasta fagioli using favas, a rough puree of favas with garlic and sage, and a vinaigrette salad, to name a few. The point is that what constitutes an exciting, exotic ingredient is very much in the eye of the beholder and that few things can be as compelling as fresh, locally grown materials that you know have been raised in a responsible way.

When I was first thinking about opening what would become Chez Panisse, my friend Tom Luddy took me to see a Marcel Pagnol retrospective at the old Surf Theater in San Francisco. We went every night and saw about half the movies Pagnol made during his long career, including *The Baker's Wife* and his Marseilles trilogy—*Marius*, *Fanny*, and *César*. Every one of these movies about life in the south of France fifty years ago radiated wit, love for people, and respect for the earth. Every movie made me cry.

My partners and I decided to name our new restaurant after the widower Panisse, a compassionate, placid, and slightly ridiculous marine outfitter in the Marseilles trilogy, so as to evoke the sunny good feelings of another world that contained so much that was incomplete or missing in our own—the simple wholesome good food of Provence, the atmosphere of tolerant camaraderie and great lifelong friendships, and a respect both for the old folks and their pleasures and for the young and their passions. Four years later, when our partnership incorporated itself, we immodestly took the name Pagnol et Cie., Inc., to reaffirm our desire to re-create a reality where life and work were inseparable and the daily pace left time for the afternoon anisette or the restorative game of *pétanque*, and where eating together nourished the spirit as well as the body—since the food was raised, harvested, hunted, fished, and gathered by people sustaining and sustained by each other and by the earth itself. In this respect, as in so many others, the producers and farmers we have come to know not only have provided us with good food but have also been essential in helping us to realize our dreams.

PAUL SCHMIDT

What Do Oysters Mean?

This is an excerpt from a book about food in fiction. It began as a cookbook, but it got more complicated and more interesting the longer I worked on it. When we think and write about food we are often thinking and writing about something else. Food always means something beyond the fact of what we put into our mouths. Food, I found, is about loving and living and dying.

Eating, like making love, is a sign we will not die. But food and death are inseparable. To prepare food is to destroy one thing in order to preserve something else. Eventually I came to realize that I was really writing about passion and death, just like Tolstoy and Dickens and Joyce and Proust—and like most cookbooks. And that struck me funny, finally.

The piece opens with part I, chapter 10 of Leo Tolstoy's Anna Karenina, *translated by myself.*

—P. S.

As Levin entered the restaurant with Oblonsky, he couldn't help noticing a certain expression, almost a contained radiance, that suffused Oblonsky's face and his whole presence. Oblonsky took off his coat, and with his hat cocked to one side he made his way to the dining room, giving orders to the Tatar waiters in tail coats who flocked about him with their napkins. He bowed right and left to friends who greeted him joyfully—here as everywhere else—and went to the hors d'oeuvres buffet, where he drank a glass of vodka, took a bite of fish, and said something to the heavily made-up Frenchwoman in her ribbons and lace behind the cashier's counter, something that made even that Frenchwoman burst out laughing. Levin drank no vodka, precisely because he found that Frenchwoman offensive; she seemed to him stuck together out of fake hair, *poudre de riz*, and *vinaigre de toilette*. He moved immediately away from her, as if she were something unclean. His entire being overflowed with the memory of Kitty, and his eyes smiled with triumph and happiness.

"This way, your Excellency, if you please; your Excellency won't be disturbed here," said an especially attentive old Tatar with white hair, whose hips were so wide the tails of his coat parted over them. "If you please, your Excellency," he said to Levin; his courtesy to Oblonsky's guest was a sign of respect for Oblonsky.

In an instant he had spread a fresh tablecloth on a table already covered with one, a round table beneath a bronze light fixture, brought up velvet-covered chairs, and stood beside Oblonsky, a napkin in one hand and a menu in the other, waiting.

"If you'd prefer, Your Excellency—a private dining room will be free in a moment; Prince Golitzin is with a lady. And we have fresh oysters."

"Ah, oysters . . ."

Oblonsky began to reconsider.

"Should we change our plans, Levin?" he said, as he took the menu. His face expressed serious indecision. "Are the oysters any good? Eh?"

"Flensburgs, Your Excellency. We don't have any Ostends."

"Flensburgs or not, what I asked was, are they fresh?"

"They arrived yesterday, sir."

"Well, then. What do you think? Should we start with the oysters, and then change our entire program?"

"It doesn't make any difference to me. I'd just as soon have cabbage soup and kasha, but I don't suppose they've got that here."

"You'd like *kasha à la russe?*" said the Tatar, bending over Levin like a nurse over a child.

"No, I'm only joking, whatever you decide is fine with me. I've just been skating, so I'm quite hungry. And don't imagine," he added, as he noticed an expression of dissatisfaction on Oblonsky's face, "that I don't appreciate your choices. I'm looking forward to a good meal."

"I should hope so! No matter what you may think, eating is one of life's pleasures," said Oblonsky. "Very well then, my good man. Give us two—no, that's not enough—three dozen oysters, then the vegetable soup . . ."

"*Printanière,*" the waiter added. But it was clear that Oblonsky did not intend to give him the pleasure of ordering in French.

"Vegetable, you know? Then the turbot with cream sauce, then . . . Roast beef, if it's any good. Then the capon, I suppose, then some fruit compote."

The Tatar, aware of Oblonsky's habit of not calling the dishes by their French names, did not repeat what he had said, but allowed himself the luxury of repeating the entire order as it appeared on the menu: "*soupe printanière, turbot sauce Beaumarchais, poularde à l'estragon, macédoine de fruits . . .*" And then immediately, like some kind of automaton, he set down one folded card and snatched up another, the wine list, which he put down in front of Oblonsky.

"What should we have to drink?"

"Whatever you like is fine with me, only not too much. Champagne," said Levin.

"What? To start with? Well, that's not a bad idea, actually. Do you like White Label?"

"*Cachet blanc,*" said the waiter.

"Well, bring us that with the oysters, and then we'll see."

"Of course, sir. And what would you like to follow it with?"

"Bring us a bottle of Nuits . . . No. A classic Chablis would be better."

"Of course, sir. And would you like your favorite cheese?"

"By all means. Parmesan. Or would you prefer something else?"

"No, that's fine with me," said Levin, who could barely keep from smiling.

The Tatar waiter rushed off, his coat tails flying; in five minutes he returned with a plate covered with oysters in their pearly shells, and a bottle.

Oblonsky opened his starched napkin and tucked it into his waistcoat, settled his arms comfortably, and began on the oysters.

"Not too bad," he said, lifting the quivering oysters from their pearly shells with a little silver fork, and swallowing them one after another. "Not too bad," he repeated, glancing with soft glittering eyes at Levin, then at the Tatar waiter.

Levin did eat his oysters, though he would have preferred bread and cheese. But he enjoyed watching Oblonsky. Even the Tatar waiter, who had drawn the cork and poured the foaming wine into tall thin wine glasses, straightened his tie and glanced at Oblonsky with an obvious smile of pleasure.

"You really don't care for oysters?" asked Oblonsky, as he drained his glass. "Or are you thinking of something else, hm?"

He wanted Levin to be happy. And it wasn't exactly that Levin wasn't happy, but he felt constrained. His feelings for Kitty made him ill at ease and uncomfortable in the restaurant, with its private rooms where men took "ladies" to dine, in the midst of this fussiness and scurrying, these bronzes, these mirrors, this gaslight, these Tatar waiters. . . .

There will always be, some evening when we are sitting in a wonderful restaurant, full of ourselves and anticipating the delights of the menu, someone sitting with us who doesn't much care what he eats. His reasons may vary, but all the same there he is—someone who rejects the excitement we expect of the evening and the sensual pleasure, the artistic pleasure even, we have been contemplating. Composing a menu can be a serious and perplexing affair, but not in the presence of people who find nothing serious or perplexing about it.

Not that they have anything against the excitement we may be feeling—Levin here is experiencing pretty much the same emotion as Oblonsky, but his is inspired by Kitty, not by food. The casual waiter, I imagine, would be unable to distinguish between the "contained radiance" that fills Oblonsky when he enters the restaurant, and the "smile of triumph and happiness" that shines in Levin's eyes. Both men glowed with excitement, and what would any waiter think but that they had come to celebrate something in common? And yet Levin is ecstatic because he is in love and contemplating marriage to Kitty, and Oblonsky is ecstatic because for a few hours he is free from his depressing marriage to Kitty's sister Dolly.

The perfection we imagine and hope we will find in a restaurant cannot be gotten at casually. It is, first of all, as much a matter of security as anything else. That first stroll—Oblonsky, hat cocked to one side, talking, smiling to friends, stopping for a glass of vodka and a bite of *zakuski* from the hors d'oeuvres buffet—that's the apotheosis of the restaurant diner. That's what he lives for. Who doesn't want to be addressed by name in a restaurant, shown to one's regular table by a respectful waiter, offered a prince's private dining room, and then sit down to the contemplation of oysters and champagne? To feel completely at home there is the first aim of anyone who likes to eat in restaurants. That is the reason for Oblonsky's familiarity with the place and the waiters who attach themselves to him, as he bows to acquaintances who greet him joyfully, as he jokes with the Frenchwoman. And that familiarity spreads: Oblonsky's guest is treated respectfully because of Oblonsky, even if that respect is a bit patronizing. The waiter treats Levin like a child, someone who is not quite up to the elaborate game that the waiter and Oblonsky are about to play.

For it is a game, and everyone in it has his role, even Levin. Tolstoy brings together the classic components of eating in restaurants: a French menu and a waiter whose airs and graces derive from it; a visitor from the country to be impressed with the splendor of the event, but who turns out to like just plain food, nothing fancy thanks; and the restaurant diner, the city mouse, who mediates between all these elements and gets out of them what he wants most—a few lavish hours with one of the great sensual pleasures in life. What greater dissatisfaction could there be in a moment like that than someone across the table who would just as soon have a hamburger and french fries, or cabbage soup and kasha?

Nothing wrong with kasha, or with cabbage soup either—*shchi*, the

Russians call it—it's just that Tolstoy introduces them into this passage quite deliberately to offset the French menu. They do that quite forcefully in the Russian, since they echo the well-known peasant proverb "Cabbage soup and kasha is the food *we* eat": *Shchi da kasha, pishche nashe*. Around the rock of that rhyme, the French phrases of the menu ripple very frivolously indeed. But Oblonsky handles the moment wonderfully, and partly for Levin's sake translates the menu back into plain Russian. This throws the burden of the moment onto the waiter, who is deprived of his private poetry, the carefully learned exoticism of the menu, and who has to wait for *his* pleasure until Oblonsky has finished ordering, when he translated the entire order back into French, like the litany of some private ritual. It is a ritual, of course, part of the game, and they all get their turn to play. Levin registers his down-home rejection of big-city frivolity; the waiter gets to show off his only show-offable talent, and Oblonsky, the perfect host, mediates between the two and still gets his oysters in five minutes.

For the oysters, after all, are the heart of the matter, and the matter is a complicated metaphor. *Anna Karenina* is a novel about adultery, and one that condemns it in no uncertain terms. It is a novel about the relationships between men and women, and the constantly problematic place of marriage and the family in those relationships. Behind these two men dining in a restaurant stand three women, and their shadows fall across those plates of oysters.

Is opening an oyster a rape? We want so much to unclamp the bivalve, to spread those hard muscles and get at the softness within. Yet Tolstoy found, as every man who loves women has found, that the situation is pretty problematic: Exterior hardness does not always hide softness within. Nor does exterior softness, for that matter. Who can believe, on passionate occasions, that softness can be so unyielding—or, alas, hardness sometimes so soft? Tolstoy was obsessed with the problem all his life. He was constantly jumping peasant girls on his own estate and hating himself for it afterward. Then at some point he transferred his hatred to women, and transferred the jumping-sin to them too, as if it were their fault and they were the ones who led him on. It was an endless Moral Drama, and Tolstoy played all the parts at once. First he was the simple, innocent country boy, lured into sin by the women who crossed his path. Then he was the rabid sinful rapist, pale with lust, but paler afterward, shaken and empty and full of remorse. And finally he played the great part: he played God Almighty to his own transgressions, the vengeful deity who would punish him for his jumping, and punish women for having attractive hidden softnesses, and punish the whole world for containing them all. Tolstoy was the stern patriarch, hard and rough and bearded, Old Oyster himself, the God who saw all and knew all, the Omniscient Narrator who would open everything to the light of day, whose all-seeing vision would pry apart the soul with the oyster knife of judgment.

The one role, alas, that Tolstoy could never play was the part of the peasant girl he jumped. Nor, for all his talent, could he ever really understand the women he described, though it was a trick the oyster might have taught him. Did he ever know that the oyster switches its sex?

At the overlapping point of all these images and metaphors of Tolstoy's imagination lies the innocent mollusk, the poor oyster, condemned on all points. Sin is hidden, then revealed? So is the oyster dredged up and pried apart. Flensburgs, Ostends—the oyster is foreign? Therefore offensive, like the perfumed and powdered Frenchwoman at the cashier's desk. The oyster is secretive, dark and hidden? Then it is sinful and must be exposed! The oyster is dumb? It cannot speak honest peasant language any more than the Frenchwoman can! The oyster says nothing? But ah, God, it smells of the sea, of all the iodine and ooze and slime and wetness of the great primeval Mother! Tolstoy's oysters are smelly, smirking signs of immorality; the glitter in Oblonsky's eyes, the gleam of silver forks and pearly shells, is the glitter of sin. The opened oyster is the mark of the adulterous affair, and it lies there looking at Tolstoy (who of course pictures himself as the innocent Levin), winking lewdly at him from its bed of ice.

And what are the moral choices? Opposed to Oblonsky's oysters are Levin's cabbage soup and kasha, honest brown mushes both of them, made of vegetables that go from open field to open pot to open bowl—a single wooden bowl set in the middle of a rough table. About that table the Russian peasant family gathered, and each member in turn dipped into the bowl with his homemade wooden spoon, just as they dipped with homemade wooden plows into the brown earth that provided the stuff in the bowls. That bowl is the foundation of the home, the center of the family circle that is so elaborately broken in this novel of adultery. Seen from the family table and the edge of the kasha pot, this scene in the restaurant is perverse. Two men sit by themselves alone at a table, beneath imported bronzes and velvets, in a nest of starched napery. Everything is light and brilliance and glittering surfaces. They tear away with silver forks at oysters, images of iniquity, complex metaphors of the whole cycle of transgression and guilt and punishment, of the temptation and fall of men and women. The two men who eat them are an adulterer and a young man about to marry, and each must surely taste them differently, though they eat them face-to-face. Is Levin's lack of interest in oysters simply a sign of his own virginity? Oblonsky's pleasure in the oysters, his glittering eyes, are signs of experience: they speak of voluptuousness, of sensuality—turned here to oysters, perhaps, for lack of anything better at home.

Because there's nothing at home but the kasha pot. Behind these two men seated at their oysters stand the two women at the back of their minds: two sisters, innocent Kitty and wronged Dolly. And behind them further still, in the darkness of Tolstoy's imagination, ready to burst upon the scene, stands the great adulteress herself, Anna the Oyster-Woman.

FRANCINE PROSE

Cocktail Hour at the Snake Blood Bar: On the Persistence of Taboo

Not long ago, at a dinner party, the conversation turned to the subject of why we generally don't eat household pets or our near-neighbors on the food chain. It was a warm summer evening; we were eating *vitello tonnato* and a tomato-arugula salad.

Almost everyone had heard the story of the formal, diplomatic dinner at which the raw, pulsing brain of a monkey was served from the still-warm monkey skull. And everyone knew of some Chinese restaurant, somewhere, suspected of serving cat meat.

A friend said that there are Cambodian restaurants in Washington, D.C., at which you can order dog meat.

He said that you have to know the code. You must ask for "traditional food."

*   *   *

The best beef I ever tasted was, perhaps needless to say, in Bombay, at a restaurant gleaming with chrome, chandeliers, and mirrored walls, not far from the central market where cows, in their capacity as manifestations of the divine, were permitted to roam freely and graze at the produce stalls.

The beef on my plate at the G. Restaurant had been considerably less lucky.

Or was it actually buffalo? The menu called it steak. Steak Honolulu, Steak Milan, Steak Peking, Steak Paris, steak prepared in the imagined, unimaginable style of a dozen distant cities where cows were not allowed to wander through the streets, and it was perfectly normal to eat them.

It was not at all normal in India in 1976, where from time to time one read accounts of Muslim butchers lynched by Hindu mobs on the suspicion of selling beef. Beef (or buffalo) was expensive, not illegal, but hard to get, except at the famous G. Restaurant, which drew a chic crowd of Anglo-Indians, Parsis, Goan Christians, liberated Hindus, and especially Bombay film stars.

Always there were a few tourists present, but fewer than one might have expected, considering that every travel guidebook enthusiastically recommended the G. Restaurant as a welcome break from vegetable curry for homesick carnivores. Perhaps most tourists suspected— wrongly, as it turned out—that the guides were describing a cultural rather than a culinary experience.

In fact it was both, and I have never again had a steak as tender and sweet as the G. Restaurant's Steak Marseilles, a plump little pillow of beef done rare and topped with a pleasantly briny sauce that claimed to be anchovies and French butter, but was probably *ghee* (clarified butter) and the omnipresent, desiccated tiny fish oddly named Bombay duck.

Of course it's impossible to gauge how much the atmosphere contributed to the deliciousness of the food: for all the place's glitter and brittle display, the mood of the patrons at the G. Restaurant was furtive and intense, and an aura of the forbidden floated over every banquette. People studied one another in mirrors, their faces bright, flushed, and slightly strained—you would have thought everyone there was engaged in some adulterous tryst.

It used to be that we knew who we were by the foods we refused to eat, and perhaps some species memory is behind the vehemence with which infants assert their autonomy by flinging dinner across the room, the righteousness with which every sentient American child goes through a phase of vegetarianism.

Claude Lévi-Strauss helped us see food preparation as a profound form of social expression, and Margaret Visser's recent book, *The Rituals of Eating*, makes it clear that even cannibalistic rites were not the stumbly chaotic bloodfeasts out of *The Night of the Living Dead* that we might have imagined. Strict rules governed whose flesh you ate, and how and when you consumed it, mostly depending on your emotional, familial, and tribal ties to the taboo or edible dead.

For centuries, Orthodox Jews and Muslims haven't eaten pork, Christians did eat pork but didn't eat meat on Friday, upper-caste Hindus and some Buddhists ate no meat, especially not beef, and Jains didn't eat anything that had ever possessed a living soul, a category that for some reason included onions and garlic. It may be that food taboos affirm special covenants with God, but they also affirm the covenant with like-minded avoidants and (perhaps most importantly) an essential, unbridgeable distance from the food tastes of the Other.

Not only does the Other blithely and greedily consume what we know is unclean; they would like nothing better than to defile us by making us eat it, too. During the early, horrific wars between Indian Sikhs and Muslims, Sikhs were said to ritually wash down mosques with the blood of freshly slaughtered pigs. During the Inquisition, secretly practicing Marrano Jews pretending to have converted were tested on how far they'd progressed by being forced to eat pork; and it seems, sadly, that the fantastic, medieval idea that Jews bake Passover matzos with the blood of Christian children is, even now, not quite so safely dead (or so far from the surface) as one might reasonably suppose.

All of us have heard gossip about the wily Asian restaurateur who kidnaps dear Fido and Mittens and tricks us into ordering and eating our darlings, served sweet-and-sour. A friend once told me that the principal (indeed the only) amusement in her small home town in Wales was beating up Tony, the Chinese waiter, every Saturday night; to work themselves into the proper violent, vengeful frenzy, local teens swapped rumors about the pets slaughtered and stir-fried that week.

Much of this, of course, is flat-out racism, but one also detects a milder note of strain and unease in our best efforts to confront the spectrum of multicultural dietary diversity—to understand and defend the right of those with cultures unlike our own to eat, if they wish, their dogs, their cats, their monkeys, and even their dead.

One needn't be an anthropologist to make the obvious associations between taboos regarding food and taboos about the body and about sex—specifically about (as they say) exogamous relations with the Other who dines on the forbidden and assimilates the unclean flesh into his or her own body.

If, as they say, we are what we eat, then the same must be true of the Other; our flesh, we imagine, is unlike their flesh, made of different stuff, characterized by different colors, tastes, and smells. I remember reading a story about a girl who grew up in China and, on first encountering a crowd of white people, nearly became sick, so repulsed was she by the sour-milk odor of people whose diet included dairy.

Our ideas about the Other's diet are allied with ideas of exotic sex, with the sexual prowess (or lack of it) of some untrustworthy group or race or tribe. Americans are curious and (in the case of environmentalists) enraged by the Chinese belief in the aphrodisiacal properties of various powdered horns and tusks.

Indulging in a taboo food, forbidden since early childhood, can often be, to judge from published accounts, at once sickening and erotic. Gandhi's autobiography contains a fascinating and highly charged description of how he once broke his vow to his mother to never eat beef—a sin for which he repented with a bout of illness and a renewed commitment to activist vegetarianism.

There is a grade-Z exploitation movie currently available in the sleazier and more politically incorrect video stores, a low-budget pseudo-documentary purporting to report on the shocking sexual customs practiced in today's "Orient": a Japanese brothel in which businessmen dress up in diapers and pretend to be infants, the sex-change-operation mill in Sri Lanka, etc. The movie is deeply frightening, though not at all in the way it intends.

In one scene, a group of worried (indeed, almost stricken-looking) Taiwanese businessmen are shown quaffing the house drink at a Taipei snake blood bar: vampirizing hapless reptiles to render themselves more amorous. The camera lingers lovingly on the nasty serpentine *kris* with which the bartender makes an incision just below the snake's head, then focuses on his rather hammy fist, squeezing out the blood—drip, drip, not a single drop wasted—into a glass. The bartender is all business, he shows neither pleasure nor disgust; for all the emotion on his face, he could be pulling draft beer from a tap.

Then the camera zooms in on the customers' faces, as if to catch some dreamy, abstracted expression; perhaps they are musing on the pleasure that the snake blood is meant to enhance? The customers (or are they actors?) nervously eye the lens; one gets the impression that this is not where they stop off on their way home to their wives. Meanwhile the sonorous voice-over narration drones solemnly on and on: these men, we hear, share the belief that the blood of certain rare vipers can prolong a single act of intercourse for upwards of seven hours.

A friend told me that he and his wife were taken to such a bar on a business trip to Taipei. Determined to be polite, and also frankly intrigued, my friend drank a shot glass of snake blood. Then the company employee assigned to shepherd him around the city asked him if, now that he was properly fortified, he would like to visit a brothel full of fresh country girls, all fourteen years old or younger.

* * *

It is necessary for us to think that such things happen only in faraway places, where the poor and benighted still observe their arcane food tastes and taboos. If we tolerate food superstitions at all, we insist they be benevolent: we like hearing about the good-luck dishes various ethnic groups cook on New Year's Day.

We do know that there are otherwise apparently sensible Muslims and Jews who *still* atavistically persist in not eating pork, Hindu friends we would never invite for a steak dinner. But most of us in the "rational" West consider ourselves light-years beyond all that. As some strictly macrobiotic neighbors once said disapprovingly of my family: They eat *everything*.

Though, naturally, there are limits.

At the dinner at which our friend explained about "traditional food," another guest said that he knew a Venezuelan artist who for a mere four hundred dollars could arrange to have a cube of fresh human flesh shipped, on ice, direct from Caracas to Manhattan. He waited. There were no takers. Was it because of the expense? The guest with the Venezuelan friend said, Wasn't it interesting that no one wanted to try it? He said that the desire to partake of human flesh is the only desire in human history that civilization has ever successfully eradicated.

But civilization (so-called) has apparently been more widely successful at eradicating other food taboos. Aside from obvious exceptions, like the ban on cannibalism, we have (or we flatter ourselves that we have) evolved beyond the forbidden. We no longer really need diet to affirm our group identity or to encourage us to despise those whose diets are different from our own—we have so many neater ways to set ourselves apart (nationalism, for example), careful methods of differentiation that don't muck about in those fuzzy, gray areas involving individual food preferences and unclean forms of animal life.

No longer deemed politically or spiritually necessary, and finally, just an inconvenience, the Church's ban on eating meat on Fridays has been lifted during our lifetimes. Few of my friends are (in any traditional sense) religious, and, though I realize that many do exist, I myself know few Jews of my generation who, were it not for the taboo on cholesterol, wouldn't happily and guiltlessly dine daily on prosciutto and Canadian bacon.

My paternal grandparents read a Socialist newspaper and kept a kosher kitchen. My mother's parents ran a small restaurant near the docks in lower Manhattan and served ham and pork to stevedores but never once (that they admitted) tasted it themselves. Their children, my parents, ate lobster, shrimp, and bacon, but never ham and pork; and my brother and I, their children, were clearly made to understand that these distinctions were all about health and not at all about religion.

My father, who was a pathologist, informed us about trichinosis, and seemed to take an almost uncanny pleasure in describing the larvae—or were they worms?—who migrated through your bloodstream and, if they didn't kill you right away, took up residence in your brain and rendered you a helpless, jumping mass of uncontrolled tics and twitches.

Yet no one appeared to worry when my brother and I went through a phase of preferring our bacon underdone, pearly and translucent. Our parents might conceivably have let us eat raw bacon if it meant we at least went off to school with something in our stomachs. No one ever suggested that undercooked bacon could harm us—as opposed to, say, dangerous Chinese-restaurant pork, fried till it was closer in texture to cellulose than protein.

During those years, it seemed, Jews who no longer believed in God learned to believe in trichinosis; fear of parasites supplanted the fear of God and the prohibitions in Leviticus. And now we have even lost our religious faith in the punishment-by-parasite for disobeying the God of our Fathers. We know about meat inspection and how the FDA, inefficient as it is, has rendered the incidence of meat contamination statistically insignificant.

Yet the spirit, if not the letter, of the dietary laws remains. The awful little secret of many mixed marriages is that the Jewish member of the couple is always accusing the Other of lethally undercooking the pork, of not roasting or broiling or frying it, until, as the prudent cookbooks say, it "loses its pink color."

If taboos no longer speak to our spiritual lives, they do still address issues of longevity and health. Perhaps now that we no longer believe in God or in an afterlife, now that we no longer expect the strict observation of dietary restrictions to assure us a berth in heaven, we must endeavor to do the next best thing—that is, live forever.

It's too drearily familiar to track the changing fortunes of various foods that, through no fault of their own, have lost their reputation as elixirs and been identified as poisons. Many of us hope wanly for the day when butter, cream, and cheese will be discovered to be better for us than their pale and ascetic low-fat equivalents.

Those who have any doubt about the extent to which health concerns and taboos have edged out simple good manners should try serving, at a dinner, anything that includes a minimal, detectable trace of animal fat. Many hosts have had the dismaying experience of seeing perfectly healthy guests (those who have not yet been warned by their doctors that overindulgence may prove fatal) push offending, suspect, or high-cholesterol items off to the edge of their plates, or conceal them under the parsley.

Such guests might do well to meditate on the example of the vegetarian Zen monk who, when asked why he'd unprotestingly eaten beef at a dinner party, replied that the cow was already dead—but his hostess wasn't.

It's no secret that patterns of dietary attraction and avoidance bear a skewed and often ironic relation to privilege and social class: in the 1980s a generation discovered that one of the perks of new money was being able to pay astronomical prices for comfy, uninspired, solid middle-class, Mom-like "home" cooking: meat loaf and mashed potatoes.

One of the luxuries of class is that we can afford to make exquisite nutritional, esthetic, and culinary distinctions—or, perversely, conversely, dispense with those distinctions altogether. The rich and the stylish often take a certain pride in being catholic in their food tastes— the earliest to "discover" this or that peculiar ingredient, the first to value the cuisine of some remote and starving province. A recent movie, *The Freshman,* turned on the conceit of an exclusive, decadent club whose members paid huge sums to dine on endangered species, rare South Seas dragon-lizards and so forth.

Often, the poor and the working class distrust the weird foods of the rich and ethnic: the brains, the sweetbreads, the snails, the bloody duck breast, the nasturtiums and edible flowers. (The obvious irony is that many such foods—tripe, organ meats, etc.—were at one time the despised and discarded scraps tossed to the poor.)

Meanwhile, the rich, who flatter themselves that nothing humanly edible is foreign to them, do in fact draw the line at the pitiful, unesthetic, unsavory food of the poor: the white bread, the processed spreads, the rat-tail-pink luncheon meat and the sugary, carnival-colored cereals. Certainly there are gourmets who would happily dine on monkey brains and Venezuelan human cube steak, but would flee in horror from the prospect of a white-bread-and-bologna sandwich.

Some will say this is personal taste, but it is a form of social taboo, or perhaps it is a social taboo masquerading as personal taste. Indeed the food taboo is very much alive and well, and has only gone into hiding under the shiny sheets of Velveeta, in the airy puff of Wonder Bread and the rare pork bleeding onto our plate.

As we lurch into the future, and the population continues to grow in advance of the food supply, it may be that the luxury of taboo becomes less and less available. By the time we're all lunching on sea kelp and cheap, plentiful science-fiction protein, fine distinctions about diet may have even vanished completely.

But that seems unlikely, and certainly inconsistent with what little we know about our own natures. It's easier to imagine our descendants establishing their identity in terms of what kind of algae they resolutely refuse to eat, or else searching out the sinful, mirrored restaurants of the future, where they'll whisper the guilty, secret code of taboo, and ask for traditional food.

BETTY FUSSELL

On Murdering Eels and Laundering Swine

Murder we must. If not cows and pigs and fish, then cabbages and rutabagas. We flay bananas, violate oysters, ravage pomegranates. Our lot is beastly and there's no help for it, for feed we must on creature kinds. Our hands are stained with carrot blood and not all the seas of Noah's Flood will wash them clean, not after God's pact with Noah: "Every moving thing that lives shall be food for you." That's a lot of territory in which to assert our puny manhood and decree that this is fit and this not, this food pure and that dirty. No, all that lives is food for man who, dead, is food for worms. That's the deal.

Some living things are harder to kill than others, even though some things beg to be killed. Snakes, for instance. Their very shape mirrors our throttled circumstances, the narrowness of our confines, the anguish of our passage. The same root, *ango*, generates *anguis* (snake) and anguish (pain). The same root generates *anguilla* (eel), a fish in snake's clothing. Its snaky form makes some eaters queasy and others ravenous, but to eat an eel you must kill him first and quite deliberately, with the zeal of an ax murderer, because he is well armed against us.

I have killed many snakes in the desert when it was their life or mine, but killing an eel in cold blood, on the fourth floor, in a New York City apartment—that's different. The eel and I were already intimate, for I had carried him in my lap in a large plastic bag on the subway from Chinatown, and he had roiled against my belly as if I were pregnant with eels. Watching the bag slither with speed across my kitchen floor, I was afraid to deliver him. I was, in fact, deathly afraid of snakes.

My father had kept them in cages in our basement, next to the laundry tub, the newfangled washing machine, and the old-fashioned clothes wringer. Dumping laundry from tub to washer to wringer to basket for hanging on the line, I kept my eye on the snakes. Whether harmless as garters or lethal as rattlers, they were the Serpent *anguiformes*, the One cursed by God to creep without legs or wings on its belly, condemned without mercy to the darkness of a basement with a burnt-out bulb. Their skins, if you touched them, were cold as death and, though dry, wet as an oyster. Because of them I was damned, as my grandfather had read me in the Book of Genesis, "For the imagination of man's heart is evil from his youth." I was young and therefore evil. The logic was impeccable: the snake and I were kin.

Nothing in my basement past, however, had prepared me for murdering an eel. I needed time to think and threw the bag in the freezer overnight. When I opened the bag in the sink next day, he looked stone cold dead. When I turned the water on to remove the slime, he came suddenly to life. I grabbed a Chinese cleaver and tried to grab his thrusting head, but he was all muscle and I was not. With both hands I slammed the cleaver down on what might have been his neck but may have been his shoulders. A mighty whack barely nicked him. I whacked again as, tail thrashing, he tried to worm his way down the minnow-sized drain. "I'm sorry," I apologized with every whack, and I was. But I needn't have been because I had not even scotched the snake, let alone killed him.

I looked for a blunt instrument and found a wooden mallet that I used for pounding meat. I cracked the mallet on his head and the wood split, but nothing else. He was breathing heavily, gulping air that filled a pouch below his jaws. Was he strangling? I didn't want to know. Like Raskolnikov, I wanted him dead. Like Rasputin, he refused to die. I looked to the freezer for respite and held the bag open for him to slither in. He went halfway, then with a quick U-turn wrapped his tail around my arm and began to slither out. Engulfing him with a second bag, I flopped the works onto the ice trays and slammed the freezer door.

I needed time for research and reflection, my brain against his muscle. I consulted books. "To kill eels instantly, without the horrid torture of cutting and skinning them alive, pierce the spinal marrow, close to the back part of the skull, with a sharp-pointed skewer," William Kitchiner advised in the *Cook's Oracle* in 1817. "The humane executioner," he added, "does certain criminals the favour to hang them before he breaks them on the wheel." A kind thought, but what if the criminal refused to hang? Madame Saint-Ange, in *La Cuisine*, advised French housewives to grab the eel's tail in a dishtowel and bash its head violently against a stone or wall. So much for sentimental Brits.

Surely there was some practical, efficient, clean—American—way to kill. The best way to kill an eel, A. J. McClane wrote in his *Encyclopedia of Fish Cookery,* was to put him in a container of coarse salt. I poured two large boxes of coarse kosher salt into a large stockpot, pulled the eel bag from the freezer, and slid the mound of icy coils into the pot. Before they could quiver, I blanketed them with salt and waited. Nothing stirred. Salt, McClane said, also "deslimes" the eel, but my hands and clothes were already covered with an ooze that would not wash off. When I finally inspected my victim, I found the deed was done, his mouth marred by a single drop of blood.

Skinning was yet to come. McClane suggested I attach his head by a string to a nail pounded in a board. I had neither nail nor board. What I wanted was an electric 7 1/4-inch circular saw with a carbide-tooth blade. What I had was a pair of poultry shears. I pierced his thick hide and cut a jagged circle below his head, then scissored the length of his belly. With one hand I held his head and with the other pulled back the skin with a pair of stout pliers. It was slow work, but the leathery hide finally slipped off the tail like a nylon stocking. Naked, he was malleable as any flesh.

With one clean stroke I severed his head and hacked him into lengths. He was a three-pound meaty boy, thick and fat. He was everything one could ask for in an eel. I put him in a pot and baptized him with white wine and vinegar, vegetables and herbs, and butter whipped to a froth. He was delicious, as fat eels always are, and crowned my murderer's feast with blessing. For the order of eels are in nature born and buried in salt. Enduring a lifetime's banishment to freshwater pastures and the long journey there and back, they return to their cradle in the salt Sargasso Sea to die in a burst of sperm and roe. "It is a covenant of salt forever": God's covenant with Levi matched the one with Noah. The salt that blesses and preserves also deslimes and kills. The eel and I were bound by the same double deal. His life for mine, salt our shared salvation.

A serpent dead, however, did nothing to scotch my deeper anguish. "Shit is a more onerous theological problem than is evil," Milan Kundera wrote in *The Unbearable Lightness of Being*. "Since God gave man freedom, we can, if need be, accept the idea that He is not responsible for man's crimes. The responsibility for shit, however, rests entirely with Him, the Creator of man." If murder is man's crime, shit is not. Shit is God's joke, yet shit we must even as we feed.

What was my relation to the ten pounds of frozen hog's guts, thawing and spreading like drowned Ophelia's hair, in my apartment bathtub? The chitterlings, ten times the length of my own inner tubing, were pastel yellow, white, and pink. They spread like dubious laundry, triggering memories of washing dirty socks and underwear in the bathtubs of innumerable French and Italian hotels that invariably forbade guests to launder. With guts as with underwear, it were better to do as a French cookbook instructs, "Take the stomach and intestines to the nearest stream or river." Women once washed guts as they washed linen, rising at dawn to carry their baskets of offal to the communal gathering place, to laugh and quarrel, a medieval poet said, as they washed "inwards" at the stream.

It is laundry that connects pig's inwards to man's outwards. The ruffles on a shirtfront were once called chitterlings, "exuberant chitterlings," as Washington Irving said, "puffed out at the neck and bosom." Our foppish frills were once the ancients' omens, when offal was deemed awe-ful and the parts most worthy of the gods. A beast's inwards then put man in touch with the stars, the outermost circle of our confinement. But we who see in serpents no more than snakes, in guts no more than garbage, in destiny no more than a gambler's shake—to our narrow and straightened palates, chitterlings are the food of slaves.

I suppose it's the smell that does it, a pervasive stink that clings to hands and hair, slightly sweet, slightly sour, like dank earth turned over, like rotting bodies in a trench, like human shit. It rubs our noses in all we would deny. Washing guts, I found clusters of fat stuck to the inner lining, along with specks of what dignified recipes call "foreign matter." Some guts are thick and rubbery, others thin and limp as wet hankies. Guts are not smooth like plastic tubing, but gathered lengthwise along invisible seams, to puff like parachute silk with gas. They are gathered the way a seamstress gathers cloth for ruffles. To reach the translucent membrane of the casing, I had to strip and strip again the clogging fat until, held to the light, the stretched skin showed leaf patterns, clouds, sea scum, palely mottled and beautiful. Only by laundering the guts of swine did I discover that shit comes wrapped in a layer of clouds trapped in a membrane resilient as nylon. Still, my lustrations were brief. Most of the cleansing had been done for me at the slaughterhouse, before the guts were frozen by the Gwaltney Company, a son of IT&T. The corporate master that sent me hog's guts puts satellites in space, making however inadvertently the cosmic connection of shit and stars.

From Lily of the Valley, Virginia, a slave's granddaughter told me that she cooks chitlins in their own yellow juice with onion and garlic and vinegar, until the guts are tender enough to chew. Chewy they are, rich on the tongue like all rejected vitals—heart, liver, lights, or haslet—all those messy inwards that remind us uneasily of our own. "Cut them chitlins in small lengths, or knot 'em, and cook 'em up with collards or rice in the pot of chitlin gravy, or fry 'em deep in bubblin' fat till they float up crisp and light," she said.

Even crisp and light, a little inwards go a long way. They go a long way as vitals, en route to shitty death. Bre'r hog knows better than I the rhythm that melds eating and shitting in every moving thing that lives, in the dung birth and death of cabbages and swine, men and snakes. "We must pitch our tents in the fields of excrement," cried Crazy Jane, who liked the way my fingers smell, my stove, my bathtub. The smell of chitterlings clings to the air the way the taste of chitterlings sticks to the tongue. It is a lingering power that gives, my Lily of the Valley friend says, satisfaction.

But I am a child of deodorized air and Lysol drains. My pasteurized senses are not ready for the excremental smell of my bathtub. I poured "Fragrant Pine" bubble bath into the water and was ashamed to read the labeled contents: sulfates, chlorides, formaldehydes, succinates, and an ingredient called "fragrance." I am too sanitized for the fragrance of pig shit. I can turn murder into blessing by symbolic salt, but excrement into sacrament is a harder trick to turn. God owes me there. My guts are serpentine as a mess of eels, but the inward darkness of Genesis shakes out as farce. Farce is my Exodus. I know that after a lifetime's wandering through a wilderness of snakes and swine, no amount of murdering, no amount of laundering, will change my promised end as meat and gravy for rutabagas, pudding for worms.

HARRY CREWS

FROM A TELEPHONE INTERVIEW AUGUST 1986

WITH BETTY FUSSELL

On Food

I still love all the stuff I grew up eating. I like weird shit, I mean if I really want to pleasure myself—I always have it in the house though I don't eat it all the time—I'll have some hog's head cheese. You know what hog's head cheese is. Take the eardrums and eyeballs out of a pig's head and scrape it good and boil it some and pick the teeth out and mix all that fat on the head with all kinds of herbs and press it into a mold and there it is.

I don't know how to say this without sounding racist, but I shop a lot where the brothers and sisters, the black folk, shop because they eat the kind of shit I eat. They just do. I'm very fond of tripe, which is cow's stomach, but most people don't like it because it's cross-grained like a piece of plywood. You have to have a good set of teeth and you have to like to chew. I've never understood people who talk about meat melting in their mouth. I don't want the shit to melt in my mouth. I want to chew, man, and I want to chew a long time. I want to fight with that sucker.

If I'm shaky from some outrage the previous night and I really got to get back onto my game quick, or if I simply want to do something to pleasure myself in the morning, what I do is I take three ounces of Jack Daniel's Black Label, or any kind of sour mash whiskey will do, and I suck a couple of eggs but I suck 'em in a strange way. You punch a little hole in either end of the egg—if you don't punch two holes the egg won't come out—and then you suck out about a quarter egg and then you fill the shell with Tabasco sauce or Red Rooster or anything comes out of New Iberia, Louisiana, and then you suck that sucker down and drain off about half of the Jack Daniel's and do the same with the other egg. And I tell you, man, you're ready to eat nails. I mean, fuck it, bring 'em down, no quarter asked and none given, the word goes out all along the line—the saber's out.

I like to hunt, I find it very relaxin'. I like to hunt rattlesnakes and I like the butcherin' of 'em and the skin that I keep and tan and use for belts and other shit. I generally like the steak which you cut so that there's two ribs in each one of the little inch-thick pieces of meat. You chop the head off about six inches behind where the fangs are and then just gut it and skin it. No skill is required. You cut it along the backbone so that two ribs are in each little thing and then dip it in whatever kind of batter pleases you. I'm strong to go to shit like garlic and Tabasco sauce and jalapeño peppers and that kind of thing. You have to deep-fry a snake.

You see, a rattlesnake—I don't know if there's a word for it, they can't control their temperature—they're as hot or as cold as wherever they find themselves. So you have to wait until a day when it's cold but above freezing. They can't be on top of the ground if it's below freezing, or they'll die. And so, here in the South, you wait until it's a good chilly day and you go up on a sandy ridge where there's blackjack oak. They live in gopher holes—or land tortoise, that's what southerners call gophers. They live down there with the gopher, they go down in the earth and it's warm down there. They don't screw with the gopher and the gopher don't screw with them. I don't know why they don't eat 'em, I don't know why they don't strike 'em, but they don't. Whatever they eat they got to eat whole because they got no teeth. They live down there in perfect harmony.

What you do when you go out lookin' for them, you take eight to ten feet—six will do but you want to take eight to ten to get all the way down—of garden hose. Push it all the way down the gopher hole, because he digs a hole way down there and you gotta git it all the way to the bottom or the snake won't come out. When it's all the way to the bottom you take about a half teaspoon gasoline, pour it in the top, blow on the garden hose and those fumes come out the bottom and in a few minutes here comes Mr. Rattlesnake, drunk and staggerin' from the gas and you just throw him in the sack, take him home, cook him up, and eat him. Really a lot of fun.

To take him out of the sack, that's a fairly simple matter. The big thing one would want to know that might not occur to you when you got one in the croaker sack—what you call burlap sack—bringin' 'im home, you don't want to throw that croaker sack over your shoulder 'cause he can strike through the sack. When you let him out of the sack—all snakes are notoriously slow, even those black racers that look like they're goin' eighty miles an hour, hell, even the slowest fattest man could get away from 'em and you can probably walk faster than a rattlesnake can crawl, so there's no problem there—a lot of people use noose sticks, a stick with a noose on the end, but I've never used that. I use a forked stick and put that behind his head and pick him up and take a machete and go to the block and there goes his head. Gut and skin 'em like an eel, same way.

Other people when somethin' good happens to them, they go out and buy a bottle of champagne, but this is the honest to God's truth here, I mean growin' up where I did in south Georgia, I go out and buy if I don't have some in the house which I probably would have, I'd go out and buy a pickled pig's foot. You see, we really like pickled pig's feet. It was a delicacy when I was a child. Like light bread. We used to get light bread about once a year when I was growin' up on a tenant farm. You know, sliced bread, light bread, and I used to think it was the greatest goddamn thing in the world and I wouldn't eat that shit on a bet today. I much prefer what we call hoecake, which was nothing but ground meal and lard and water, and they call it hoecake because slaves used to fry it on a hoe at the end of the row.

Grits I eat every day of my life. I still love backbone and rice, that's pig backbone. Backbone is great with any kind of greens except turnip, but mustard and greens like that. You get to suck and chew and gnaw around on it a lot. A thing that I'm very very fond of—you almost can't do this in a butcher shop even if you know the butcher, hell he can git it for you but you won't see it there in the store—is something that I grew up eating. What we used to call liver and lights. Lights is lungs. You can also put the heart in there but you gotta have an absolutely freshly slaughtered pig. You can't do it if it's old. Never mind freezing, but if it's been killed for any length of time, it doesn't taste the way it's supposed to taste.

Where I live in Gainesville, it's easy enough to go to a slaughter-house and git what you want. You can cook it up any damn way you want for stew. But the way I cook it: first and foremost, *always* if it's at all possible or compatible when I'm cooking, I've got more cloves of garlic in there than anyone wants to think about and I do onions and bell pepper and carrots, you know, all that shit up there, all those spices and whatever I'm feeling like, that's what I do. I pretty much wait until I get the stuff on the plate to do anything with hot sauce, but I also put jalapeño peppers right in the stew, a liquidy stew, absolutely, but you can make it thick or not.

Another thing I love—it's good for you, it's good lean stuff, and you can ask your butcher to order you one—is beef tongue. A lot of people don't want to screw with beef tongue. First thing you do is get that membrane off, and if you boil it that membrane comes right off. Otherwise you have to take it tediously off the tongue. But the membrane, that thick kind of thing, I guess it's the taste buds or bumps on the damn tongue, and most people don't want to screw with it because they can't stand looking at the damn thing because it looks just like what it is—a beef tongue. What I would do, after I've boiled it, I'd put it in the oven and put some new potatoes, that I'd already boiled, in the little tray with the tongue. And I'd put a lot of lemon or grapefruit slices. The thing about tongue, it's like a solid muscle, marvelous consistency, good chewable solid stuff and however you cook it you can put what you don't eat in the icebox and it makes tremendous sandwiches.

Speaking of tongue, there's another thing I grew up eating—brains and eggs. Pork brains, I'm talking about. You grow up doin' a thing and for various reasons you get away from it, most people do. I think I got away not only from the way I talked but where I came from and the stuff I ate because when I left Georgia at seventeen and was thrown into the Marine Corps with a bunch of guys from Jersey and New York, a bunch of Yankees, I was like fuckin' ashamed of where I came from and how I talked and I made this conscious effort. But it wasn't long before I come full circle.

I've never managed to cook cornbread like my mama does. Most restaurants here in the South, you get a cornbread that's not as sweet as you see up North, but it's too light. My mama's cornbread is dry and coarse and thick, and sort of got this crust around the edge. I love that stuff. When I was on the farm right until the time I left, there was a gristmill and we'd shell the corn and took it to town once a month and had it ground for meal and grits right there at the gristmill.

Turtles? Oh yeah, at home I catch 'em on a trotline, you know what a trotline is, you put out a line in the water and it's legal where I am if you don't put no more than sixteen hooks on a line. You have to have a commercial license to put sixteen hooks on the line. You bait it with various things depending on what you want to catch during the night. And you'll get three or four turtles a week. The shell's not hard, I just do it with a goddamn hatchet, it's the easiest fuckin' way to do it, the bottom of the shell comes right off. "Sorry turtle, here I come." Let him keep his fuckin' head in, I don't care. I just turn him on his side and cut him open like a goddamn nut.

They also have a license for harvesting of gators down South where

I am. They draw lots and bullshit, but if I want gator tail I just go out and take it. You can shoot it but there's a problem with that. Game wardens all over the place down there. They're brighter than they used to be and I just don't care to fuck with the law. You can always tell where they're gonna be or not gonna be, and the problem with a gun is the sound. So you set what's called a brush hook and a brush hook is where you find a limb that's going out over the water where gators are. The water can be deep or shallow it doesn't matter, and what you do is run a line from the limb down to the water, but not all the way to the water, and put a good piece of rotten meat on the end of it. They love things that are full of putrefaction, gators do. A gator'll eat any goddamn thing he can get his mouth on, including each other, they're into cannibalism.

Now, if you want to catch a little gator, you put your hook six inch off the water and you'll probably get a small gator. If you want a bigger gator, the bigger gator you want the higher you raise your hook off the water, but with this shit hangin' on it. A small gator can't rise up out of the water. You put the hook a foot or eighteen inches off the water, you'll get a good-sized gator. Easy enough to do it, makes no sound. Once the gator's taken the hook, a very large hook, he goes back in the water and then it's cool. The line is good and stout and you drag him out of the water and kill him. You bash him. That's all it is. They're not difficult to kill.

If you want to take the hide and fuck with that, well that's more difficult than it sounds. Tryin' to cure a gator skin is a hopeless and thankless task, but gator tail itself is absolutely wonderful. A small gator, say a five-foot gator—a gator grows a foot a year so you're talkin' about a five-year-old gator—you'd get about fifteen pounds of good, solid, edible, wonderful flesh. Gator can be barbecued, but the best way to do gator tail is to put it in an egg and flour batter and deep-fry it. Cut it into small bite-sized pieces, put it in deep fat and fry it up.

I'm very fond of doves. Usually I eat the doves I shoot, but there is a guy nearby raises doves commercially and I went over and got some doves and brought 'em home and all you do is pull their little heads off and dip 'em in boiling water and pull the feathers out and split 'em open and put 'em under the broiler and they come out wonderful if you cook 'em just right. Put 'em pretty close to the fuckin' flame and don't leave 'em too long. That's the mistake everybody makes because they say fowl's got to be done. I'm with you but they don't got to be cooked to death.

That's the mistake people make with liver. Nobody wants to eat liver. But if they would just marinate the fuckin' liver in milk for about fifteen minutes before they cook it and then put a whole pan—I'm talking about a big black skillet—full of onions in there, and do those guys right by themselves until they're all cooked in their own water —and maybe just a tiny little bit of flour in there until they're brown— get those guys done, take 'em out of the skillet, put the liver right in the frying pan where the onions were, where that juice is—you can put garlic or whatever's to your taste, whatever you dig—with the skillet really hot, cook it one minute on one side. Turn that sucker off, turn the fellow over, the liver over, turn the fire off. Put the onions back in, leave 'em about four minutes, take the whole thing out and you've got great liver. I mean it's going to be a little bloody, but it's *done*. Liver you buy everywhere is like shoe leather. I don't blame anyone for not eating it.

I tell you the honest to God truth I don't eat sweets hardly at all. In my childhood we didn't get much of that, no. We might git a cake once a year maybe. Something that I still love to this day is to take peanuts and syrup, that we make ourself—just grind the cane, cook it in a vat and it cooks right down to sugarcane syrup—and you take what we call a cookie pan, with the little sides, not a sheet but a pan. And you put about a half inch of syrup in there, then you just put mature raw peanuts, the early ones, in there in the syrup and bake it and just keep on baking it, about 350 degrees, until you can reach in there with your finger and touch it when it's beginning to set up—it's not setting up but a bunch of shit evaporates out of it, right? And then when it sets up it's not exactly hard like peanut brittle, it almost is, but it's firm enough so it's chewy, like toffee. Other than that and punchin' a hole in a biscuit with your finger and pourin' syrup in there until it soaks it up, other than shit like that, we didn't get anything sweet. There just wasn't nothing there. We were on a tenant farm, Macon County, Georgia, and that's where I come from.

ALEXANDRE DUMAS

TRANSLATED FROM THE FRENCH BY ALAN AND JANE DAVIDSON

Mustard

"Mustard" *is an elegant essay of more than five thousand words, supposedly written in response to an anonymous correspondent who had conveniently requested Dumas to deal with the subject historically, etymologically, botanically, and in the context of cookery. Dumas did so, in such an orderly and coherent way as to startle any reader familiar with the looser and more jumbled essays in the dictionary. Extracts only are given here; but we have taken care to include the final page, in which the purpose of the whole essay is revealed as an advertisement for Bornibus Mustard.*

You ask me, my dear anonymous correspondent, how far back in history mustard goes. Let me, then, deal with the egg before I come to the chicken, and with the seed before the plant.

The Greeks and Romans, who were not familiar with mustard in pots or in "bricks," as it is sold nowadays, knew it in the form of mustard grains, which they used in stews, and as a powder, which they employed with roasts, just as we use our modern mustard.

Greeks and Romans had but the one word for mustard, which proves clearly that this condiment came from Greece to Italy, from Athens to Rome. They used the name *sinapis* without distinction for both mustard grain and powdered mustard.

[After further comments on mustard in classical times, Dumas describes the Dark Ages when much knowledge and many recipes were lost.]

Dijon alone, the city which the Romans called Divio, had kept the original recipe of Palladius, and can be credited, if not for inventing mustard, at least for restoring it to us.

Since when have the Dijonnais had the honour of providing this indispensable condiment for our table?

It is impossible to say. All that is known is that Etienne Boileau, who was Provost of Paris under Saint Louis, granted to the vinegar-makers, in his regulations about guilds and corporations, the right to make mustard.

In the *Cris de Paris* of the thirteenth century, we find:

> "Vinaigre qui est beau et bon!
> Vinaigre de moutarde."

During that period, the sauce-vendors *(sauciers)* used to carry sauces to people's houses at dinner-time, and would run through the streets of Paris, crying: "Mustard sauce! . . . Garlic sauce! . . . Onion sauce! . . . Verjuice sauce! . . . Ravigote sauce! . . ." Anyone who was disinclined to eat his meat without sauce would open his window or door and summon the vendor, whereupon he would be served at once with the sauce of his choice.

It is readily understandable that these sauce-vendors resorted to imitation in an effort to make mustard their own product and to exploit it; but Dijon maintained her supremacy in its manufacture.

[After explaining that attempts in the south of France to supplant the vinegar in mustard with wine-must were unsuccessful, Dumas returns to the Paris scene.]

At nine o'clock in the morning and six o'clock in the evening the only people one met in the streets of Paris were children on their way to buy a pennyworth of mustard. If one asked what time it was, the reply would not be "nine o'clock" or "six o'clock," but "it's the time for children to be fetching the mustard."

The first cookery book to appear in France, *Le Viandier* by Taille-vent, head chef of King Charles VII, contains a long and unaffected eulogy of mustard. Here is what he wrote, in French which is difficult to read, but which we render in a manner comprehensible to all.

"One evening, following a great battle against the English, King Charles VII and his three inseparable companions, Dunois, La Hire, and Xaintrailles, came to lodge for the night in the little town of Sainte-Menehould, in which only five or six houses survived, the town having been burned. The king and his suite were dying of hunger. The ruined and ravaged countryside was lacking in everything. Finally, they managed to get hold of four pig's feet and three chickens.

"The king had with him no cook, male or female; so the wife of a poor edge-tool maker was charged with cooking the chickens. As for the pig's feet, there was nothing to do but put them on the grill. The good woman roasted the chickens, dipped them in beaten egg, rolled them in breadcrumbs with fines herbes, and then, after moistening them with a mustard sauce, served them to the king and his companions, who devoured the pig's feet entire and left only the bones of the chickens.

"King Charles, who had supped to perfection, asked on more than one occasion subsequently for *des poulets à la Sainte-Menehould.* Taillevent, who knew what he meant, served him chickens like those which the wife of the poor tool-maker had prepared for him."

Louis XI, who liked to invite himself to supper at short notice with his cronies, the *bons bourgeois* of Paris, used almost always to carry with him his own pot of mustard. According to the *Contes* of J. Riboteau, the Receiver-General of Bourgogne, he ordered from an apothecary of Dijon, in 1477, twenty pounds of mustard for the personal use of the king.

Finally, and to end this chronological history of mustard with an anecdote which I believe to be little known, we shall relate that among the various Popes who held such a brilliant court at Avignon, Pope John XXII was one of those who did not disdain the pleasures of the table. He was passionately fond of mustard, put it in everything, and not knowing what to do with one of his nephews who was a good-for-nothing, made him his *premier moutardier* (head mustardier). Hence comes the practice of saying of a conceited fool that he thinks himself "the Pope's head mustardier."

[Dumas explains how the dominant position of mustard was threatened by the influx of new spices and condiments from, e.g., the East Indies.]

Mustard, attacked by this invasion of eastern and western spices, fought a brave battle. Dijon, the great centre for its manufacture, thought that the product needed statutes which would completely reassure the public about the way in which mustard was handled and about the ingredients of which it was composed. As a result, the mustard-makers and the vinegar-makers of Dijon were given, in 1634, statutes which brought them into line with the other trades of the town and gave to them alone the right to make mustard.

Twenty-three vinegar-mustard makers of Dijon adhered to the new regulations. Among their signatures is to be seen that of Naigeon.

But, despite all this, the fashion for mustard was continuing to decline. People found that it left something to be desired, as a source of acidity and variety in their food. Then there arrived on the scene Jean Naigeon, great grandson of the one who had signed the regulations of the twenty-three. By changing one single element in the manufacture of mustard he brought about a recrudescence of sales and a renewal of the favour which mustard had enjoyed.

What did he need for this? An inspiration, a flash of genius. He was the first to substitute verjuice for vinegar, verjuice being the juice pressed from the grape before it is ripe. The result of this was that mustard no longer contained any sugar or acetic acid, but only tartaric, citric and malic acids.

[Meanwhile, however, there was a new development.] Paris had begun to be a serious competitor of Dijon. This revolution began in 1742. A vinegar maker of Paris, called Capitaine, began to use white vinegar instead of red vinegar for his infusions, and to introduce capers and anchovy essence into mustard of high quality. These innovations found great favour.

Ten years later, another vinegar-maker, called Maille, established a European reputation for his speciality. Having been named purveyor "by appointment" to the Marquise de Pompadour, he assumed the title, just a shade ambitious, of vinegar-maker and distiller to the King of France and the emperors of Germany and Russia. A man of ready wit, who understood his own epoch, which was one of full sensuality, he began by composing some vinegars for the use of women and others for men. His clientele soon included all the smartest people and the dandies of the aristocracy, duchesses, marquises, countesses, young beaux and abbés who moved in society. To work for the boudoir was a sure means of arriving in the kitchen. Before the emergence of Maille there were only nine kinds of vinegar. He added ninety-two, all of fine quality and good for the health.

He multiplied to a similar extent the number of vinegars used at table. He had twenty-four mustards: red mustard, fine mustard with capers, fine mustard with anchovy, mustard powder, garlic mustard, tarragon mustard, nasturtium mustard, lemon mustard, Choiseul mustard, Choisy mustard, mustard *à la conserve, aux fines herbes, à la grecque, à la maréchale, à la marquise, à la reine, à la romaine,* and finally mustard with truffles. These were all his own, except for the versions with capers and with anchovy. The most fashionable were mustard *à la ravigote,* with garlic, with truffles, with anchovy, and with tarragon.

Bordin flourished at the same time as Maille and, like him, had his role in the period. He invented the mustard called *de santé* (for the health) and composed recipes for forty different kinds of mustard—imperial mustard, mustard *au vin de Champagne, à la rocambole, aux champignons, à la rose, à l'italienne,* and *à la vanille.*

In 1812, counting the twenty-nine new kinds of mustard invented by Acloque, the pupil and successor of Maille, but not counting the mustards of Capitaine and of Dijon, France possessed eighty-four kinds of mustard. At this point Grimod de la Reynière announced three new mustards, which brought the total up to ninety-three [?]. These three were those of Châlon-sur-Saône, Besançon, and Saint-Brieuc.

Here is what was said about them by this famous connoisseur, on whose part we must notice a marked preference for Messieurs Maille and Bordin, who were, I suspect, regular and profitable subscribers to the *Almanach des Gourmands*.

"An apothecary and chemist of Saint-Brieuc has recently constructed a factory for the production of a mustard which is not without merit and which has above all great strength and pungency. It is beginning to penetrate the old region of Armorique and to arrive as far as le Contentin. M. Maout (for this is the name of the manufacturer, who was predestined to make mustard, since his name includes the first five letters of *moutarde*) plans to set up an establishment at Paris."

However, this brief comment on the product of M. Maout was enough to attract attention to him. Doctor Gastald, Portalis and Cambacérès declared themselves in favour of the mustard of Maout, and wherever one supped in France, that is to say wherever one ate with a certain delicacy, this "Celtic" mustard appeared on the table beside those of Maille and of Bordin. This triumvirate reigned for more than half a century on the tables of France.

[Dumas next deals with his anonymous correspondent's question about the etymology of the word *moutarde*, before proceeding to treat it from the botanical point of view; and then passes to its role in cuisine.]

You ask me, finally, which of the preparations I prefer from the culinary point of view.

Until I tasted and appreciated the mustard of M. Alexandre Bornibus, I used to prefer to all others the aromatic mustards of Maille and Bordin. But once chance had caused me to taste the Bornibus mustard I realized that the day would come when it would be the champion.

I speak of chance, for here is how it happened. I was writing a novel of which the main scene took place at Bourg-en-Bresse. I obtained information about the shortest way of visiting this town, the stage on which my characters were to perform, and was told: "Go to Mâcon, a branch line from there will take you straight to Bourg."

I arrived fast asleep at Dijon, heard the cry "Dijon! Dijon!" and then fell into confusion. Was it at Dijon or was it at Mâcon that there was a branch line to Bourg? I no longer had any idea. Since I had only one travelling-bag with me, I jumped down on to the platform from my coach, made for the exit, and asked for the branch line to Bourg. The ticket-collector, who did not understand what I was trying to say, did not reply, and I found myself outside in the courtyard. I addressed myself to a coachman who was conveniently waiting there.

"The branch line for Bourg?" I asked him.

"For what *bourg* (place)?"

"For Bourg-en-Bresse."

"Ah, well, you're not in the right place. That is at Mâcon."

I made to re-enter the station. The ticket-collector asked me for my ticket.

"My ticket? I've just given it to you. Look among the tickets which you've just collected and you'll find one for Mâcon."

While he was looking for it, the locomotive coughed, spat, sneezed, and departed.

"Goodness me," laughed the ticket-collector, "you'll be the first arrival for tomorrow's train."

"But still," said I, "if I'm going to leave tomorrow you'll have to give me back my ticket."

"And here indeed it is," quoth he. "My goodness, yes! It's for Mâcon, all right. Bah! . . . Stay the night here."

"So be it," I replied, "and I'll take the opportunity to visit the cathedral and to pay a call on my poor friend Louis Boulanger."

Louis Boulanger, one of those painters whose first works were the most promising, was director of the museum at Dijon, and I was delighted to have this opportunity of seeing him. The only trouble was that I could hardly burst in on him at eleven o'clock in the evening. So I had myself taken to the Hôtel du Parc.

I asked for supper. They served me two mutton cutlets and half a cold chicken.

"What mustard do you want?" asked the waiter.

"That of Dijon, of course."

"I know," said he, with the air of someone who was saying to himself "what an imbecile!," "but I'm asking whether you prefer men's mustard or ladies'."

"Oh, oh," said I in turn, "and what difference is there between men's mustard and women's?"

"Ladies'."

"All right, ladies'."

"The fact is, sir, that since a lady's palate is more delicate than a man's, the ordinary mustard of Dijon is too strong and too pungent for the ladies, so much so that M. Bornibus has invented a separate mustard for them."

"Who is this M. Bornibus?"

"Oh, sir, he's all the rage as mustard-maker. People here talk of no mustard but his."

"It's true, I know him by reputation, but I don't yet know his mustard. It would be interesting to taste it here in Dijon. Will you give me some, then?"

"Which of the two?"

"Both of them."

"So monsieur will eat the ladies' mustard?"

"Yes, on the principle of *a fortiori*."

And the waiter served me the two mustards with my cutlets.

I am not a great lover of mustard. Since nature has furnished me with an excellent stomach, I have never made much use of this "preface to the appetite," as Grimod de la Reynière calls it. But I must say that on this occasion, prompted only by the fine canary colour of this good apéritif, I plunged the wooden spoon into the mustard pot and made two pyramids on my plate, one of the men's mustard and one of the ladies'. And I must also say that from this moment I shed my former self and joined the supporters of Bornibus mustard.

On my return to Paris, I went to visit the premises of M. Bornibus at 60, Boulevard de la Villette. He gave me a tour of the establishment, in the most obliging manner, and explained to me that the superiority of his products derived from the perfection of the handling machinery which he had himself invented, and above all from the way in which he chose and combined his primary ingredients.

There, my dear anonymous correspondent, I think you have all that you sought from me, chronologically, etymologically, botanically, and from the culinary point of view.

MADELEINE KAMMAN

Of Gardens, Herbs, and Wines

It was a big bunch of fragrant herbs and some fresh eggs that ended for me, in the spring of 1946, that wintering of the taste buds known as World War II.

When fresh herbs and eggs reappeared in French markets, my mother cooked a most delicious omelet chockful of *fines herbs*— parsley, tarragon, chervil, and chives—and I can honestly say that this simple fare, accompanied by a glass of Beaujolais, started me on my way to creating food for enjoyment rather than nourishment alone.

Because of the great influence of the classic cuisine of France on American cookery at the end of the eighteenth century, these *fines herbes* have long been favorites among American cooks. When it comes to matching food prepared with herbs with the right wine, it is my personal view that there are no set rules and no foolproof system. I think each and every combination of wine and herbs requires a fresh review of the elements involved. I came to this conclusion after I arrived in this country and began using more American (more precisely, Californian) rather than European wines. Soon I realized I needed to reevaluate my whole approach to the subject of "herb usage" within the context of wine service.

Chives, scallion greens, and garlic chives form a group I like to call the *passe partout* or "go-with-everything" herbs because their onion-like taste complements any type of food and wine; they tend to "agree with" all vegetables and meats (both white and red meats and fish) and, used in moderation, with all classes of wines (red, white, or rosé; mellow, dry, or sweetish). The *passe partout* herbs are best used in combination with other herbs.

A second category, the "parsleys," are important refreshers of the palate, and their grassy taste helps link the grassy and herbal flavor in a wine to the dish it accompanies. These herbs are "blenders" or "tamers" of the more pungent herbs, softening pronounced perfumes and flavors that could damage the taste of the wine. (They will, for example, tone down the strong, licoricy herbs.)

The parsleys include both the curly-leaved and flat Italian types as well as Chinese parsley which, in Central America, is called cilantro. Be careful with cilantro. Many winemakers cite its ability to "wreck" a wine. Certainly it will destroy any fine white wine. I usually serve dishes flavored with plain cilantro with pleasant but lesser wines, be they white, pink, or red, but if you blend this herb with another flavor like orange rind it becomes much more manageable, lending itself nicely to a light fruity red wine. Used with cheese as in a dish of pasta, it adapts well to a good solid red wine. Both orange rind and cheese act here as bridges between the pungent herb and wine.

Then there are the "turpentine" herbs. The Mediterranean and California bay leaf, the thymes, savories, sages, marjoram, oregano, rosemary, and lavender all originally kept company in the same soils flavored by pine trees and they have acquired some of the same taste characteristics as pine resins. The rule here is: Watch your step because a little goes a long way. I have tasted too much lovely lamb marinated in rosemary for too long, the dish becoming rosemary-with-lamb instead of lamb-with-rosemary. Used without restraint, the herb no longer works as a bridge between meat and wine but overwhelms the palate, masking the nuance and fine flavor of a Cabernet Sauvignon; but this is not the only wine successful with the "turpentine" herbs; try the new California Syrahs from recent years for a real taste revelation. Our climate, after all, is a Mediterranean one.

The mints form a taste category of their own and can require some special handling. Some of our California Cabernets are said to have a "mint" aftertaste, and I enjoy sustaining this ever-so-delicate herbal note in the wine by adding some mint to the dish I will serve with it. A pan-fried beef steak dry-marinated with a mixture of mint, parsley, and garlic is wonderful for this. Always minimize mint to a faint hint and always use it in combination with compatible "blenders" like parsley and garlic. For red meats presented with mint, I like to add a bit of allspice to the marinade or sauce to tie the tastes of the mint, meat, and wine together.

Basil, a member of the mint family, behaves in recipes much like that herb when placed in combination with wine. Favorite preparations featuring basil's irreplaceable flavor, such as pesto and bouillabaisse, as a rule employ other ingredients to modify its very dominant taste (pignoli and cheese in the pesto; fennel, saffron, and orange rind in the bouillabaisse). This modification allows basil's strong flavor to blend well with a variety of wines.

Yet another herb category provides tastes of anise or licorice or a mixture of both. Members of this group come in the form of seeds such as fennel, anise, dill, caraway, and coriander. These are easy to powder and introduce into dressings and sauces or crush and add to a reduction of white wine. Again, use just a little for a subtle hint rather than a dominant note. I prefer these with fish or white-meated poultry accompanied by white wines that have undergone malolactic fermentation and been aged into a rounded mouthful. Fresh herbs of these anisey flavors such as tarragon, chervil and fennel and angelica greens are harder to handle because they assert themselves so radically; too much tarragon in a sauce or dry marinade will sink your wine into the flavor of the herb. Your recourse is to blend these herbs with parsley and one of the onion-flavored herbs.

And what of the peppery flavors from horseradish, nasturtiums, and the sweet and hot peppers? Personally, I am not partial to any frankly peppery taste with wine. I like to enjoy either one or the other. But I must admit that finely chopped nasturtiums introduced into a reduction of excellent Chardonnay and finished with butter and a bit of cream can be quite good.

In Europe the art of marrying wines and herbs is simple: use the herbs produced by a region with the beverages enjoyed in that region— chives with Normandy cider, for instance, or herbs for bouillabaisse (fennel, basil, thyme, bay leaf, saffron, orange rind) with a wine of the Mediterranean region (a Cassis, a Bandol, or a white Châteauneuf-du-Pape). This way you can be certain both herbs and wine will harmonize, exhibiting characteristics of the same soils.

But in California things get a lot more complicated. Here in the Napa Valley, for example, where we have sixty-four different types of soils, the Chardonnay or Sauvignon Blanc grown in one soil differs from that grown in another, and our herbs display similar differences in taste. Quite a quandary for the cook! My response to this more complex picture is to divide my herbs into basic taste categories, appraise the strength of each herb within its category, and work from there.

HARRY MATHEWS

Country Cooking from Central France: Roast Boned Rolled Stuffed Shoulder of Lamb (Farce Double)

FOR MAXINE GROFFSKY

Here is an old French regional dish for you to try. Attempts by presumptuous chefs to refine it have failed to subdue its basically hearty nature. It demands some patience, but you will be abundantly rewarded for your pains.

Farce double—literally, double stuffing—is the specialty of La Tour Lambert, a mountain village in Auvergne, that rugged heart of the Massif Central. I have often visited La Tour Lambert: the first time was in late May, when *farce double* is traditionally served. I have observed the dish being made and discussed it with local cooks.

The latter were skeptical about reproducing *farce double* elsewhere—not out of pride, but because they were afraid the dish would make no sense to a foreigner. (It is your duty to prove them wrong—and nothing would make them happier if you did.) Furthermore, they said, certain ingredients would be hard to find. Judicious substitution is our answer to that. Without it, after all, we would have to forgo most foreign cooking not out of a can.

The shoulder of lamb itself requires attention. You must buy it from a butcher who can dress it properly. Tell him to include the middle neck, the shoulder chops in the brisket, and part of the foreshank. Without them, the stuffing will fall out of the roast.

In Auvergne, preparing the cut is no problem, since whole lambs are roasted: the dish is considered appropriate for exceptional, often communal feasts, of a kind that has become a rarity with us.

All bones must be removed. If you leave this to the butcher, have him save them for the deglazing sauce. The fell or filament must be kept intact, or the flesh may crumble.

Set the boned forequarter on the kitchen table. Do not slice off the purple inspection stamps but scour them with a brush dipped in a weak solution of lye. The meat will need all the protection it can get. Rinse and dry.

Marinate the lamb in a mixture of 2 quarts of white wine, 2 quarts of olive oil, the juice of 16 lemons, salt, pepper, 16 crushed garlic cloves, 10 coarsely chopped yellow onions, basil, sage, rosemary, melilot, ginger, allspice, and a handful of juniper berries. The juniper adds a pungent, authentic note. In Auvergne, shepherds pick the berries in late summer when they drive their flocks from the mountain pastures. They deposit the berries in La Tour Lambert, where they are pickled through the winter in cider brandy. The preparation is worth making, but demands foresight.

If no bowl is capacious enough for the lamb and its marinade, use a washtub. Without a tub, you must improvise. Friends of mine in Paris resort to their bidet; Americans may have to fall back on the kitchen sink, which is what I did the first time I made *farce double*. In La Tour Lambert, most houses have stone marinating troughs. Less favored citizens use the municipal troughs in the entrance of a cave in the hillside, just off the main square.

The lamb will have marinated satisfactorily in 5 or 6 days.

Allow yourself 3 hours for the stuffings. The fish balls or quenelles that are their main ingredient can be prepared a day in advance and refrigerated until an hour before use.

The quenelles of La Tour Lambert have traditionally been made from *chaste*, a fish peculiar to the mountain lakes of Auvergne. The name, a dialect word meaning "fresh blood," may have been suggested by the color of its spreading gills, through which it ingests its food. (It is a mouthless fish.) It is lured to the surface with a skein of tiny beads that resemble the larvae on which it preys, then bludgeoned with an underwater boomerang. *Chaste* has coarse, yellow-white flesh, with a mild but inescapable taste. It has been vaguely and mistakenly identified as a perch; our American perch, however, can replace it, provided it has been caught no more than 36 hours before cooking. Other substitutes are saltwater fish such as silver hake or green cod. If you use a dry-fleshed fish, remember to order beef-kidney fat at the butcher's to add to the fish paste. (Be sure to grind it separately.)

To a saucepan filled with 2½ cups of cold water, add salt, pepper, 2 pinches of grated nutmeg, and 6 tablespoons of butter. Boil. Off heat, begin stirring in 2½ cups of flour and continue as you again bring the water to a boil. Take off heat. Beat in 5 eggs, one at a time, then 5 egg whites. Let the liquid cool.

Earlier, you will have ground 3¾ pounds of fish with a mortar and pestle—heads, tails, bones, and all—and forced them through a coarse sieve. Do *not* use a grinder, blender, or Cuisinart. The sieve of La Tour Lambert is an elegant sock of meshed copper wire, with a fitted ashwood plunger. It is kept immaculately bright. Its apertures are shrewdly gauged to crumble the bones without pulverizing the flesh. Into the strained fish, mix small amounts of salt, white pepper, nutmeg, and chopped truffles—fresh ones, if possible.

Stir fish and liquid into an even paste.

Two hours before, you will have refrigerated 1 cup of the heaviest cream available. Here, of course, access to a cow is a blessing.

The breathtakingly viscid cream of La Tour Lambert is kept in specially excavated cellars. Those without one use the town chiller, in the middle depths—cool but not cold—of the cave mentioned earlier. Often I have watched the attendant women entering and emerging from that room, dusky figures in cowls, shawls, and long gray gowns, bearing earthenware jugs like offerings to a saint.

Beat the cool cream into the paste. Do it slowly: think of those erect, deliberate Auvergnat women as they stand in the faint gloom of the cave, beating with gestures of timeless calm. It should take at least 15 minutes to complete the task.

At some previous moment, you will have made the stuffing for the quenelles. (This is what makes the stuffing "double.") It consists of the milt of the fish and the sweetbreads of the lamb, both the neck and stomach varieties. (Don't forget to mention *them* to your butcher.) The milt is rapidly blanched. The sweetbreads are diced, salted, spiced with freshly ground hot pepper, and tossed for 6 minutes in clarified butter. Both are then chopped very fine (blender permitted) and kneaded into an unctuous mass with the help of 1 cup of lamb marrow and 3 tablespoons of aged Madeira.

I said at the outset that I am in favor of appropriate substitutions in preparing *farce double:* but even though one eminent authority has suggested it, stuffing the quenelles with banana peanut butter is not appropriate.

The quenelles must now be shaped. Some writers who have discoursed at length on the traditional Auvergnat shape urge its adoption at all costs. I disagree. For the inhabitants of La Tour Lambert, who attach great significance to *farce double*, it may be right to feel strongly on this point. The same cannot be said for families in Maplewood or Orange County. You have enough to worry about as it is. If you are, however, an incurable stickler, you should know that in Auvergne molds are used. They are called *beurdes* (they are, coincidentally, shaped like birds), and they are available here. You can find them in any of the better head shops.

But forget about bird molds. Slap your fish paste onto a board and roll it flat. Spread on stuffing in parallel ½-inch bands 2 inches apart. Cut paste midway between bands, roll these strips into cylinders, and slice the cylinders into sections no larger than a small headache. Dip each piece in truffle crumbs.

I refuse to become involved in the pros and cons of presteaming the quenelles. The only steam in La Tour Lambert is a rare fragrant wisp from the dampened fire of a roasting pit.

We now approach a crux in the preparation of *farce double:* enveloping the quenelles and binding them into the lamb. I must make a stern observation here; and you must listen to it. You must take it absolutely to heart.

If the traditional ways of enveloping the quenelles are arduous, they are in no way gratuitous. On them depends an essential component of *farce double,* namely the subtle interaction of lamb and fish. While the quenelles (and the poaching liquid that bathes them) must be largely insulated from the encompassing meat, they should not be wholly so. The quenelles must not be drenched in roasting juice or the lamb in fishy broth, but an exchange should occur, definite no matter how mild. Do not *under any circumstance* use a baggie or Saran Wrap to enfold the quenelles. Of course it's easier. So are TV dinners. For once, demand the utmost of yourself: the satisfaction will astound you, and *there is no other way.*

I mentioned this misuse of plastic to a native of La Tour Lambert. My interlocutor, as if appealing for divine aid, leaned back, lifted up his eyes, and stretched forth his arms. He was standing at the edge of a marinating trough; its edges were slick with marinade. One foot shot forward, he teetered for one moment on the brink, and then down he went. Dripping oil, encrusted with fragrant herbs, he emerged briskly and burst into tears.

There are two methods. I shall describe the first only briefly: it is the one used by official cooks for public banquets. Cawl (tripe skin) is scraped free of fat and rubbed with pumice stone to a thinness approaching nonexistence. This gossamer is sewn into an open pouch, which is filled with the quenelles and broth before being sewn shut. The sealing of the pouch is preposterously difficult. I have tried it six times; each time, ineluctable burstage has ensued. Even the nimble-fingered, thimble-thumbed seamstresses of La Tour Lambert find it hard. In their floodlit corner of the festal cave, they are surrounded by a sizable choir of wailing boys whose task is to aggravate their intention to a pitch of absolute, sustained concentration. If the miracle always occurs, it is never less than miraculous.

The second method is to seal the quenelles inside a clay shell. This demands no supernatural skills, merely attention.

Purveyors of reliable cooking clay now exist in all major cities. The best are Italian. In New York, the most dependable are to be found in east Queens.

Stretch and tack down two 18-inch cheesecloth squares. Sprinkle until soaking (mop up puddles, however). Distribute clay in pats and roll flat until entire surface is evenly covered. The layer of clay should be no more than 1/16 inch thick. Scissor edges clean.

Drape each square on an overturned 2-quart bowl. Fold back flaps. Mold into hemispheres. Check fit, then dent edge of each hemisphere with forefinger so that when dents are facing each other, they form a 3/4-inch hole.

Be sure to prepare the shell at least 48 hours in advance so that it hardens properly. (If you are a potter, you can bake it in the oven; if not, you risk cracking.) As the drying clay flattens against the cheesecloth, tiny holes will appear. Do *not* plug them. Little will pass through them: just enough to allow the necessary exchange of savors.

Make the poaching liquid—3 quarts of it—like ordinary fish stock. The wine used for this in Auvergne is of a local sparkling variety not on the market; but any good champagne is an acceptable substitute.

By "acceptable substitute," I mean one acceptable to me. Purists have cited the fish stock as a reason for not making *farce double* at all. In La Tour Lambert, they rightly assert, the way the stock is kept allows it to evolve without spoiling: in the amphora-like jars that are stored in the coldest depths of the great cave, a faint, perpetual fermentation gives the perennial brew an exquisite, violet-flavored sourness. This, they say, is inimitable. *I* say that 30 drops of decoction of elecampane blossoms will reproduce it so perfectly as to convince the most vigilant tongue.

Fifteen minutes before roasting time, put the quenelles in one of the clay hemispheres. Set the other against it, dent to dent. Seal the seam with clay, except for the hole, and thumb down well. Hold the sphere in one hand with the hole on top. With a funnel, pour in *hot* poaching liquid until it overflows, then empty 1 cup of liquid. This is to keep the shell from bursting from within when the broth reaches a boil.

Be sure to keep the shell in your hand: set in a bowl, one bash against its side will postpone your dinner for several days at least. In La Tour Lambert, where even more fragile gut is used, the risks are lessened by placing the diaphanous bags in woolen reticules. It is still incredible that no damage is ever done to them on the way to the stuffing tables. To avoid their cooling, they are carried at a run by teen-age boys, for whom this is a signal honor: every Sunday throughout the following year, they will be allowed to wear their unmistakable lily-white smocks.

Earlier in the day, you will have anointed the lamb, inside and out: inside, with fresh basil, coriander leaves, garlic, and ginger thickly crushed into walnut oil (this is a *must*); outside, with mustard powder mixed with—ideally—wild-boar fat. I know that wild boars do not roam our woods (sometimes, on my walks through Central Park, I feel I may soon meet one): bacon fat will do—about a pint of it.

You will have left the lamb lying outside down. Now nestle the clay shell inside the boneless cavity. Work it patiently into the fleshy nooks, then urge the meat in little bulges around it, pressing the lamb next to the shell, not against it, with the gentlest possible nudges. When the shell is deeply ensconced, fold the outlying flaps over it, and shape the whole into a regular square cushion roast. Sew the edges of the meat together, using fine nylon thread. (Nylon is acceptable. It has even been adopted in La Tour Lambert, partly for its efficacy, partly because local materials became scarce after a murderous outbreak of cat leprosy in 1962.) The seams must be hermetically tight.

If the original roasting conditions will surely exceed your grasp, a description of them may clarify your goals.

In Auvergne, the body of the lamb is lowered on wetted ropes into a roasting pit. It comes to rest on transverse bars set close to the floor of the pit. Hours before, ash boughs that have dried through three winters are heaped in the pit and set ablaze: by now they are embers. These are raked against the four sides and piled behind wrought-iron grids into glowing walls. The cast-iron floor stays hot from the fire. When the lamb is in place, a heated iron lid is set over the pit. The lid does more than refract heat from below. Pierced with a multitude of small holes, it allows for aspersions of water on coals that need damping and the sprinkling of oil on the lamb, which is thus basted throughout its roasting in a continuous fine spray. Previously, I might add, the lamb has been rapidly seared over an open fire. Four senior cooks manage this by standing on high stepladders and manipulating the poles and extensible thongs used to shift the animal, which they precisely revolve over the flames so that it receives an even grilling.

Thus the onslaught of heat to which the lamb is subjected is, while too restrained to burn it, intense enough to raise the innermost broth to the simmering point.

Carefully lower the lamb into a 25-inch casserole. (If you have no such casserole, buy one. If it will not fit in your oven, consider this merely one more symptom of the shoddiness of our age, which the popularity of dishes like *farce double* may someday remedy.) Cover. You will have turned on the oven at maximum heat for 45 minutes at least. Close the oven door and lower the thermostat to 445°. For the next 5 hours, there is nothing to do except check the oven thermometer occasionally and baste the roast with juices from the casserole every 10 minutes. If you feel like catnapping, have no compunctions about it. Do *not* have anything to drink—considering what lies in store for you, it is a foolish risk. The genial cooks of La Tour Lambert may fall to drinking, dancing, and singing at this point, but remember that they have years of experience behind them; and you, unlike them, must act alone.

One song always sung during the roasting break provides valuable insight into the character of the Auvergnat community. It tells the story of a blacksmith's son who sets out to find his long-lost mother. She is dead, but he cannot remember her death, nor can he accept it. His widowed father has taken as second wife a pretty woman younger than himself. She is hardly motherly toward her stepson: one day, after he has grown to early manhood, she seduces him—in the words of the song, "she does for him what mother never did for her son." This line recurs throughout as a refrain.

It is after the shock of this event that the son leaves in quest of his mother. His father repeatedly tries to dissuade him, insisting that she is dead, or that, if she is alive, it is only in a place "as near as the valley beyond the hill and far away as the stars." In the end, however, he gives his son a sword and a purse full of money and lets him go. The stepmother, also hoping to keep the son from leaving, makes another but this time futile attempt to "do for him what mother never did for her son."

At the end of three days, the son comes to a city. At evening he meets a beautiful woman with long red hair. She offers him hospitality, which he accepts, and she attends lovingly to his every want. Pleasure and hope fill his breast. He begins wondering. He asks himself if this woman might not be his lost mother. But when night falls, the red-haired woman takes him into her bed and "does for him what mother never did for her son." The son knows she cannot be the one he seeks. Pretending to sleep, he waits for an opportunity to leave her; but, at midnight, he sees her draw a length of strong, sharp cord from beneath her pillow and stretch it toward him. The son leaps up, seizes his sword, and confronts the woman. Under its threat, she confesses that she was planning to murder him for the sake of his purse, as she has done with countless travelers: their corpses lie rotting in her cellar. The son slays the woman with his sword, wakes up a nearby priest to assure a Christian burial for her and her victims, and goes his way.

Three days later, he arrives at another city. As day wanes, a strange woman again offers him hospitality, and again he accepts. She is even more beautiful than the first; and her hair is also long, but golden. She lavishes her attentions on the young man, and in such profusion that hope once again spurs him to wonder whether she might not be his lost mother. But with the coming of darkness, the woman with the golden hair takes him into her bed and "does for him what mother never did for her son." His hopes have again been disappointed. Full of unease, he feigns sleep. Halfway through the night he hears footsteps mounting the stairs. He scarcely has time to leap out of bed and grasp his sword before two burly villains come rushing into the room. They attack him, and he cuts them down. Then, turning on the woman, he forces her at swordpoint to confess that she had hoped to make him her prisoner and sell him into slavery. Saracen pirates would have paid a high price for one of such strength and beauty. The son slays her, wakes up a priest to see that she and her henchmen receive Christian burial, and goes his way.

Another three days' journey brings him to a third city. There, at end of day, the son meets still another fair woman, the most beautiful of all, with flowing, raven-black hair. Alone of the three, she seems to recognize him; and when she takes him under her roof and bestows on him more comfort and affection than he had ever dreamed possible, he knows that this time his hope cannot be mistaken. But when night comes, she takes him into her bed, and she, like the others, "does for him what mother never did for her son." She has drugged his food. He cannot help falling asleep; only, at midnight, the touch of cold iron against his throat rouses him from his stupor. Taking up his sword, he points it in fury at the breast of the woman who has so beguiled him. She begs him to leave her in peace, but she finally acknowledges that she meant to cut his throat and suck his blood. She is an old, old witch who has lost all her powers but one, that of preserving her youth. This she does by drinking the blood of young men. The son runs her through with his sword. With a weak cry, she falls to the floor a wrinkled crone. The son knows that a witch cannot be buried in consecrated ground, and he goes his way.

But the young man travels no further. He is bitterly convinced of the folly of his quest; he has lost all hope of ever finding his mother; wearily he turns homeward.

On his way he passes through the cities where he had first faced danger. He is greeted as a hero. Thanks to the two priests, all know that it was he who destroyed the evil incarnate in their midst. But he takes no pride in having killed two women who "did for him what mother never did for her son."

On the ninth day of his return, he sees, from the mountain pass he has reached, the hill beyond which his native village lies. In the valley between, a shepherdess is watching her flock. At his approach she greets him tenderly, for she knows the blacksmith's son and has loved him for many years. He stops with her to rest. She has become, he notices, a beautiful young woman—not as beautiful, perhaps, as the evil three: but her eyes are wide and deep, and her long hair is brown.

The afternoon goes by. Still the son does not leave. At evening, he partakes of the shepherdess's frugal supper. At nighttime, when she lies down, he lies down beside her; and she, her heart brimming with gladness, "does for him what mother never did for her son." The shepherdess falls asleep. The son cannot sleep; and he is appalled, in the middle of the night, to see the shepherdess suddenly rise up beside him. But she only touches his shoulder as if to waken him and points to the starry sky. She tells him to look up. There, she says, beyond the darkness, the souls of the dead have gathered into one blazing light. With a cry of pain, the son asks, "Then is my mother there?" The shepherdess answers that she is. His mother lives beyond the stars, and the stars themselves are chinks in the night through which the fateful light of the dead and the unborn is revealed to the world. "Oh, Mother, Mother," the young man weeps. The shepherdess then says to him, "Who is now mother to your sleep and waking? Who else can be the mother of your joy and pain? I shall henceforth be the mother of every memory; and from this night on, I alone am your mother—even if now, and tomorrow, and all the days of my life, I do for you what mother never did for her son." In his sudden ecstasy, the blacksmith's son understands. He has discovered his desire.

And so, next morning, he brings the shepherdess home. His father, when he sees them, weeps tears of relief and joy; and his stepmother, sick with remorse, welcomes them as saviors. Henceforth they all live in mutual contentment; and when, every evening, the approach of darkness kindles new yearning in the young man's heart and he turns to embrace his wife, she devotedly responds and never once fails, through the long passing years, to "do for him what mother never did for her son."

The connection of this song with *farce double* lies, I was told, in an analogy between the stars and the holes in the lid of the roasting pit.

When your timer sounds for the final round, you must be in fighting trim: not aggressive, but supremely alert. You now have to work at high speed and with utmost delicacy. The meat will have swelled in cooking: it is pressing against the clay shell harder than ever, and one jolt can spell disaster. Do not coddle yourself by thinking that this pressure is buttressing the shell. In La Tour Lambert, the handling of the cooked lamb is entrusted to squads of highly trained young men: they are solemn as pallbearers and dexterous as shortstops, and their virtuosity is eloquent proof that this is no time for optimism.

Slide the casserole slowly out of the oven and gently set it down on a table covered with a thrice-folded blanket. You will now need help. Summon anyone—a friend, a neighbor, a husband, a lover, a sibling, even a guest—so that the two of you can slip four broad wooden spatulas under the roast, one on each side, and ease it onto a platter. The platter should be resting on a soft surface such as a cushion or a mattress (a small hammock would be perfect). Wait for the meat to cool before moving it onto anything harder. Your assistant may withdraw.

Meanwhile attend to the gravy. No later than the previous evening, you will have made 1½ quarts of stock with the bones from the lamb shoulder, together with the customary onions, carrots, celery, herb bouquet, cloves, scallions, parsnips, and garlic, to which you must not hesitate to add any old fowl, capon, partridge, or squab carcasses that are gathering rime in your deep freeze, or a young rabbit or two. Pour out the fat in the casserole and set it on the stove over high heat. Splash in enough of the same good champagne to scrape the casserole clean, and boil. When the wine has largely evaporated, take off heat, and add 2 cups of rendered pork fat. Set the casserole over very low heat and make a quick *roux* or brown sauce with 3 cups of flour. Then slowly pour in 2 cups of the blood of the lamb, stirring it in a spoonful at a time. Finally, add the stock. Raise the heat to medium high and let the liquid simmer down to the equivalent of 13 cupfuls.

While the gravy reduces, carefully set the platter with the roast on a table, resting one side on an object the size of this cookbook, so that it sits at a tilt. Place a broad shallow bowl against the lower side. If the clay shell now breaks, the poaching broth will flow rapidly into the bowl. Prop the lamb with a spatula or two to keep it from sliding off the platter.

Slit the seams in the meat, spread its folds, and expose the clay shell. Put on kitchen gloves—the clay will be scalding—and coax the shell from its depths. Set it in a saucepan, give it a smart crack with a mallet, and remove the grosser shards. Ladle out the quenelles and keep them warm in the oven in a covered, buttered dish with a few spoonfuls of the broth. Strain the rest of the liquid, reduce it quickly to a quarter of its volume, and then use what is left of the champagne to make a white wine sauce. Nap the quenelles with sauce, and serve.

If you have worked fast and well, by the time your guests finish the quenelles, the lamb will have set long enough for its juices to have withdrawn into the tissues without its getting cold. Pour the gravy into individual heated bowls. Place a bowl in front of each guest, and set the platter with the lamb, which you will have turned outside up, at the center of the table. The meat is eaten without knives and forks. Break off a morsel with the fingers of the right hand, dip it in gravy, and pop it into your mouth. In Auvergne, this is managed with nary a dribble; but lobster bibs are a comfort.

(Do not be upset if you yourself have lost all desire to eat. This is a normal, salutary condition. Your satisfaction will have been in the doing, not in the thing done. But observe the reaction of your guests, have a glass of wine [see below], and you may feel the urge to try one bite, and perhaps a second . . .)

It is a solemn moment when, at the great communal spring banquet, the Mayor of La Tour Lambert goes from table to table and with shining fingers gravely breaks the skin of each lamb. After this ceremony, however, the prevailing gaiety reasserts itself. After all, the feast of *farce double* is not only a time-hallowed occasion but a very pleasant one. It is a moment for friendships to be renewed, for enemies to forgive one another, for lovers to embrace. At its origin, curiously enough, the feast was associated with second marriages (some writers think this gave the dish its name). Such marriages have never been historically explained; possibly they never took place. What is certain is that the feast has always coincided with the arrival, from the lowlands, of shepherds driving their flocks to the high pastures where they will summer. Their coming heralds true spring and its first warmth; and it restores warmth, too, between the settled mountain craftsmen of La Tour Lambert and the semi-nomadic shepherds from the south. The two communities are separate only in their ways of life. They have long been allied by esteem, common interest, and, most important, by blood. Marriages between them have been recorded since the founding of the village in the year one thousand; and if many a shepherd's daughter has settled in La Tour Lambert as the wife of a wheelwright or turner, many an Auvergnat son, come autumn, has left his father's mill or forge to follow the migrant flocks toward Les Saintes-Maries-de-la-Mer. Perhaps the legend of second marriages reflects a practice whereby a widow or widower took a spouse among the folk of which he was not a member. The eating of *farce double* would then be exquisitely appropriate; for there is no doubt at all that the composition of the dish—lamb from plains by the sea, fish from lakes among the grazing lands—deliberately embodies the merging of these distinct peoples in one community. I should add that at the time the feast originated, still another group participated harmoniously in its celebration: pilgrims from Burgundy on their way to Santiago de Compostela. Just as the people of La Tour Lambert provided fish for the great banquet and the shepherds contributed their lambs, the pilgrims supplied kegs of new white wine that they brought with them from Chassagne, the Burgundian village now called Chassagne-Montrachet. Their wine became the invariable accompaniment for both parts of *farce double*; and you could hardly do better than to adopt the custom. Here, at least, tradition can be observed with perfect fidelity.

It is saddening to report that, like the rest of the world, La Tour Lambert has undergone considerable change. Shepherds no longer walk their flocks from the south but ship them by truck. The lakes have been fished out, and a substitute for *chaste* is imported frozen from Yugoslavia. The grandson of the last wheelwright works in the tourist bureau, greeting latter-day pilgrims who bring no wine. He is one of the very few of his generation to have remained in the village. (The cement quarry, which was opened with great fanfare ten years ago as a way of providing jobs, employs mainly foreign labor. Its most visible effect has been to shroud the landscape in white dust.) I have heard, however, that the blacksmith still earns a good living making wrought-iron lamps. Fortunately, the future of *farce double* is assured, at least for the time being. The festal cave has been put on a commercial footing, and it now produces the dish for restaurants in the area all year round (in the off season, on weekends only). It is open to the public. I recommend a visit if you pass nearby.

Eat the quenelles ungarnished. Mashed sorrel goes nicely with the lamb.

Serves thirteen.

CHARLES LAMB

A Dissertation Upon Roast Pig

Mankind, says a Chinese manuscript, which my friend M. was obliging enough to read and explain to me, for the first seventy thousand ages ate their meat raw, clawing or biting it from the living animal, just as they do in Abyssinia to this day. This period is not obscurely hinted at by their great Confucius in the second chapter of his Mundane Mutations, where he designates a kind of golden age by the term Chofang, literally the Cooks' Holiday. The manuscript goes on to say, that the art of roasting, or rather broiling (which I take to be the elder brother) was accidentally discovered in the manner following. The swine-herd, Ho-ti, having gone out into the woods one morning, as his manner was, to collect mast for his hogs, left his cottage in the care of his eldest son Bo-bo, a great lubberly boy, who being fond of playing with fire, as younkers of his age commonly are, let some sparks escape into a bundle of straw, which kindling quickly, spread the conflagration over every part of their poor mansion, till it was reduced to ashes. Together with the cottage (a sorry antediluvian make-shift of a building, you may think it), what was of much more importance, a fine litter of new-farrowed pigs, no less than nine in number, perished. China pigs have been esteemed a luxury all over the East, from the remotest periods that we read of. Bo-bo was in the utmost consternation, as you may think, not so much for the sake of the tenement, which his father and he could easily build up again with a few dry branches, and the labour of an hour or two, at any time, as for the loss of the pigs. While he was thinking what he should say to his father, and wringing his hands over the smoking remnants of one of those untimely sufferers, an odour assailed his nostrils, unlike any scent which he had before experienced. What could it proceed from?—not from the burnt cottage—he had smelt that smell before—indeed this was by no means the first accident of the kind which had occurred through the negligence of this unlucky young fire-brand. Much less did it resemble that of any known herb, weed, or flower. A premonitory moistening at the same time overflowed his nether lip. He knew not what to think. He next stooped down to feel the pig, if there were any signs of life in it. He burnt his fingers, and to cool them he applied them in his booby fashion to his mouth. Some of the crumbs of the scorched skin had come away with his fingers, and for the first time in his life (in the world's life indeed, for before him no man had known it) he tasted—*crackling*! Again he felt and fumbled at the pig. It did not burn him so much now, still he licked his fingers from a sort of habit. The truth at length broke into his slow understanding, that it was the pig that smelt so, and the pig that tasted so delicious; and surrendering himself up to the new-born pleasure, he fell to tearing up whole handfuls of the scorched skin with the flesh next it, and was cramming it down his throat in his beastly fashion, when his sire entered amid the smoking rafters, armed with retributory cudgel, and finding how affairs stood, began to rain blows upon the young rogue's shoulders, as thick as hail-stones, which Bo-bo heeded not any more than if they had been flies. The tickling pleasure, which he experienced in his lower regions, had rendered him quite callous to any inconveniences he might feel in those remote quarters. His father might lay on, but he could not beat him from his pig, till he had fairly made an end of it, when, becoming a little more sensible of his situation, something like the following dialogue ensued.

"You graceless whelp, what have you got there devouring? Is it not enough that you have burnt me down three houses with your dog's tricks, and be hanged to you! but you must be eating fire, and I know not what—what have you got there, I say?"

"O father, the pig, the pig! do come and taste how nice the burnt pig eats."

The ears of Ho-ti tingled with horror. He cursed his son, and he cursed himself that ever he should beget a son that should eat burnt pig.

Bo-bo, whose scent was wonderfully sharpened since morning, soon raked out another pig, and fairly rending it asunder, thrust the lesser half by main force into the fists of Ho-ti, still shouting out, "Eat, eat, eat the burnt pig, father, only taste—O Lord!"—with such-like barbarous ejaculations, cramming all the while as if he would choke.

Ho-ti trembled every joint while he grasped the abominable thing, wavering whether he should not put his son to death for an unnatural young monster, when the crackling scorching his fingers, as it had done his son's, and applying the same remedy to them, he in his turn tasted some of its flavour, which, make what sour mouths he would for a pretense, proved not altogether displeasing to him. In conclusion (for the manuscript here is a little tedious), both father and son fairly set down to the mess, and never left off till they had dispatched all that remained of the litter.

Bo-bo was strictly enjoined not to let the secret escape, for the neighbours would certainly have stoned them for a couple of abominable wretches, who could think of improving upon the good meat which God had sent them. Nevertheless, strange stories got about. It was observed that Ho-ti's cottage was burnt down now more frequently than ever. Nothing but fires from this time forward. Some would break out in broad day, others in the night-time. As often as the sow farrowed, so sure was the house of Ho-ti to be in a blaze; and Ho-ti himself, which was the more remarkable, instead of chastising his son, seemed to grow more indulgent to him than ever. At length they were watched, the terrible mystery discovered, and father and son summoned to take their trial at Pekin, then an inconsiderable assize town. Evidence was given, the obnoxious food itself produced in court, and verdict about to be pronounced, when the foreman of the jury begged that some of the burnt pig, of which the culprits stood accused, might be handed into the box. He handled it, and they all handled it; and burning their fingers, as Bo-bo and his father had done before them, and nature prompting to each of them the same remedy, against the face of all the facts, and the clearest charge which judge had ever given,—to the surprise of the whole court, townsfolk, strangers, reporters, and all present—without leaving the box, or any manner of consultation whatever, they brought in a simultaneous verdict of Not Guilty.

The judge, who was a shrewd fellow, winked at the manifest iniquity of the decision: and when the court was dismissed, went privily and bought up all the pigs that could be had for love or money. In a few days his lordship's town-house was observed to be on fire. The thing took wing, and now there was nothing to be seen but fire in every direction. Fuel and pigs grew enormously dear all over the district. The insurance-offices one and all shut up shop. People built slighter and slighter every day, until it was feared that the very science of architecture would in no long time be lost to the world. Thus this custom of firing houses continued, till in process of time, says my manuscript, a sage arose, like our Locke, who made a discovery that the flesh of swine, or indeed of any other animal, might be cooked (*burnt*, as they called it) without the necessity of consuming a whole house to dress it. Then first began the rude form of a gridiron. Roasting by the string or spit came in a century or two later, I forget in whose dynasty. By such slow degrees, concludes the manuscript, do the most useful, and seemingly the most obvious, arts make their way among mankind——

Without placing too implicit faith in the account above given, it must be agreed that if a worthy pretext for so dangerous an experiment as setting houses on fire (especially in these days) could be assigned in favour of any culinary object, that pretext and excuse might be found in ROAST PIG.

Of all the delicacies in the whole *mundus edibilis*, I will maintain it to be the most delicate—*princeps obsoniorum.*

I speak not of your grown porkers—things between pig and pork—those hobbydehoys—but a young and tender suckling—under a moon old—guiltless as yet of the sty—with no original speck of the *amor immunditœ*, the hereditary failing of the first parent, yet manifest—his voice as yet not broken, but something between a childish treble and a grumble—the mild forerunner or *prœludium* of a grunt.

He must be roasted. I am not ignorant that our ancestors ate them seethed, or boiled—but what a sacrifice to the exterior tegument!

There is no flavour comparable, I will contend, to that of the crisp, tawny, well-watched, not over-roasted, *crackling*, as it is well called—the very teeth are invited to their share of the pleasure at this banquet in overcoming the coy, brittle resistance—with the adhesive oleaginous—O call it not fat! but an indefinable sweetness growing up to it—the tender blossoming of fat—fat cropped in the bud—taken in the shoot—in the first innocence—the cream and quintessence of the child-pig's yet pure food—the lean, no lean, but a kind of animal manna—or, rather, fat and lean (if it must be so) so blended and running into each other, that both together make but one ambrosian result or common substance.

Behold him, while he is "doing"—it seemeth rather a refreshing warmth, than a scorching heat, that he is so passive to. How equably he twirleth round the string!—Now he is just done. To see the extreme sensibility of that tender age! he hath wept out his pretty eyes—radiant jellies—shooting stars—

See him in the dish, his second cradle, how meek he lieth!—wouldst thou have had this innocent grow up to the grossness and indocility which too often accompany maturer swinehood? Ten to one he would have proved a glutton, a sloven, an obstinate, disagreeable animal—wallowing in all manner of filthy conversation—from these sins he is happily snatched away——

Ere sin could blight or sorrow fade,
Death came with timely care—

his memory is odoriferous—no clown curseth, while his stomach half rejecteth, the rank bacon—no coal-heaver bolteth him in reeking sausages—he hath a fair sepulchre in the grateful stomach of the judicious epicure—and for such a tomb might be content to die.

He is the best of sapors. Pine-apple is great. She is indeed almost too transcendent—a delight, if not sinful, yet so like to sinning that really a tender-conscienced person would do well to pause—too ravishing for mortal taste, she woundeth and excoriateth the lips that approach her—like lovers' kisses, she biteth—she is a pleasure bordering on pain from the fierceness and insanity of her relish—but she stoppeth at the palate—she meddleth not with the appetite—and the coarsest hunger might barter her consistently for a mutton-chop.

Pig—let me speak his praise—is no less provocative of the appetite, than he is satisfactory to the criticalness of the censorious palate. The strong man may batten on him, and the weakling refuseth not his mild juices.

Unlike to mankind's mixed characters, a bundle of virtues and vices, inexplicably intertwisted, and not to be unravelled without hazard, he is—good throughout. No part of him is better or worse than another. He helpeth, as far as his little means extend, all around. He is the least envious of banquets. He is all neighbours' fare.

I am one of those, who freely and ungrudgingly impart a share of the good things of this life which fall to their lot (few as mine are in this kind) to a friend. I protest I take as great an interest in my friend's pleasures, his relishes, and proper satisfactions, as in mine own. "Presents," I often say, "endear Absents." Hares, pheasants, partridges, snipes, barndoor chickens (those "tame villatic fowl"), capons, plovers, brawn, barrels of oysters, I dispense as freely as I receive them. I love to taste them, as it were, upon the tongue of my friend. But a stop must be put somewhere. One would not, like Lear, "give everything." I make my stand upon pig. Methinks it is an ingratitude to the Giver of all good flavours to extra-domiciliate, or send out of the house slightingly (under pretext of friendship, or I know not what) a blessing so particularly adapted, predestined, I may say, to my individual palate—It argues an insensibility.

I remember a touch of conscience in this kind at school. My good old aunt, who never parted from me at the end of a holiday without stuffing a sweetmeat, or some nice thing into my pocket, had dismissed me one evening with a smoking plum-cake, fresh from the oven. In my way to school (it was over London Bridge) a grey-headed old beggar saluted me (I have no doubt, at this time of day, that he was a counterfeit). I had no pence to console him with, and in the vanity of self-denial and the very coxcombry of charity, schoolboy-like, I made him a present of—the whole cake! I walked on a little, buoyed up, as one is on such occasions, with a sweet soothing of self-satisfaction; but before I had got to the end of the bridge, my better feelings returned, and I burst into tears, thinking how ungrateful I had been to my good aunt, to go and give her good gift away to a stranger that I had never seen before, and who might be a bad man for aught I knew; and then I thought of the pleasure my aunt would be taking in thinking that I—I myself, and not another—would eat her nice cake—and what should I say to her the next time I saw her—how naughty I was to part with her pretty present!—and the odour of that spicy cake came back upon my recollection, and the pleasure and the curiosity I had taken in seeing her make it, and her joy when she sent it to the oven, and how disappointed she would feel that I had never had a bit of it in my mouth at last—and I blamed my impertinent spirit of alms-giving, and out-of-place hypocrisy of goodness; and above all I wished never to see the face again of that insidious, good-for-nothing, old grey impostor.

Our ancestors were nice in their method of sacrificing these tender victims. We read of pigs whipt to death with something of a shock, as we hear of any other obsolete custom. The age of discipline is gone by, or it would be curious to inquire (in a philosophical light merely) what effect this process might have toward intenerating and dulcifying a substance, naturally so mild and dulcet as the flesh of young pigs. It looks like refining a violet. Yet we should be cautious, while we condemn the inhumanity, how we censure the wisdom of the practice. It might impart a gusto—

I remember an hypothesis, argued upon by the young students, when I was at St. Omer's, and maintained with much learning and pleasantry on both sides, "Whether, supposing that the flavour of a pig who obtained his death by whipping (*per flagellationem extremam*) superadded a pleasure upon the palate of a man more intense than any possible suffering we can conceive in the animal, is man justified in using that method of putting the animal to death?" I forget the decision.

His sauce should be considered. Decidedly, a few bread crumbs, done up with his liver and brains, and a dash of mild sage. But banish, dear Mrs. Cook, I beseech you, the whole onion tribe. Barbecue your whole hogs to your palate, steep them in shallots, stuff them out with plantations of the rank and guilty garlic; you cannot poison them, or make them stronger than they are—but consider, he is a weakling—a flower.

EDWARD STEINBERG

The Vines of San Lorenzo: A Proposal

This book is about the making of a great wine.

The primary narrative thread follows one wine from birth to bottle. Through the enlivening particular the reader learns about the general. "In the end," writes Émile Peynaud, the most influential enologist of our time, "it's everywhere like in Bordeaux." In spite of the infinite variations possible, the story of the growing of grapes on one plot of land in a given year and their subsequent transformation is the story of Everywine.

Our wine is Italian: the 1989 vintage of Angelo Gaja's Sorì San Lorenzo, a vineyard in the village of Barbaresco. Further essential geography includes the region of Piedmont, the town of Alba and the area around it called the Langhe, the Tanaro River.

Why Italy? Italy is going through a vinous revolution to overthrow an oppressive heritage and is in many ways more interesting than other choices, such as France, with its long-standing successful tradition and California, which was "born free."

Why Sorì San Lorenzo? It certainly is a great wine. When the 1985 vintage made its debut, two of Germany's leading wine writers wrote about "multifaceted structure, enormous extract, concentrated fruit, unbelievable richness, magnificent finish." Their most famous American colleague described the wine as "exotic, compelling, and incredibly complex" and its bouquet as "reminiscent of what a fictional blend of Romanée-Conti and Mouton-Rothschild might taste like." Sorì San Lorenzo is made with a native Italian grape, Nebbiolo. Gaja was in the vanguard of the revolution. He grows many grape varieties, planted in various vineyards, which makes revealing comparisons possible.

What does it take to make a great wine? In 1977, André Mentzelopulous bought one of the most famous wine estates in Bordeaux, Château Margaux, which had not produced a great wine since 1961. He engaged as a consultant the enologist referred to earlier, Émile Peynaud, and told him that he wanted to make the best wine in the world. "That's not so hard," Peynaud replied. "All you have to do is give me the best grapes in the world."

Peynaud's reply took many things for granted that will be an important part of our story. But there is no doubt that it all begins in the vineyard, with the grapes.

Our main guide here is Federico Curtaz. Just over thirty, born to the north in the Valle d'Aosta and partly bred in the nearby town of Asti, Federico started to work for Gaja in 1983. As a schoolboy, he had participated precociously in the radical politics and strenuous ideological confrontations of the seventies. "If you want war," Angelo told him, "you'll have it."

Federico has worked on a farm in England, growing hops and squash. While harvesting, he talks about jazz or the cartoons by Raphael in the Victoria and Albert Museum in London. We see him walking among his vines, examining a leaf here, removing one there. His attitude is at once clinical and paternal. When he kneels down and scoops up a handful of earth, he talks about soil structure as passionately as wine lovers discuss the differences between Pauillac and Pomerol. He observes that the soil of a vineyard Angelo has just bought has been overfertilized. "We have to make those vines suffer," he says deadpan. "I've read de Sade."

Most people are more familiar with table grapes than with the great wine varieties. The latter are smaller, juicier, less crunchy. They have a higher ratio of skin to pulp and can look rather miserable to an untrained eye, as Angus Reach noted almost a century and a half ago in his book *Claret and Olives*. Observing the "unpromising" grapes at Château Margaux, he saw in them a "homily against trusting to appearances. If you saw a bunch in Convent Garden you would turn from them with the notion that the fruiterer was trying to do you with overripe black currants."

There are many varieties of all plants. A passionate potato-lover, Donald Maclean, once had more than 400 varieties growing in his collection, but just six of them account for over 80 percent of America's commercial production. Who writes about the difference between the common Russet Burbank and the rare Pink Fir Apple, and how many consumers are ready to pay the difference in price?

Wine grapes are one of the few crops capable of fetching a price that rewards growing fussy, low-yielding varieties such as Nebbiolo. "Nebbiolo," says research agronomist Lorenzo Corino, whom we meet in Asti, "is a discouraging grape." Indeed, when Barbaresco growers met in 1908 to discuss fraud and other problems, they protested against their Nebbiolo vineyards being put in the highest tax bracket. "Given that the fastidiousness of that variety does not ensure a constant income," they noted, "in no vineyard is Nebbiolo grown by itself, but together with Barbera, Freisa and Dolcetto," lesser but hardier varieties. "With Nebbiolo," says Aldo Vacca, who works in the office at the Gaja winery, but comes from a family of Barbaresco growers, "you're always in the vineyard."

The importance of site was expressed prosaically in the seventeenth century by the English philosopher John Locke (who marveled during a visit to Bordeaux that the mere "width of a ditch" separated the great vineyard of Haut-Brion from a lesser one) and poetically in our own by the French writer Colette ("The vine makes the true savor of the earth intelligible to man. It senses, then expresses in its clusters the secrets of the soil").

When we observe Sorì San Lorenzo at sunrise and sunset from the hill across the valley, Fasèt, it is like a stage where the lights go on early and are turned off late. On a cold morning in January 1989, Fasèt is still covered by the snow that fell yesterday. On the slope of Sorì San Lorenzo it has completely melted, while there are still patches here and there on contiguous plots. We are reminded that when the cooperative winery was founded at Barbaresco in 1894, it classified as first-class those vineyards of its members where the snow melted first. We begin to understand the local dialect: *sorì*, a slope facing south, a slope that catches the most sun.

That same morning, Federico and his crew are at San Lorenzo to do the winter pruning. We observe him sizing up a vine before clipping off the "past" (the canes that bore last year's crop) and trimming the "present" (the one that will bear this year's) and the "future" (the spurs that will provide the fruiting cane next year). Federico comments; we learn about the vine.

Even the noblest wine varieties are marked by their origins as forest creepers. Under natural conditions a vine must compete with other plants. Since it does not have a thick trunk to hold it above the ground, it has evolved other means to ensure itself a place in the sun. It grows rapidly and over a long period; tendrils enable it to climb to the top of trees. Nathaniel Hawthorne was fascinated by such a sight in Tuscany in 1858. "Nothing can be more picturesque," he wrote in his notebook, "than the spectacle of an old grape-vine . . . stretching out its innumerable arms on every bough." But the writer also recorded his suspicion that "the vine is a pleasanter object of sight under this mode of culture than it can be in countries where it produces a more precious wine, and therefore is trained more artificially."

Hawthorne's suspicion was well founded. Great wine is a product of strenuous viti*culture*, of nature highly nurtured. With vines as with us, culture directs the course of nature toward certain goals.

Federico chuckles at the thought of what would happen if vines were allowed to follow their natural tendencies. "The vine doesn't know it's supposed to produce the kind of grapes we want," he says. "You have to discipline it pretty brutally." He pauses. "After all, pruning is a mutilation."

We learn about various training systems (which give the vine's permanent and semipermanent parts a certain form) and pruning (which regulates annual growth and thus the quantity and quality of the grapes produced in a given year). The aim of the latter is to get the vine to channel its energy into the nourishment of a limited amount of grapes instead of wasting it on excessive vegetation or the production of more grapes than it can bring up properly.

The pruners regulate production by the number of eyes they leave on each vine. Quality and quantity are at odds here. Angelo says that when his father would talk about a certain year as being exceptional, it always turned out that the harvest had been small, as in 1961, when hail reduced the crop by more than half. In the early sixties, Angelo worked in the vineyards and decided to halve production by pruning more severely. The workers couldn't believe what they were being told to do. They talked about it at the local tavern and soon the whole village thought Angelo was crazy. "One day my father rushed into the house all upset. 'Everyone is saying that we have so few grapes we're going to go bankrupt!' he exclaimed. 'How are we going to pay the workers?' "

Pruning is over, but the crew cut will not last long.

As we observe San Lorenzo during the growing season, we learn about other factors affecting the growth of a vine and the quality of its grapes. We notice from Fasèt that the vines of another vineyard are closer together (density of planting). The rows of vines at San Lorenzo follow the curve of the hill *(girapoggio)*, while others run straight up and down the slope *(rittochino)*. One vineyard is covered by grass; another does not have a single blade. Federico explains how thinking about vineyard management has changed since the sixties, when a "body building" concept was dominant. Strolling through San Lorenzo during a prolonged spell of drought, we notice that the vines in one section seem more wilted than those in another (age of vine). We also notice, just above the ground on the trunk of each vine, the slight bulge that reminds us that, because of the phylloxera louse, the proud aristocrat is unable to stand on its own feet and needs the help of a plebeian American immigrant to survive (rootstock).

We follow as the various vineyard tasks are performed far from the limelight of cellar and tasting room by Federico and his men. We get to know some of them, hear their voices. Federico talks about the problems many workers have when they start at the winery. "They have no idea what quality is all about." Like the vines they tend, the workers have their roots deep in the soil of history, of culture. Last year he sent a couple of men to thin out the clusters in another vineyard in order to reduce the yield. "They tided up the shoots and cleaned around the vines," he says, "but they didn't remove a single bunch." Federico respects them. "They come from families that have stared hunger in the face." He mentions the solitude of some of the older workers. "There are those who suffer if they have to pair off with others." He nods in the direction of an old man. "Beppe couldn't have muttered more than three words all morning. Even having to *listen* to others is painful to him."

Federico is proud of his work, but expresses its goal in modest terms: "to enable the winemaker to *choose* when to harvest," rather than having to because the grapes would rot if they stayed on the vine any longer. This means keeping the vines healthy. It means keeping the skins of the grapes intact. Federico winces. "Once the skin breaks, that's the ball game."

The vine must be protected from harm. The seriousness of disease and pest control is eloquently expressed by the Italian terms *difesa* (defense) and *lotta* (fight). Of the three plagues that America inadvertently visited upon European vineyards in the nineteenth century—phylloxera, oidium, and downy mildew *(peronospora)*—the latter two still require constant vigilance and often intensive spraying. The traditional preventive for *peronospora* is based on copper sulfate. Growers became so fond of seeing the leaves of their vines turn blue from this spray that more recent ones have been dyed the same color. We hear how, during World War II, growers melted down pots, pans, and even coins in order to obtain the necessary copper. We visit consultant Paolo Ruaro, shy and deliberate as he speaks, with whom we discuss such matters as organic cultivation. We watch Federico using pheromones in his fight against the grape moth larva.

The buds break, the vine flowers, the fruit sets. Angelo is all smiles:

"The vineyard is way ahead of schedule." That means an early harvest, while the weather is sure to be good. But it is hard to believe that those hard green pinheads will ever be transformed into any kind of wine. In August they suddenly become credible, turning red overnight (the *invaiatura*) and starting to swell.

A shaded leaf annoys Federico. "It's not working for its keep," he snorts. It will also cause problems for the winemaker. He admires a cluster: not too big, not too tight, small grapes.

In the spring we saw a vineyard that had been destroyed by hail; now we drive by one where rows of vines have been knocked down by a violent storm. With Aldo Vacca, who wrote his thesis at the University of Turin on clonal selection, we go to an experimental vineyard devoted to that process. Aldo talks about clones while the differences stare us in the face. In Gaja's new vineyard at Serralunga, in the Barolo area on the other side of Alba, Federico points out the effects of management concerned with high yields and insensitive to the needs of the soil. In Asti, we visit Lorenzo Corino. "We're ahead of the French because we fell behind," he says with an impish grin about soil conservation. "We tried to keep up. Luckily, we had some problems."

After the *invaiatura* the grapes ripen rapidly. They swell and are more vulnerable. Drought is worrisome, but so is humidity. The difference between maximum and minimum temperatures is sometimes more than 20°C. ("Fantastic!" exults Federico.) At dinner the subject of mechanical harvesting comes up. Angelo rolls his eyes. "Machines don't think. How can they select grapes?"

As the harvest approaches, the winemaker leaves his cellar and takes to the vineyard more and more frequently. We meet Guido Rivella, born and bred in Barbaresco. We'll be seeing Guido scurrying like a monkey up ladders and across catwalks between fermentation tanks. Measuring one or another component of a wine like a doctor listening to a patient's heart.

On the far side of forty, with thinning hair, Guido seems to be thinning all over. He is hard on himself. His wines get reviewed, compared, and even graded throughout the world. Given Gaja's reputation and prices, expectations are high. "It's like the Juventus," he sighs, referring to Italy's most prestigious soccer team. "The Juve *has* to win." Calm and prudent, Guido is a foil to Angelo's passionate activism. "I come home from abroad wanting to change everything," says Angelo. "Guido puts on the brakes, plays the devil's advocate."

Times have changed since Guido was growing up in Montestefano, a cluster of houses less than a mile from the village itself. He recalls playing with his uncle's truffle dogs. Now and then they would dig up one of the tubers. Guido shrugs his shoulders. "I never cared much for them." His uncle didn't even sell them. The only merchant was in Alba, and the little he paid did not make buying a train ticket and taking several hours off from work worthwhile. "Wine was just a beverage in those days," remarks Guido. At the school in Alba where he studied enology and viticulture "they were mainly concerned about avoiding spoilage."

We follow Guido in his gray smock as he strides through Sorì San Lorenzo, picking grapes here and there at random and crushing them on his refractometer. He holds it up to the light and reads off a number on the Babo scale, named after a nineteenth-century Austrian. It's Baumé in France, Brix in the United States, and Oechsle in Germany, but what they all tell you in the end is how much sugar the grapes contain. "Twenty-two." "Nineteen." "Just under twenty-one." As the French thinker Pascal wrote back in the seventeenth century, "Are there ever two grapes exactly alike in a cluster?" Each grape has its own place in the vineyard pecking order according to its vine, its cluster (the nearer the trunk, the more sugar), its position in the cluster (the nearer the top, the more sugar).

We are reminded again that Nature could not care less about wine. From her point of view, the most important part of the grape is the seeds, which ensure the survival of the species. But the more seeds a grape has, the less sugar and more acidity it contains. In a sense, the sugar is merely a surplus left over after the seeds have received all the nourishment they need.

Now and then, Guido tastes a grape, examines the skin, crushes it in his hand. ("The juice comes out already colored!"). He could pick now, but since it is so early (October is still a week away and the harvest usually takes place well into that month) and the grapes are healthy, he could also wait. Federico and his crew have accomplished their mission: Guido has a choice.

In his book *Le vin et les jours (Wine and Days)*, Peynaud has an amusing chapter on "all those good reasons for harvesting early" ("The weather forecast is bad: I'd better hurry before it's too late." "The forecast is good: I'd better take advantage of it while it lasts."), for that has always been the great temptation. Yet the concept of ripeness is not a simple one. Sometimes less is more.

In 1978 the weather was so good that Angelo and Guido delayed the harvest in another vineyard, Sorì Tildìn, until November 11. "We were just showing off more than anything else," Guido confesses. "The old-timers were always saying that grapes weren't what they used to be, that you had to bring them in earlier nowadays." But he regrets that decision. The '78 Sorì Tildìn is still hard and unyielding.

Guido has noticed that the first batches of grapes from San Lorenzo produce more supple wines, with deeper color and a finer bouquet, than later ones. The skin is firmer and releases less pectin, which makes the wine hard. He also wants grapes with more malic acid, which will later be converted into lactic acid and thus make the wine more supple. "In the past, we lacked the knowledge, and maybe the courage, to harvest earlier," says Guido. "If the weather's good, we tend to feel it's a shame not to wait a bit longer."

Tomorrow is the day. "We'll start at seven-thirty in the morning," says Federico. "If there's no dew."

We start at the bottom of the slope. ("If it happens to rain later on, it'll be nastier at the bottom when we start working again.") We catch some of the banter as we work our way up Sorì San Lorenzo. ("When's Gaja going to install a sky-lift?") Angelo Lembo, who came north to work at the Fiat automobile factory in Turin and has lived in Barbaresco for twenty years, instructs a newcomer: "It's better to lose a few grapes than to let one rotten one slip through." The clusters are put into plastic containers. ("They might not be as attractive as wicker baskets," remarks Federico, "but they're a lot more hygienic.")

We sit on the tractor as it hauls away the first load of grapes toward the winery.

As the grapes move through the ideally cool morning air, the mind imagines their magical metamorphosis into a glass of Sorì San Lorenzo 1989. But it will be three years and many transformations later when bottles start to appear in wine shops around the world. The only other product of Barbaresco soil comparable in renown and price is the white truffle, which you can dig up, wipe off, and eat.

Making wine ("the fermented juice of grapes") is simplicity itself; making great wine involves a seemingly infinite number of details and decisions. One could argue that winemakers do not actually make wine (those alchemical agents, yeasts, do), but this is true only in the sense that cooks do not cook food (heat does).

Yet much of winemaking can be seen as controlling the effect of a few crucial factors such as microorganisms (yeast and bacteria), oxygen, and temperature. Guido explains how winemaking has evolved in recent times. There is both greater knowledge of the conditions affecting the major processes and the technology to control them. "Sure, great wines were made here in the past," he acknowledges, "but only when luck had it that certain conditions occurred spontaneously."

We follow the grapes as they are destemmed and crushed. The latter term is misleading. "It's like squeezing an orange," Guido explains. "If you press too hard, you get bitter substances from the skin in your juice." Indeed, the traditional crusher, the human foot, was a much more gentle piece of equipment than the first mechanical ones.

We observe Guido in his tiny laboratory with a beaker full of pale pink juice (in technical language, must). He measures the sugar and pH. We listen as he explains the importance of the latter.

Since sulfur dioxide is added to the grapes after crushing, we have a look at its functions in winemaking. Guido is amused by the "contains sulfites" warning familiar to American consumers. The warning would have to remain even if no sulfur dioxide were added to wine because it is a natural product of fermentation. But he is serious about using as little as possible. "With present-day knowledge and technology, there is no need to use even half the amount that was common not so long ago." Guido has made wines without sulfur dioxide, but prefers those with minimal amounts because they are "cleaner," have fewer off odors and flavors. "After all," he exclaims, "you don't want to throw out the quality baby with the sulfur dioxide bath."

The grapes are conveyed into large stainless-steel tanks. We learn about yeast: their role in the making of other beverages (beer) and foods (bread); the characteristics of different species and strains (baker's yeast, for instance, should be a strain that produces exceptionally large amounts of carbon dioxide so the dough will rise better); the isolation and cultivation of selected yeast strains that was begun by Emil Christian Hansen at the Carlsberg Brewery in Copenhagen in the late nineteenth century.

Yeasts produce more than alcohol. ("Thank God they do," exclaims Albino Morando, a researcher friend of Guido's. "Otherwise we'd have weak vodka instead of wine." Morando has the mind of a scientist and the hands of a farmer. He can talk for hours about manure, but he's also slung it.) They metabolize small quantities of other products, which contribute, favorably and otherwise, to a wine's character. Selected strains are the same the world over; wild ones reflect the local conditions in which they evolved. Similarly, the ripening agents of cheeses used to be specific to particular locations, such as the Emmental region in Switzerland and the caves at Roquefort in southern France. Selected cultures of molds and bacteria have made possible the production of "Swiss" and "blue" cheese in other locations, and are generally used even in their places of origin to ensure consistent results.

Guido sees the choice between using selected yeast and giving the wild ones a free hand as one of the many occasions when a winemaker has to choose between safety and a little more complexity. "You have to walk a tightrope," he explains. He will be pleased when he decides that Sorì San Lorenzo 1989 does not need the help of selected yeast, because "there *is* a difference, however slight."

Yeasts work better in some conditions than others. "They're only human," says Guido with a shrug. They need certain nutrients, even vitamins, and dislike extremes of temperature. When stressed, they produce higher levels of off odors and flavors.

We see again how the aims of nature have nothing to do with wine. Yeasts ferment sugar to obtain energy for reproduction. Alcohol, which they produce in anaerobic conditions (in the absence of oxygen), is simply a waste product, and a toxic one for them at that.

In the frenzy of fermentation, yeasts produce much more energy than they need and the excess is given off as heat. As the temperature rises, they find it harder and harder to work. Sometimes they stop working altogether and the fermentation gets "stuck." No longer protected from oxygen by the carbon dioxide also produced by the yeast, the must is vulnerable to spoilage bacteria. In this way, even so prestigious an estate as Château Lafite found itself temporarily in the vinegar business in the scorching Bordeaux fall of 1921.

The tanks in the Gaja winery are equipped with thermostats that automatically switch on a cooling system when the temperature reaches a certain point. When Guido started to work for Angelo in 1970, fermentation took place in either large wooden barrels or even larger concrete vats built into the wall, neither of which dispersed heat. In 1971 the fermentation was galloping out of hand because of the heat. Angelo rented a minibus that sped back and forth between the slaughterhouse in Alba and the winery with huge blocks of ice. "They weighed about a hundred pounds each," says Guido, shuddering at the thought. "And we carried them on our shoulders down to the cellar." There he pumped the must through a tube wrapped around the ice to cool it down.

We note how modern cooling systems are another instance of wine's indebtedness to its country cousin, beer.

Much of what we learn about yeast comes from Vincenzo Gerbi at the University of Turin's Institute of Microbiology. We visit him with Aldo Vacca, who has brought Guido's pH meter to be calibrated.

The lab is full of sophisticated equipment, scholarly journals, test tubes full of wine. We look at yeast cells through an electronic microscope that magnifies them 740 times. (This sight was first beheld by the Dutchman Anton van Leeuwenhoek in the seventeenth century, but it was not until Louis Pasteur and the birth of microbiology two centuries later that the phenomenon of fermentation was understood.) Gerbi talks about yeast research and sets some common misconceptions straight. In his white lab coat, with his measured and precise gestures, Gerbi is the very image of the scientist. It is to scientists that we owe our understanding of the processes involved in winemaking, but, like stainless-steel tanks and plastic containers, they still have no place in our vinous imagery.

We cannot see what is going on inside the tank, but there are signs that the fermentation is under way. The thermometer is rising. Guido opens a valve and a blast of acrid carbon dioxide assaults the unwary nose.

Guido puts a tall glass tube on a table in his lab and pours some must and skins into it. This microcosm will be our visible version of what is happening inside the fermentation tank. We observe how the impetuous bubbles of carbon dioxide push most of the solid matter toward the surface of the liquid. We learn about the problems created by the formation of this "cap" and the various ways of dealing with them.

Another crucial process, maceration, is taking place simultaneously with fermentation. The challenge for the winemaker is to extract the pigments and savory substances contained in the skins without extracting the astringent and bitter ones as well.

A similar problem is involved in making coffee, when only a fraction of the solubles contained in the coffee beans winds up in your cup. The method of extraction (filter, percolator, espresso, etc.), the fineness of the grind, the temperature of the water and the length of time the process lasts all influence how the coffee tastes.

We have a look at phenol compounds, the most important substances contained in the skins of our grapes, and especially anthocyanins (which give red wine its color) and tannins. Nebbiolo has an enormous amount of the latter (much more than Cabernet Sauvignon, for example) and relatively little of the former (similar in this respect to Pinot Noir). Guido exploits the fact that anthocyanins are water soluble, while tannin is extracted only by alcohol. He shoots the temperature up high at the beginning of fermentation (before the yeast cells have multiplied to the point where a significant amount of alcohol has been produced) and then lowers it, thereby extracting a lot of color without excessive tannin. The longer the wine remains in contact with the skins, the more tannin is extracted. Guido drains off the Sorì San Lorenzo 1989 after twelve days, as soon as the fermentation is over.

After the "free run" wine has been drained off, the skins are pressed. "Press wine" is dark and dense. From a second, harder pressing it is too coarse to drink. By tasting samples we understand better what was still left in the skins.

Like Barolo, Barbaresco has long had a reputation for toughness. "Toughness is indeed the essence of Nebbiolo," declares even wine writer Jancis Robinson, who rates the variety as one of the greatest. Angelo recalls tasting Barbarescos that were "so astringent they had grown old without ever reaching maturity." We look at the tradition of what Guido calls "macho macerations." It was as a follower of tradition that Guido's predecessor, Luigi Rama, let the skins and pips macerate with the new wine for up to two months. We also look at the tradition before the Tradition. In his book on viticulture and enology in the province of Cuneo (which includes Alba and the Langhe), written a century ago, agronomist Lorenzo Fantini describes Barbaresco as "ready at two years, perfect at three." Domenico Cavazza, the founder and first enologist of the cooperative winery, drained off the new wine after twelve and a half days in 1905, "a typical year."

The question is complex. Tannin is a catchall term, covering substances that can be savory or bitter, that undergo radical changes in barrel and bottle, that can make a wine velvety or harsh. Greater understanding of phenolic compounds is "the new frontier of red wine making," says Guido, who is not satisfied with the merely empirical knowledge derived from experience. We go with him to Asti, where Rocco Di Stefano receives us in his laboratory and talks about his research on this still-wild frontier.

After the wine has been drawn off the skins into a large barrel, we learn about a third process that is crucial for red wines, the malolactic fermentation. Sharp malic acid (the acid of apples, *malus* in Latin, when they are still green) is converted by bacteria into softer lactic acid and the wine becomes less astringent. We note other lactic acid fermentations, such as yogurt and sauerkraut. (Even the holes in Swiss cheese are due to the prodigious amount of carbon dioxide produced by a particular strain of bacteria.) Guido explains how the harshness and off odors of many older Barbarescos were frequently due to malolactic fermentations that took place in the worst possible conditions, after the wine had been bottled.

The phenomenon of malolactic fermentation was not understood until recently. Pasteur himself had created a kind of dualism, with yeasts as the good guys who make wine and bacteria as the bad guys who spoil it. "Rehabilitation" of the latter got under way only at the beginning of this century with the work of the great German microbiologist Robert Koch, discoverer of the tuberculosis bacterium. The textbook that Guido used at his school in Alba, a massive work of 1,500 pages, has little to say about the subject and reflects the hazy and contradictory notions of the times. Malolactic fermentation is actually discussed in a section on "the ailments of wine," so it would seem that all bacteria are still bad guys. But no: by reducing the total acidity, they can bring about "an improvement in the quality of the wine." On the practical side, the text offers little help. It does note that a low pH hinders the process, but "other factors are little known at the present."

Guido's real malolactic education began right after he started to work with Gaja. He recalls a trip to Burgundy in 1970. "Beaune was my first contact with a real wine culture," he exclaims as his face lights up. "You breathed it in the air, you saw it in the way they poured the wine in restaurants." He noticed the attention winemakers were giving to the malolactic fermentation and discovered the chromatography paper used to test the presence and amount of malic acid. "At the school where I studied," he says as he prepares the test, "they had never heard of this paper." Guido ordered a supply from France and translated the section on malolactic fermentation from one of Peynaud's books.

Like yeast, malolactic bacteria metabolize a variety of products, good and bad, according to species and conditions. The buttery flavor that many people find in Chardonnay (and is found in commercial buttermilk, which is not a by-product of making butter) comes from diacetyl, one of those products, and has nothing to do with the grape itself.

As far as working conditions are concerned, malolactic bacteria are even choosier than yeast. "You have to really pamper them," says Guido. Since they will not work if it is too cold, Gaja had a heating system installed in the cellar. In 1974 it was very cold after the new wine had been racked off the skins and the heating was turned on. It took a long time to bring the contents of the huge, insulated barrels up to the critical temperature. "You should have seen Angelo's father!" Guido almost cracks up. "He was running all around the cellar making sure all the doors were closed tight, trying to shut out even the slightest draft." Those were inflationary times, and the price of heating oil was rising fast.

When the malolactic fermentation is over, Guido gets rid of his microscopic workers as quickly as he can. "Just think!" he exclaims with his eyes flashing. "Millions, billions, trillions of bacteria out on the street, starving and unemployed." If they attack other substances, they can ruin the wine. Guido racks the wine off into small casks on the lowest level of the cellar, where it is too cold for the bacteria to work.

If, during the summer of 1989, you had looked down from the courtyard onto the area outside the lowest level, you would have seen work to enlarge the cellar going on to your left. Next to a construction crane were steel girders and bags of cement; stacks of lumber covered most of the rest of the area. A sharp eye might have noticed that the stacks to the right, the ones farthest from the crane, looked somewhat different from the others. The boards were uniform in length, and smaller; their color varied from pinkish to dull gray; they were stacked more methodically. Now only those stacks to the right are still there. They are what the French call *merrain*, roughhewn staves. They will be used to make Gaja's small casks.

Such casks date back to B.C. times and have long been part of our traditional wine imagery. An attentive visitor to Trajan's Column in Rome, for example, will notice a scene portraying a boat transporting three of them; a stained-glass window in the cathedral at Chartres shows a cooper in the process of making one.

It is ironic that just as wood was ceasing to be the universal container of wine, awareness of its importance began to grow rapidly throughout the world. As with our awareness of grape varieties, California played a major role in the process. In his effort to re-create the wines of Burgundy at the Hanzell Winery, in 1956 James D. Zellerbach ordered casks for his Chardonnay and Pinot Noir from a Burgundian cooper, Yves Sirugue. Other producers followed suit. The oaking of the world had begun. Hundreds of thousands of French oak casks later, the container has achieved near equality with the contents. Many Americans assume the flavor of oak to be the flavor of Chardonnay or even Cabernet Sauvignon, and winemakers around the world are catering to that assumption.

To say that a wine was aged in wood is about as meaningful as to say that it was made from grapes. Guido's textbook does not dedicate much space to the aging of wine, but what it does say merely reflects the situation in Italy when Angelo Gaja began to take charge at the winery. "Wines to be aged should be put into old barrels with a capacity of 3,000 to 10,000 liters." Oak is indeed the best wood, and it comes from Yugoslavia. Small casks are mentioned, but only as a container for transportation.

The contrast with Ottavio Ottavi, a Piedmontese who founded Italy's first enological journal and wrote a number of books in the second half of the nineteenth century, is striking. Ottavi's views are detailed and cosmopolitan. "Casks are the most important cellar instrument," he writes, and it is important to "pay close attention to the choice of staves." The combination of 225-liter casks, thin staves, and new wood used in the aging of fine Bordeaux allows "the slow oxidation of wine through the pores of the wood."

Toward the end of the sixties, Angelo was looking for a way to age Barbaresco that would give it more finesse. He had not read Ottavi, but he had been to France. We follow his long experimentation with small casks, beginning with those he bought in 1969 from one of the first-growth châteaux of Bordeaux. "I was ripped off," he says. "They were supposed to be two years old. Fifteen would have been more like it."

Angelo and Guido took nothing for granted. They had casks made from all kinds of wood. ("Some of the wines tasted like sawdust.") They wanted to find a way to treat the casks so they would confer neither too much of their own tannin nor too much oak flavor on the wine. They hit upon pressurized steam and varied the length of time the casks were steamed to see which gave the best results. When Robert Mondavi, whom Gaja had met in California, heard about what they were doing, he could not believe his ears: they were actually trying to get rid of some of the flavor that American consumers couldn't get enough of!

Advice was sought from famous coopers and winemakers in France. One day Jacques Puisais, "the Pope of the palate," came to visit. Guido was impressed. "He could enchant you for half an hour just talking about a glass of water." But when asked specific questions about small-cask aging, Puisais would always give the same answer: "You have to ask the wine." Guido's face lights up in amusement; he gestures in imitation. "*Il faut le demander au vin.*" "I thought he was putting me on," he says thoughtfully. "It took me quite a while to realize just how right he was." Every wine is different, and Nebbiolo is more different than others. Long experience is the only guide.

We are introduced to small casks and oak. The latter, like grapes and all plants, varies greatly according to species, soil, climate, and cultivation. Some casks in the cellar look as if they had bled. Guido says that they were made from sawed wood: splitting spares the vascular rays of the wood, but sawing cuts across them and makes leakage more likely.

Placed by the side of the 7,000-liter barrel where the wine has just finished its malolactic fermentation, one of the small casks looks insignificant. We learn how wines age differently in the two. We also learn about the substances that are extracted from new oak by the wine, including the lignin that gives it a vanilla-like flavor. (Indeed, vanilla extract is sometimes produced from lignin.) A new cask releases most of these substances during its first year of use and after two years has very little left to give.

Guido is putting Sorì San Lorenzo 1989 into casks that are 40 percent new and 60 percent one year old. He will see after a while if he wants to increase or decrease the percentage of new oak.

Strolling between the long rows of casks, we notice various names branded on them; many are French. The newer the cask, the greater the frequency with which one name appears, and it is Italian: Gamba.

The "prize-winning Angelo Gamba Cooperage" is located in the nondescript town of Castell'Alfero, a few miles north of Asti. There we visit Eugenio Gamba, with whom we follow the transformation of a pile of staves into a finished cask. He explains, among other things, the different degrees of char that are given to casks ("rare, medium, well done"). Gamba's casks are a cross between the *barrique* of Bordeaux and the *pièce* of Burgundy: more elongated than the latter, but plumper in the middle than the former.

Gamba was just another cooper until the late seventies. The big name in Italy was Garbellotto, in the Veneto, who made all of Gaja's large barrels. But when Garbellotto started to make small casks, they stuck to their traditional supplier of oak, nearby Slovenia. The Yugoslavs, however, do not split.

The turning point for Gamba came when French customers ordered some large barrels from him, but demanded that they be made of French oak. (Large barrels are much more difficult to make than small ones, and French coopers had little experience with them.) Until then Gamba, like all Italian coopers, had always used Yugoslav oak, so he set out for France with his "four or five words of junior high school French" to scout for suppliers. He gradually lengthened his list of *fendeurs* (splitters). When the small-cask movement began to turn into a mass phenomenon, he was ready.

We drive with Angelo and Gamba through the Mont Blanc Tunnel toward the heart of France. Gaja has established relations with a few *fendeurs* and wants to consolidate them. He is convinced that, of all the myriad factors affecting the quality of a stave, seasoning is one of the most important. But it is a process that ties up capital for a long time (Gaja insists on three years), and the temptation is to cut corners. Kiln drying is out of the question ("It's like pasteurizing wine." It also causes microscopic splits in the fibers.) The only solution is for him to season the wood himself.

We drive through the forest of Tronçais, a unique sylvan *cru*. All other *merrain* is referred to in much broader geographical terms, such as Allier, the department in which the forest is located. In one of the older sections the trees on either side of the narrow road are so tall that it is like driving through a tunnel. Younger sections are planted so densely you cannot see the ground. Gamba explains that the forest is managed according to the principle of natural selection. The aim is to produce tall, straight oaks with no branches and thus no knots in the wood. In the youngest sections of the forest there are well over 100,000 young oaks per hectare. The weaker plants die off or are cut down. A stand with trees over two hundred years old, a *haute futaie*, has only 100 to 150 of them left.

The Tronçais forest owes its preeminence to a decree issued in 1670 by Jean Baptiste Colbert, Louis XIV's chief minister. Colbert wanted to ensure an adequate supply of timber for the naval construction upon which France's commercial ambitions rested. Similar considerations earlier in the century had led King James I of England to forbid the burning of wood for the manufacture of glass, a measure that led to the use of coal and the birth of the modern wine bottle. The ways of the Lord have not neglected the aging of wine.

We stop to buy a map and Gamba asks if there are any *fendeurs* in the vicinity. To his surprise, the shopkeeper mentions an unfamiliar name, and off we dash to Vitray, a hamlet on the edge of the forest.

The ruddiness of Monsieur Daffy's face is set off by the whiteness of his hair and mustache. A third-generation *fendeur*, he has been plying his craft since he was thirteen. We note how he splits the logs. "There's less and less good wood," he says. "Ten years ago you could get a cubic meter of staves from three of *grume* (unhewn wood). Now you need six or even seven." Gamba has been chewing a chip of wood. "Taste how sweet this is!" He is impressed by what he has seen, but then comes the bad news: Daffy sells all his *merrain* to a cooper in Bordeaux.

We head north again, into the Cher and past Bourges. In the little town of Méry-ès-Bois, near the forest of St. Palais, we drive into the sizable establishment of Camille Gauthier.

Gauthier has an authoritarian, but roguish air. With brisk gestures and index finger continually raised, "the professor of oak" (as Angelo calls him) enlightens us. He has a worker bring out five staves. "Which is the heaviest?" he asks as he sizes you up. "Yes, indeed!" he roars triumphantly. "That's Limousin, a *gros grain*." Limousin grows rapidly in rich soil and is coarse grained. "And the lightest? Yes, indeed! That's Tronçais, a *grain fin*." Tronçais grows slowly in poor soil and is fine grained. The Tronçais has a pinkish tinge. Intermediate is *mi-fin*, semi-fine. "A *grain fin* should be at least one hundred fifty years old for *merrain*; Limousin grows so much faster it can be eighty."

Gauthier shows us around. "There were some Australians here yesterday." A couple of weeks earlier, an American had passed by. "And you know what he wanted?" the professor asks incredulously. "*Grume!*"

We learn how to stack staves properly. We observe that the ground is black. "That's all the bitter tannin from the staves," Gauthier cackles. "Better on the ground here than in your wine!"

Inside his shop, we meet a bearded young researcher from Beaune, who is carrying out an experiment concerning the effect on wine of such variables as the height on the tree at which wood grows and the direction it faces.

Gauthier tells us about the auctions where the government, proprietor of most of the forestland in France, sells lots every year. The auction for forests in the Cher takes place in October in Bourges.

On the evening before the auction, the Gauthier household is excited. Gauthier shows us a booklet put out by the National Forest Bureau. It describes the lots to be auctioned and is covered with annotations. He and his wife have been around sizing up quantity and quality. Gamba complains that he is unable to get all the wood he needs. Mrs. Gauthier, a quick, ironic woman, tells him that the French do not like to sell *merrain* to Italians. "Casks, sure. That's okay. But not staves."

We follow the auction. The auctioneer starts at a given price, then lowers it until someone shouts "*Prends!*" ("I'll take it!") There is no time to hesitate; he moves from one price to another in less than a second. The thirty-eighth lot starts off at 410,000 francs. Just as the auctioneer is about to say "Three hundred and sixty thousand," Gauthier leaps to his feet. "*Prends!*" He buys three lots in all.

Gauthier is only partially satisfied. The best lots were very expensive, and he cannot compete with big furniture manufacturers like

Chaussière, "who have customers in Switzerland and own real estate in Paris."

On the road home, Gamba stops off to visit a couple of famous French coopers. He examines a stack of staves and turns up his nose. "Most of them are sawed," he whispers. "They've put a few split ones on top."

Back in the Gaja cellar, we taste Sorì San Lorenzo and other wines from various casks and note the differences. Guido is wary of generalizations about different forests. "It's difficult to do rigorous experiments," he says. Even within the same forest, some sections are better than others. If you want to compare Bordeaux and Burgundy, you can't taste a Mouton-Rothschild against a village Nuits-St.-Georges. "To be absolutely sure of what I'm getting," he exclaims, "I'd have to cut down the tree myself and haul it back to Barbaresco!"

(Like certain wines, perhaps this synopsis has spent too much time in wood. We shall be much briefer from this point on.)

Sometime later this year (summer is best), Sorì San Lorenzo 1989 will be bottled. At this point in a ball game, the crowd might think it is all over but the shouting and start heading for the exits. Bottling is a critical operation, however. It can even ruin a wine. Guido explains what goes on (including prebottling filtration, a controversial issue); Angelo has stories about the old days. We note briefly how bottle and cork were married in the late seventeenth century and have a critical look at the "and lived happily ever after" aspect of the story.

Ottavio Ottavi noted over a century ago that "the choice of a bottle has an influence on the wine's future that is far from being unimportant." We go with Angelo to the Trentino region, where we are shown around the Nordvetri bottle factory by Franco Marchini. He explains the progress that has been made since Ottavi's time, as exemplified by the bottle Gaja uses for Sorì San Lorenzo. We notice a bottle with an unusually thin neck. "That's for a producer who was convinced by an expert that the less cork you put there, the better." Marchini turns reproachfully to Angelo. "But you drove us even crazier with that cork of yours."

When you pull the cork from a bottle of Sorì San Lorenzo, you notice at once that it is exceptionally long. As is the story behind it.

As long ago as 1973 a reader of France's leading wine journal, *Revue des vins de France*, would have come across photos of thirty-three-year-old Angelo, his father, his grandfather, and his great-grandfather. In an advertisement with the title "The passion of four generations hangs on the quality of a . . . cork," Angelo explains that he is looking for "a really exceptional cork."

On the island of Sardinia, we drive with Angelo through forests of the cork oak, *Quercus suber*, which is hardly recognizable as a relative of its more aristocratic northern cousins. These trees seem dumpy and gnarled in comparison. Those that have recently been stripped of their bark look like they have been caught with their pants down.

We enter Calangianus: 5,000 inhabitants, 250 cork producers, 90 percent of Italy's cork production. Peppino Molinas shows us around his highly automated factory. One machine punches the corks directly out of strips of bark; another classifies them electronically. Molinas explains the various stages of production. He drives us to an old-fashioned work-shop where craftsmen called *quadrettisti* cut parallelepipeds from the strips of cork by hand. We learn how corks made this way differ from those produced in the factory.

The cork is the last link in the long chain of production factors that is behind the quality of the wine you pour in your glass. When he talks about cork, even a gentle person like Guido looks like he could get violent. "All that work and just like that"—he snaps his fingers—"it's ruined by the cork." We look at some of the problems caused by defective corks.

Like grapes and oak, cork varies greatly according to the conditions in which it grows. With more and more wine being bottled all over the world, the demand for cork has grown rapidly. We examine why quality has suffered. "Producers do a good job of actually making corks," says Angelo, "but it's like with wine: you can't make up in the cellar for poor raw material. They're like growers who don't know what it means to select grapes."

Angelo's way of dealing with the problem was to ask suppliers for corks sixty-three millimeters long, an unheard of length when he first used them in 1981. Since no existing machine could cork a bottle with them, he had to have one made to order. "There's no proof that such long corks protect the wine any better," Angelo says, "but they do oblige the producer to select his best raw material."

The problem does not end with defective corks. Cork itself is an issue. We go with Aldo Vacca to visit an old schoolmate of his who works as an enologist at the huge Martini (of cocktail fame) and Rossi estab-lishment near Torino. Alberto Orrico explains that he periodically takes fifty bottles of wine off the bottling line and closes them with corks from different shipments as well as with crown caps, screw caps, and other devices. After three months the wines are tasted blind by a large group. "Everyone always agrees that the wines closed with corks are the least good," he says. "And each one tastes different."

Guido is convinced there are better alternatives, but they are not part of our traditional wine imagery. "It's a very touchy subject," Angelo confesses. "The idea of a crown cap on a bottle of Château Lafite is hard to swallow."

Sorì San Lorenzo 1989 will rest for a year in the Gaja cellar before making its debut in wine society. We have seen what has gone into the making of this wine. In another sense, the making of the wine takes us further back into history, a strand that in the book will be interwoven with the first one.

The purchase of Sorì San Lorenzo in 1964 was part of a strategy to ensure the winery a reliable supply of top-quality grapes. Three years earlier they had stopped buying grapes from other growers, including those from the then much better known Barolo area. Angelo explains why.

Sorì San Lorenzo was farmed by a sharecropper, who grew wheat and other crops between the rows of vines and used part of the land as a pasture for his livestock. Angelo shakes his head. "Can you imagine a great vineyard in Burgundy reduced to that condition?"

Our vineyard was on the wrong side of the Alps. We take a brief historical look at how the wines of France had achieved preeminence by cornering the all-important English market, with Bordeaux leading the way and others following.

Barbaresco's affinities were with Burgundy rather than Bordeaux: numerous small growers; small, fragmented properties; a demanding grape variety. Wine had a long tradition in Barbaresco. In the choir of the cathedral of Alba, one of the stalls dating from 1490 has an inlaid wood decoration depicting the village and its ancient castle under a bowl of grapes. But what historical association could Barbaresco boast to rival that of the great Burgundian vineyard Chambertin with Napoleon? The only one cited in writings on Barbaresco in an effort to give its tradition a bit of luster concerns a General von Melas, who, on November 6, 1799, ordered wine from the village to celebrate an Austrian victory over the French in a nearby battle. The order was actually a humiliating military requisition by a foreign power, and, symbolically enough, in a much more important battle seven months later at Marengo (of chicken à la fame), von Melas was defeated by none other than Napoleon himself.

France established the international vinous canon; Bordeaux, Burgundy, and Champagne became colors as well as wines. Modern taste was founded on those flavors. New World wines could become famous overnight by "beating" famous French ones in international competitions, but the condition for entering the competition was making your wine with one of the major French grape varieties. Cabernet and Chardonnay became the vinous equivalents of the English language. Making wine with Nebbiolo was like writing verse in Finnish.

During its frequent wars with France, England would seek other sources of wine (which is how port, for example, got its foot in the door). Early in the eighteenth century, if not Barbaresco, at least nearby Barolo got its chance. Documents in the National Archives in Turin reveal that English merchants were interested in a deal, but getting the wine to them was a problem. There was no road leading to the then Piedmontese port of Nice that was suitable for the transportation of heavy barrels, and the even closer ports of the Republic of Genoa would have taxed the wine out of the market.

Geographical isolation and Italy's lack of political unity sealed the fate of wines like Barbaresco. The Langhe remained a region of backward farmers making wine for a strictly local market. Lorenzo Fantini describes the situation in the middle of the nineteenth century: "a miserable state of winemaking" ("with procedures that go back to the good patriarch Noah") due to "the almost total lack of trade," which in turn was due to "the scarcity and sometimes total lack of roads." A vicious circle. "In those times, to speak of exporting was like speaking Sanskrit!" he writes. "Frequent were the years in which producers were forced to drink their wines themselves for want of buyers, and that explains the phenomenal generosity with which our grandfathers poured wine for their friends."

Mixed crops in even prime vineyard sites were a consequence of such a precarious situation: farmers always wanted to "grow a little of everything" so as not to put all their eggs in the wine basket. Sharecropping was another consequence and another obstacle to progress. ("A sharecropper who is a good viticulturist is as rare as the phoenix.") Indeed, Fantini sees the small farmer himself, the *contadino*, as an obstacle. Without education, he writes, he will continue to be "an inefficient machine and nothing more," "a seriously ill patient who needs an operation to get well."

France was way ahead. Writing to his father from Toulouse, Pietro Musso, a young *contadino* from Barbaresco, described the marvels of technology used to prepare the ground for a new vineyard: "Here there are two large pulleys that draw a big plow back and forth. You're not always just digging away with a hoe like we do. The ground is broken up by a machine, and in a few days it's ready to be planted." His father admonished him not to tell anybody about it when he came home. "People wouldn't believe you, and we'd soon be the laughingstock of the town."

We hear about the wines of a century ago from Ottavi. "The French are way ahead of us in the art of making fine wine," he observes. "It is an undeniable fact that at present we make little fine wine, much poor wine, and a lot of vinegar." He lists the major defects of Italian wines in general, but notes a number of promising signs, especially in Piedmont.

Times were not propitious, however. World War I hit hard. Outside the minuscule town hall of Barbaresco, a marble plaque dedicated to the village's "brave sons who fell for their country" has fifty-four names engraved on it. The autarkic fantasies of Mussolini's "Battle for Grain" encouraged growers to plant even more cereal crops in their vineyards. World War II brought German occupation, Allied bombings, and civil war. The death rate in the Langhe was almost twice that of Italy as a whole. Luigi Cavallo, foreman of Gaja's vineyard crew until his retirement in 1983, tells of the three corpses he dug up while working. A Fascist roundup in Barbaresco led to forty people, including Gaja's cellarman, being taken off to Turin.

There were amusing notes, though, as the Langhe met America toward the end of the war. A photo shows local eyes bulging as two black GIs stroll though Alba. "They had more stuff in one of their packsacks than in all of ours put together," chuckles a former partisan. Another recalls the U.S. Air Force parachuting supplies to the partisans. It was not long before "balconies all over the Langhe displayed homemade nylon lingerie in a riot of colors."

Even a year after the war was over, food was still a serious problem. Thus the narrator of a novel by Beppe Fenoglio: "Lunch and dinner were almost always dried corn mush. To give it a bit of flavor, we took turns rubbing it with an anchovy hanging from a string tied to a beam. Even when the anchovy no longer had even the semblance of one, we still went on rubbing it for several days."

The big change took place in the fifties. Alba had been the least industrialized town in the province of Cuneo; by the end of the decade it had more people employed in industry than any other. This meant prosperity for Angelo's father, who was in the construction business, enabling him to purchase Sorì San Lorenzo and other outstanding vineyards. It also meant a shortage of agricultural labor, as *contadini* became *cittadini* (townspeople).

What is perhaps the last generation of the old *contadino* culture lives on in Barbaresco today. Luigi Cavallo lives at number 1 on via Torino, Turin Street. He has never been to Turin. "I've always been here," he says, bringing to mind that as late as the early years of this century people in the Langhe talked about Piedmont as if it began, or ended, just across the Tanaro River, which flows by Barbaresco. "I'm going to Piedmont," they would say. "In Piedmont they do this and that."

Just a few yards up the street, at number 36, is the Gaja winery, a world of phone calls to New York and Amsterdam, of faxes to Tokyo, of BMWs with German license plates parked in the courtyard. Angelo is off to Burgundy for a meeting of French and American Chardonnay producers, but he and Guido talk about it in dialect. The language of Luigi Cavallo.

When Angelo, a Taurus who looks it, started to work at the family winery in 1961, it was the leading one in Barbaresco, but sales were mainly in Piedmont and direct to consumers in large, anonymous containers. Barbaresco was obscured not only by the shadow of French wine, but also by the more local one of Barolo: our vineyard was not only on the wrong side of the Alps, but on the wrong side of Alba as well.

Reading what the leading English-language food authorities were writing at the time would have been discouraging. Elizabeth David's classic *Italian Food* advises readers to approach Italian wine "in a spirit of optimism and amiable inquiry rather than with harsh comparisons to the wines of France" and mentions Barbaresco only as "another of the good wines of Piedmont" and "interesting to try." Somewhat later, in his *The Food of Italy*, Waverly Root damned Italian wines with his defensive claim that they were better than French ones with Italian food ("Who would think of drinking a fine Médoc with a dish of spaghetti and tomato sauce?") and assigned Barbaresco its routine place as "probably the second best wine of Piedmont." The first edition of Hugh Johnson's *The World Atlas of Wine* dedicated a whole chapter of seventy-two pages to France ("the undisputed mistress of the vine") and thirteen pages to Italy as part of a catchall chapter on Southern and Eastern Europe and the Mediterranean; Barbaresco was presented as "less fully ripened than Barolo." Even the *Random House Dictionary of the English Language,* published in 1966, had an entry for "barolo," but none for Barbaresco!

The occasional English visitors were put off by the yellowish hue of oxidated old Barolos and Barbarescos; they spoke of "salame skin" and "chicken skin." If the larger world had little interest in Barbaresco, the world Angelo grew up in had little interest in it. "It was almost impossible to find even a bottle of Chianti in Alba," he recalls.

Trips abroad opened his eyes. He attended courses for growers in southern France. "They were Third World, too, dealing with the same problems we had." Bordeaux and Burgundy showed him that quality paid. But the winery's cellerman in the sixties, Luigi Rama, had no contact with the outside world. "He lived in a world all his own," says Angelo. "He was the depositary of Tradition."

But there is always a tradition prior to Tradition. Nebbiolo, for instance, had a long tradition in Piedmont, where the earliest documented reference to it goes back to 1286. Passing through Turin in 1787, Thomas Jefferson noted in his journal that he had tasted "a red wine of Nebiule," but his tasting note ("sweet," "astringent," and "brisk as Champagne") might strike us as quite untraditional. Yet when Barbaresco growers met over a hundred years later to form their association, they acknowledged that the wine their village had produced in the past "was little better than those sweetish, sickly sweet, semi-sparkling or frothy Nebbiolos that delighted the unsophisticated palates and stronger stomachs of our forefathers" and that the new tradition of a consistently dry wine dated from the founding of the cooperative winery in 1894.

Barbaresco had been transformed before; Angelo would transform it again. He was also getting ready to see what he could do with canonical grapes.

A trip to California in 1973 made a deep impression on him. "People were in wine by choice," he says. "They were real pros." Above all, "they were showing you could beat the French at their own game."

To make way for Cabernet Sauvignon, Nebbiolo vines were ripped up below the Gaja home on the Bricco, the most prominent spot in the village. "I didn't want to sneak it in through the back door," says Angelo. It was as if Nebbiolo had driven Pinot Noir out of a major vineyard in Burgundy. As the work proceeded, Angelo's father would shake his head and mutter *"Darmagi,"* dialect for "What a shame!" and thus, along with the vermouth Punt e Mes, the label of Angelo's Cabernet Sauvignon now propagates Piedmontese throughout the world.

We look briefly at the history of "foreign" grape varieties in Italy and note the long line of Piedmontese who have played a major role in experimentation with them, beginning with Manfredo Bertone di Sam-buy, who, in the 1830s, planted the first Cabernet Sauvignon in Italy. By the end of the century, experimentation was thriving in many regions, as we see from a book on the subject by Salvatore Mondini, published in 1903. (There was even a famous Cabernet vineyard in what is now a fashionable residential section of Rome, Parioli!) This innovative and cosmopolitan tradition was all but destroyed by phylloxera, Fascism, and two world wars. Like two other Piedmontese, Mario Incisa della Rocchetta and Giacomo Tachis, leaders of the Tuscan wine revolution with their creations Sassicaia and Tignanello, Angelo was in on the revival.

Sorì San Lorenzo and other Gaja wines have become part of the world's vinous elite in terms of both price and critical acclaim, as have the wines of other producers in Piedmont and elsewhere in Italy. Having turned Fantini's vicious circle into a virtuous one, Angelo spends a lot of time on the road keeping them there.

He slams on the brakes as he spots a highway patrol car lying in wait farther up the road. "Italian style," he says sheepishly as the speedometer plunges. Angelo is a man in a hurry. "You should have seen him tear into town on his tractor when he was still working in the vineyards," says Guido. Perhaps he is trying to make up for more than two centuries of lost time. Fantini, obsessed by the lack of roads and thus of trade, would have understood him.

Angelo is on his way home from a visit to Europe's largest vine nursery, at Rauscedo, near the Yugoslav border. During our visits to Sorì San Lorenzo, we noticed numerous gaps where vines have been rooted up; many others "have reached the end of the line," as Federico puts it. Plans for replanting the vineyard are being made, and Angelo has been looking into rootstocks. The considerations are many. Resistance to phylloxera, of course. And to drought. Vigor. Will it perform well in Sorì San Lorenzo's calcareous soil? Does it have rooting problems?

In the distance, hilltop Barbaresco comes slowly into focus. The cranes at the Gaja winery loom above the village coequally with its ancient tower.

Angelo's mind is racing faster than his car. It's a critical decision. Those roots will be there for thirty years or more, entrusted with the "savor of the earth," the "secrets of the soil." And in the end, that is where it all begins: with the best grapes in the world.